MW00424113

FROM THE GRIDIRON TO THE BATTLEFIELD

FROM THE GRIDIRON TO THE BATTLEFIELD

Minnesota's March to a College Football Title and into World War II

Danny Spewak

ROWMAN & LITTLEFIELD
Lanham • Boulder • New York • London

Published by Rowman & Littlefield
An imprint of The Rowman & Littlefield Publishing Group, Inc.
4501 Forbes Boulevard, Suite 200, Lanham, Maryland 20706
www.rowman.com

6 Tinworth Street, London SE11 5AL

British Library Cataloguing in Publication Information Available

Library of Congress Cataloging-in-Publication Data

Names: Spewak, Danny, 1991– author.
Title: From the gridiron to the battlefield : Minnesota's march to a college football title and into
     World War II / Danny Spewak.
Description: Lanham : Rowman & Littlefield, [2021] | Includes bibliographical references and
     index. | Summary: "This book tells the story of the University of Minnesota's remarkable 1941
     football season as they chased a second consecutive national championship even as a divided
     country veered closer to total war, and chronicles the young players' contributions to the war
     effort in the months and years that followed"—Provided by publisher.
Identifiers: LCCN 2021013177 (print) | LCCN 2021013178 (ebook) | ISBN 9781538157626
     (cloth) | ISBN 9781538157633 (ebook)
Subjects: LCSH: University of Minnesota—Football—History—20th century. | Minnesota Golden
     Gophers (Football team)—History—20th century. | World War, 1939–1945. | Football and
     war—United States.
Classification: LCC GV958.U529 S64 2021 (print) | LCC GV958.U529 (ebook) | DDC 796.332/
     6309776579—dc23
LC record available at https://lccn.loc.gov/2021013177
LC ebook record available at https://lccn.loc.gov/2021013178

For my grandparents, Jack and Virginia Spewak

CONTENTS

ACKNOWLEDGMENTS

First, I would like to say that I am indebted to many of the players' families for sharing their stories with me. June Smith, for example, graciously invited me into her home in August 2019 and recalled delightful memories of her older brother Bruce. In all, I interviewed nearly two dozen of the players' relatives and friends for this book, either in person or over the phone depending on the distance. In a few cases, my communication was limited to emailed information. I would like to thank the following for all of their contributions: June Smith, Bruce Smith, Bonnie Smith Henderson, Scott Smith, Peter Levy, Rand Levy, Michael Sweiger, Cindy Sweiger, Bob Garnaas, Bruce Odson, Dave Wildung, Hal Wildung, Jane Wildung Lanphere, Charles Ringer, Deb Welch, Kristy Bierhaus, Charlie Vail, Ann Lauterbach Waits, Joe Lauterbach, Sara Lauterbach Glenn, Gary Glenn, Dave Nolander, Bruce Pukema, Dianne Plunkett Latham, and Christine Van't Hull Park.

During more than two years of research and writing, I relied on hundreds of primary documents to help me understand the 1941 Minnesota Golden Gophers and their impact on the community. Newspapers played an integral role in this process, particularly the local publications in the Twin Cities that thoroughly covered the Gophers every single day during the fall months. The *Minneapolis Tribune*, *Minneapolis Star Journal*, *St. Paul Pioneer Press*, and the *St. Paul Dispatch* provided the most comprehensive coverage and helped me tremendously in crafting game narratives. Not much film exists from the 1941 season, but clips included in the DVD "Smith of Minnesota" helped

supplement these descriptions, allowing me to view part of "The Talking Play" against Northwestern and Bill Daley's touchdown run on the
first offensive play against Illinois, among others. The University of
Minnesota's "Brickhouse" website, devoted to preserving Memorial
Stadium's history, also offered a chance to view the entire Minnesota–Wisconsin game from 1941.

Media outlets on campus, including the *Minnesota Daily* and the
Minnesota Alumni Weekly, helped me understand what daily life would
have felt like at the University of Minnesota in the months before,
during, and after the war. For coverage of Minnesota's eight opponents
in 1941, I reviewed newspapers from each region in the days leading up
to the games. Those publications include but are not limited to the
Spokesman-Review (Spokane, Washington), *Chicago Tribune*, *Pittsburgh Press*, *Pittsburgh Sun-Telegraph*, *Detroit Free Press*, the *State
Journal* (Lincoln, Nebraska), *Des Moines Register*, *Des Moines Tribune*,
the *Courier* (Waterloo, Iowa), and the *Capital Times* (Madison, Wisconsin). I found student newspapers quite helpful as well, such as the
Daily Illini, the *Pitt News*, the *Michigan Daily*, the *Daily Nebraskan*,
and the *Daily Iowan*. I appreciate each university making those publications searchable and available online for the general public. The culmination of my newspaper research helped me vividly describe the
games, practices, and weekly preparations.

To access all newspapers, I utilized a combination of ProQuest,
Chronicling America, and the Library of Congress, the News-
papers.com subscription service, microfilm at the Minnesota History
Center in St. Paul, and microfilm at the University of Minnesota's libraries. I wish to thank the staff at each of those physical locations for
helping me identify the newspaper titles that could assist me in this
research. I also wish to thank the University of Minnesota's Elmer
Andersen Library and specifically Erik Moore for helping me locate
important documents in the university archives, including game programs, yearbooks, and personnel files. They were all valuable sources
and I benefited greatly from the library's willingness to help.

Other universities and institutions responded to my requests for
documents as well. I would like to thank the generous staff at the
University of Illinois Archives, the University of Montana Mansfield
Library Archives, and the University of Michigan Bentley Historical
Library for sending digital versions of documents I requested for this

project. The Minnesota Historical Society was another outstanding resource, providing me access to newspapers on microfilm, rare book copies (like the one written by Bernie Bierman in 1937), and other old papers that likely have not been read by humans in decades. The Saint Paul Public Library and Hennepin County Library also carried relevant book titles, and the Hennepin County Library's digital high school yearbook collection from the late 1930s helped me immensely. On a local level, I am extremely grateful to Susan Garwood of the Rice County Historical Society for helping me search through the Smith family archives in Faribault, as well as Roger Paschke of the Melrose Area Historical Society for providing resources and expertise related to Bill Daley. Also, Kate Dietrick of the Upper Midwest Jewish Archives, housed in the Elmer Andersen Library at the University of Minnesota, kindly helped me access Butch Levy's fascinating papers.

Thank you to Rowman & Littlefield Publishing Group, and editor Christen Karniski, for believing in this book and providing an opportunity to present the story of the 1941 Golden Gophers to the world.

I could not have completed this project without the full support of my own family: my parents, Bob and Nancy, my brother Mike and sister-in-law Katelyn, my brothers Mark, and Andy, my Uncle Dave and Aunt Bridget, cousins Colin, Tracy, and Annie, Uncle Steve and Aunt Lynn, and, most importantly, my wife, Callan. Instead of laughing at my idea of writing a book, they offered nothing but encouragement and kept me in good spirits throughout the entire process. They also provided input on my book proposal and manuscript, vastly improving the overall quality of the work.

Mostly, I owe the inspiration for this book to my grandfather, Jack Spewak. Although he died when I was only nine years old, his story motivates me to this day: born in Minneapolis to Jewish immigrant parents, my grandfather played college football at the highest possible level, served in the Army Air Corps during World War II, graduated with a degree in business, raised three boys with my grandmother, and worked his way from an entry-level job to become president of a company named Senack Shoes. I have long admired his work ethic and could only smile when I came across a May 12, 1943, edition of the *Minneapolis Tribune*, in which sportswriter Bernard Swanson described Jack Spewak as "one of the hardest working boys on the Gopher squad."[1] I can only wonder what he and my grandmother, Virginia, would think about their grandson moving back to the Twin Cities seven decades after they left. I only wish that they both could have lived long enough to read this book.

INTRODUCTION

On the evening of December 9, 1941, a few hours before midnight on the East Coast, the American people froze all activity and huddled around their radios to listen to the president of the United States. They clustered outside cigar stands on the streets of Pensacola, Florida, crowded a banquet hall in Salinas, California, and congregated inside a social club in Casper, Wyoming. Traffic immobilized entirely in downtown Muncie, Indiana. The once-bustling Fourth Street in Louisville, Kentucky, fell to a hushed silence, and in Fremont, Ohio, fourteen couples pulled themselves away from the dance floor at a Christmas party. Church groups, booster clubs, city councils, and school boards adjourned early. From the Pacific to the Atlantic, the largest radio audience in U.S. history to that point—totaling an estimated sixty to ninety million listeners—waited patiently to hear Franklin Delano Roosevelt address the nation in his first fireside chat since the attack on Pearl Harbor.[1]

The president, sporting a black bow tie and striped jacket, had finished dinner that Tuesday night with advisor Harry Hopkins before reporting to the White House doctor's office about a half hour prior to his scheduled 10:00 p.m. speech.[2] Americans needed a healthy commander in chief at this extraordinary moment in history. With total war threatening every corner of the globe, Roosevelt's inner circle carefully revised multiple drafts of his fireside chat, striving to balance a bold but reassuring tone with an American public still weary and unsettled by the catastrophic news cycle of the past two days. Leading up to the radio address, speechwriter Samuel Rosenman even appeared to alter the very first line, replacing the phrase "acts of assassination" with "criminal attacks."[3] Every single word mattered. The president knew that when he walked into the Diplomatic Reception Room near the South Lawn, a table full of microphones, network correspondents, and the most expansive listening base since the invention of radio would await him.

As Roosevelt sweated out the final moments before his fireside chat, an unassuming senior halfback from the University of Minnesota sat anxiously inside the Downtown Athletic Club in Lower Manhattan, about two hundred miles northeast of the White House, feeling similar pressure under the national microscope. Bruce Smith, homegrown in a town named Faribault and captain of the undefeated Golden Gophers of 1941, prepared that very same Tuesday evening to receive the Heisman Trophy, awarded annually to the most outstanding player in college football. The prestigious honor required the winner to deliver an acceptance speech on the national Mutual Broadcasting System at 9:45 p.m.—about fifteen minutes before the start of Roosevelt's address in Washington. Smith faced an enormous responsibility. The Mutual network carried some of the most powerful radio affiliates in the country, including WGN in Chicago, WOR in New York, WAAB in Boston, and WLOL in the Twin Cities, where Smith's home market planned to listen intently. So, with microphones rolling, and tens of millions of his fellow Americans locked in place next to their radios anticipating the bellowing tones of Franklin Roosevelt, Smith made a move. The sturdy, blond-haired Gopher football star rose from his chair inside the thirty-eight-story Downtown Athletic Club, overlooking the Hudson River and the Statue of Liberty, and walked to the front of the banquet room to deliver his own public address during a time of national emergency. The president would have to wait.

* * *

Eight decades have passed since Bruce Smith shared the airwaves with FDR in New York City. All five hundred adults in the room—including Smith, his father, one of his siblings, and his Hall of Fame head coach Bernie Bierman—have long since passed. Just a handful of photographs remain from the event, and the sparse Paramount Pictures newsreels vanished years ago. Only the original written transcript and grainy audio recording, stored by the Rice County Historical Society in Faribault, survived for future generations.

The remaining evidence offers a glimpse into America's soul during a time of profound crisis. Two days after the Japanese attack on Pearl Harbor, this mild-mannered, twenty-one-year-old college senior from a small town in Minnesota captivated the nation, providing a needed distraction from the lingering uncertainty. By the time Smith took that stage, lawmakers in Washington had already moved rapidly the day before to approve the declaration of war against Japan, knowing that Axis powers Italy and Germany would soon retaliate.

With instructions to keep his appearance brief ahead of President Roosevelt's fireside chat, the kid they called "Boo" gave a rousing speech to accept the Heisman Trophy on that bleak December evening in America's largest city. Thrust into the spotlight, Smith used this rare prime time opportunity to promise fellow Americans that his generation would not back away from the challenge, while fully acknowledging that he and his Minnesota teammates would play an essential role in the war effort. "I think America will owe a great debt to the game of football when we finish this thing off," Smith told the Downtown Athletic Club audience and countless radio listeners. He continued: "It teaches team play and cooperation and exercise to go out and fight hard for the honor of our schools, and likewise, the same skills can be depended on when we have to fight like blazes to defend our country."[4]

His words resonated with the public, and they mattered. As the leader of the 1941 Minnesota Golden Gophers, a team selected in a landslide as the national champions of college football for a second straight season, Bruce Smith further cemented his legacy as one of the most admired and respected athletes of his time. In an Associated Press poll taken in December 1941, sportswriters voted Smith the sixth-most prominent American athlete of the year. For perspective, consider the fact that Joe DiMaggio topped the list after tallying a fifty-six-game hitting streak for the New York Yankees that year, Ted Williams finished second after batting .406 for the Boston Red Sox, and heavyweight boxing champion Joe Louis finished third. Smith had joined elite—no, historic—company in the year 1941. And so had his Gophers. Those same AP experts chose Minnesota's football squad as the second-best sports team of 1941 behind only the Yankees.[5]

University of Minnesota senior Bruce Smith accepts the Heisman Trophy on December 9, 1941, just two days after the attack on Pearl Harbor. Millions of Americans listened to his radio address that evening, ahead of President Roosevelt's fireside chat. *AP Photo*

Under the careful tutelage of Bernie Bierman, the preeminent college football coach of his era, the Gophers claimed their seventh shared or outright Big Ten title and fifth national championship since the start of the Roosevelt administration, dazzling capacity crowds on a weekly basis from late September through Thanksgiving weekend. Nearly a half-million fans handed over hard-earned cash to see them perform during a flawless eight-game schedule, which included five home games in Minneapolis and three grueling road trips to Seattle, Ann Arbor, and Iowa City. Grantland Rice, a widely respected voice at that time and perhaps the most distinguished sportswriter to ever live, said after the season that Smith was the finest individual player he saw all year and that the Gophers were, without question, the class of college football in

1941. "Minnesota," Rice said, "is the only college team of today which I believe would have a chance against the Chicago Bears."[6]

Gifted with an enormous frontline, versatile backfield, and tough-as-nails defense, the Golden Gophers played vintage Bierman-style football in 1941 by exploiting their size and outlasting opponents with mental and physical discipline. Facing an overwhelming burden already as the defending national champions of 1940, they had chased perfection again and achieved it, running their overall winning streak to an astounding seventeen games as fears of conflict and war grew louder and louder with every passing week. It all culminated in the attack on Pearl Harbor just fifteen days after the Gophers finished their regular season schedule.

College football programs felt the tension all season, long before those bombs fell on Hawaii. With the nation's first-ever peacetime military draft well underway by the autumn of 1941, coaches across the country whispered about the possibility of losing their upperclassmen to the military. The players monitored their draft numbers as though their lives depended on it, because they did. Even Bierman himself, a veteran of World War I, remained a member of the Marine Corps reserves and knew active duty might become a possibility.

These Gophers came along at a remarkable time. For almost three months, they competed at the highest level of American sports, playing in front of sellout crowds and national radio audiences as they earned coast-to-coast newspaper headlines—all while the country braced for its second world war in fewer than three decades. Bruce Smith scored touchdowns as lawmakers vigorously debated the merits of U.S. involvement in the conflict; Bernie Bierman studied formations as American forces engaged in undeclared North Atlantic shooting wars against the Germans and as the Roosevelt administration held unraveling peace talks with Japanese diplomats. "Yes, indeed it would take something superhuman to stop Bernie Bierman and the Golden Gophers," Howie Larson of the *Minnesota Daily* wrote in the campus newspaper after the season. "Toward the end of the year 1941 something superhuman did happen."[7]

❊ ❊ ❊

I have a close personal connection to the Gophers' wartime program. My grandfather, Jack Spewak, played football for the University of Minnesota from fall 1941 through the spring of 1943 before his induction into the Army Air Corps. Under Big Ten Conference rules at the time, freshmen were not eligible to play varsity sports, so he competed on the Gophers' freshman practice squad during the undefeated 1941 national championship season. He played center on the varsity team as a sophomore in 1942, appearing in at least one regular season game, and then started at center in the Gophers' annual spring game in May 1943 before heading off to war. Although I was always vaguely aware that my grandfather had played college football at Minnesota, I never asked him much about his football career while he was still alive.

I was only nine years old when my grandfather died on May 20, 2000, in St. Louis, Missouri, my hometown and the place where he and my grandmother, Virginia, had moved a half-century earlier. At the time, it would have seemed inconceivable that I would move back to their birthplace of Minneapolis. Yet, in May 2018, fate landed me in the Twin Cities when I accepted a news reporting job at a local television station. I instantly felt a connection to the region, beginning with the moment I caught a glance of the Minneapolis skyline. Unexpectedly, I found myself immersed in the history of my late grandparents' lives: I drove by their old houses and schools, walked their neighborhoods, and, eventually, grew more interested in my grandfather's football career. It had never occurred to me, until moving here, that he joined the Minnesota program at the pinnacle of Bernie Bierman's dynasty.

Like hundreds of players before and after him, Jack Spewak stayed home to play football for his state university. Born at Minneapolis General Hospital in 1923, he was the first and only member of his immediate family to attend college and the only American-born sibling. Fleeing pogroms and anti-Jewish violence, his parents, his older brother, and his older sister had emigrated from a small village near Odessa, Russia (now Ukraine), providing my grandfather the opportunity to grow up in post–World War I America. He spent all of his formative years in the Near North section of Minneapolis, a mostly Jewish and African American neighborhood just a few blocks off Plymouth Avenue, where he attended North High School and participated in wrestling and football for the Polars. In 1941, the Mercury Club honored him as the

Outstanding Jewish Athlete of the Year, which he parlayed into a spot on the University of Minnesota freshman football team that fall.

His role in the program in 1941 was mostly limited to serving as a tackling dummy in scrimmages against varsity. Still, that minor connection sparked my interest in the 1941 Gophers as a whole. I thought about all the locker room secrets and firsthand observations my grandfather could have revealed, had I known to ask at a younger age before he died. He actually *watched* Bruce Smith's momentous march to the only Heisman Trophy in Minnesota history, and he experienced for himself the methodical tactics employed by Bernie Bierman and his coaching staff. Jack Spewak lined up on the same practice field with multiple All-American and All-Conference standouts, including but not limited to Smith, Urban Odson, Leonard "Butch" Levy, Dick Wildung, Bob Sweiger, Bill Daley, and Bill Garnaas.

Against his rookie peers, meanwhile, my grandfather flourished during his first year of college football. Minnesota freshman coach Dallas Ward highlighted him in November 1941 as the top center prospect on the team, among the few interior linemen who "impressed their coach the most."[8] Built stoutly with a five-foot-ten, 190-pound frame, it appeared my grandfather had a strong future in his three remaining years of varsity eligibility. Weeks later, as his first semester of college drew to a close, a fleet of Japanese aircraft attacked Pearl Harbor. The date was December 7, 1941.

My grandfather did not head overseas right away. He dressed for every game during the 1942 season, wearing number "48" as the backup varsity center for the Gophers, before making the first start of his career in a 1943 "Army–Navy" spring scrimmage at Memorial Stadium. It would be the last game he ever played. "It's throwing hand grenades instead of footballs for Pvt. Jack Spewak, former Minnesota center who was inducted at Fort Snelling last week," the *Minneapolis Tribune* wrote in a May 1943 caption, accompanied by a picture of my grandfather in a uniformed military stance. "Spewak starred at center on the Navy team last Saturday in the spring game."[9]

The "Navy" team was just a football assignment; his real assignment landed him with the Army Air Corps, where he completed basic training at Jefferson Barracks in St. Louis before deploying on a non-combat tour to Australia, New Guinea, and the Philippines under the command of General Douglas MacArthur. After returning home unscathed, he

This photograph of my grandfather, Jack Spewak, appeared in the *Minneapolis Tribune* in May 1943 after his induction at Fort Snelling. My grandmother proudly kept a copy of the picture in her archives, with the handwritten label "Minneapolis Tribune 1943," for more than seventy years. *Star Tribune*

married my grandmother, finished his degree, started a family of three boys including my father Bob, and pursued a successful career in the shoe business. The war put an end to football. If not for the outbreak of

World War II, my grandfather's playing career may have looked very different.

❋ ❋ ❋

The war changed the trajectory of life for every member of that 1941 team. Within months of winning the Heisman Trophy, Bruce Smith and his fellow graduating seniors competed on military bases for special wartime football teams, as they began their physical training for Uncle Sam. Other players left the game altogether to enlist. They put their careers on hold and quickly confronted horrific combat over the next four years. Reserve fullback Mike Welch sailed in June 1944 to occupied France, where he earned a Purple Heart for saving five shipmates after his USS *Tide* hit a mine and exploded off the coast of Normandy. Halfback Gene Bierhaus fought in Iwo Jima the next year and watched U.S. Marines raise the first flag on Mount Suribachi. His backfield mate Joe Lauterbach, a Navy ensign, lost his left leg in the same battle. All-American tackle Urban Odson sailed into Tokyo Bay with the USS *Amsterdam* after the Truman administration dropped two atomic bombs.

Football and war are not equivalent. Marv Levy, the former head coach of the Buffalo Bills and a World War II veteran himself, denounced such analogies in his sport as insensitive and demeaning to the soldiers who fought real wars. "A must-win?" Levy scoffed in January 1993 after a reporter pressured him about the stakes ahead of Super Bowl XXVII. "World War II was a must-win."[10] With that perspective in mind, the 1941 Golden Gophers still deserve acknowledgment for their place in history. At a time of unimaginable tension, this team brought nationwide recognition to the state of Minnesota and served as a tremendous source of local pride. In the absence of major professional football in the Twin Cities before the war, the Gophers were an essential component of the community's social fabric, and they provided a crucial morale boost as battles raged overseas.

Based on nearly two dozen interviews with the players' family members, a trove of archived documents, scrapbooks, memoirs, and hundreds of contemporary newspaper reports, this book offers a moment-by-moment account of the historic 1941 season as the country veered toward conflict. Although I was unable to locate any surviving players—

it appears the last remaining few have all died within the past decade—the legacy of this team must be preserved. An argument can be made that these young men left a mark unlike any other in their sport: they won eight games, lost zero, and two weeks later found themselves in the middle of a war that would determine the course of civilization. There is simply no modern college football comparison to the undefeated Minnesota Golden Gophers of 1941.

I

RIGHT MAN FOR THE JOB

Only the Mississippi River could divide war from football on Mother's Day weekend in 1941. As sons and daughters scrambled across Minneapolis on Saturday, May 10, searching for that perfect gift or a last-minute flower arrangement, the sixteenth-largest city in the United States prepared to host two major events on opposite ends of the water. On the eastern side of the Mississippi, at two o'clock in the afternoon, several thousand giddy football fans planned to bask in the grandstands of Memorial Stadium, the brick-layered shrine on the edge of the University of Minnesota's campus, to catch an early glimpse of the 1941 Minnesota Golden Gophers in their annual spring scrimmage. Wearing rusty practice jerseys and faded leather helmets, the defending Big Ten and national champions would split into two squads—the "Maroons" and "Golds"—to offer fans some low-key, entertaining competition at a modest price of fifty-five cents for a general admission seat. The Gophers would not play another full, four-quarter football game until the season opener in September 1941. "A little bit of autumn," Bob Beebe of the *Minneapolis Tribune* wrote, "will be dropped into Memorial Stadium this afternoon."[1]

Just a few hours after the conclusion of the spring game, on the western side of the Mississippi, the second major occasion of the weekend would begin inside the Minneapolis Auditorium on Second Avenue. At precisely 7:30 p.m., just one minute after anticipated sunset in the Twin Cities, a world-famous aviator by the name of Charles A. Lindbergh intended to deliver another anti-war message on behalf of the America First Committee.[2] Fourteen years after he etched his name into history with the first solo transatlantic flight from New York to Paris, the Minnesota native and *Spirit of St. Louis* pilot had resurfaced as the controversial face of the America First movement, which steadfastly argued against U.S. involvement in the deteriorating European crisis. Lindbergh's Minneapolis speech, in front of a fervent crowd in his home state, would undoubtedly draw the ire of President Roosevelt and many other detractors. These critics largely viewed Lindbergh as a dangerous apologist for the evils of Nazi Germany and Hitler, who had launched the war in September 1939 by invading Poland and subsequently stormed through Western Europe in 1940 before signing the Tripartite Pact with Japan and Italy.

The feud between Roosevelt and Lindbergh was no secret. At the start of 1941, Lindbergh made national headlines when he railed against the president's signature Lend-Lease proposal to provide military supplies primarily to the British, and just twelve days before he arrived in Minneapolis, he escalated his dispute with the White House on April 28 by unceremoniously resigning from the Army Air Corps Reserve. Lindbergh quit because Roosevelt mocked his stance on "negotiated peace" with Hitler, which FDR viewed as a betrayal on the level of the "Copperheads" who opposed fighting the Confederacy during the Civil War.[3] But Lindbergh, a graduate of central Minnesota's Little Falls High School and the son of a former federal representative from the state's Sixth Congressional District, refused to let the criticism disrupt his America First rally in the Twin Cities. Tapping into the instincts of some war-weary Americans, Lindbergh prepared a speech that would repeat the same themes he had uttered just one week earlier in St. Louis, when he declared: "Why must all this be brought to America?"[4]

These two events on Saturday, May 10, 1941—the spring scrimmage and the Lindbergh speech—drew an estimated seventeen thousand people combined to Minneapolis. The five thousand fans who chose football that afternoon saw halfback Bruce Smith, the Gophers' newest captain and All-American candidate for 1941, score an eight-yard touchdown in the first quarter as he powered his "Maroons" to a 20–0 victory; the twelve thousand people who chose Lindbergh, meanwhile, cheered the bold words of a leading isolationist figure as he pleaded with his government to remain neutral.[5] "Are we to take the policing of our entire world upon our shoulders?" Lindbergh asked the crowd at the Minneapolis Auditorium that evening, speaking while German bombs obliterated London across the Atlantic Ocean in another over-night blitz. "Must our children fight again when the next European war takes place?"[6] Staggered five and a half hours apart and located just four miles away from each other, these near-simultaneous gatherings on each side of the Mississippi River targeted vastly different audiences, but they illustrated how closely athletics, politics, and military life would intertwine throughout the rest of the calendar year. The Lindbergh appearance would not be the last time war overshadowed the 1941 Minnesota football season.

* * *

The Golden Gophers' head coach, Bernie Bierman, said nothing of Lindbergh on that second Saturday in May and probably paid little notice to the political rally on the other side of town. The thin, silver-haired forty-seven-year-old—known affectionately by the nicknames "Silver Fox" and "Grey Eagle"—was far too preoccupied with his team's "pathetic exhibition," as he so elegantly told a newspaper reporter while watching from the press box in the first half. "I'm glad I was here to see it or I wouldn't have believed it," Bierman said, displeased by mental miscues, fumbles, and an overall lackadaisical effort that had plagued the team all spring. "Defensively all right in spots, but no punch in the offense."[7]

As the humid afternoon turned to evening, and as the city's attention turned from football to an America First anti-war rally, the frustrated coach might have grabbed his trademark fedora and trudged home from Memorial Stadium on foot. Bierman and his wife, Clara, lived with their two teenage sons inside a spacious house on Malcolm Avenue, a reclusive and shaded residential street about one mile from campus.[8] The short commute down University Avenue didn't leave much time for reflection, but Bierman was probably still fuming over the Gophers' disappointing spring scrimmage. With two-dozen lettermen returning from an undefeated 1940 squad, including half of the starting lineup, Bierman saw an unfocused team that might crumble in 1941 under the weight of enormous outside expectations from fans, pundits, and oppos-ing Big Ten coaches. "Minnesota will be the best football team in the country this fall," one rival from the University of Michigan said. "If any team can go through the season unbeaten it will be Bernie Bierman's outfit."[9] The national press agreed. "Nothing short of black magic," sports journalist Francis Powers wrote in *Football Illustrated*, "can stop the '41 Golden Gophers in their drive for national honors."[10]

Bierman disagreed with the hype. He happened to see "black magic" everywhere, including the war overseas that had prompted political spats across the United States and led to the implementation of Selective Service the previous fall. A large chunk of the Gopher upperclassmen fit the twenty-one-year-old age requirement and would spend the summer nervously checking their mailboxes for military correspondence. "There is the draft to be considered," Bierman said during the spring of 1941. "That will probably affect us some, although we don't know how much."[11] Bierman must have dreaded the walk to his own mailbox, too. He could only pray that he would not find a letter from the United States Marine Corps. "Bernie Bierman is a captain in the Reserves," the *Minnesota Alumni Weekly* reported a year earlier, noting that the World War I veteran served a two-week stint at the Marine Corps base in Quantico, Virginia, as recently as June 1940. "As yet however he has received no word that he will be called."[12] The risk remained in 1941.

Bierman would face the most daunting coaching job of his career as he entered a tenth season at his alma mater, but few could doubt his skills as a football tactician. His record of 55–12–5 since 1932 far exceeded most of his coaching peers, and he had already steered Minnesota to four national titles and six shared or outright Big Ten championships. Bierman's teams finished undefeated in 1934 and 1935, captured the top spot in the inaugural Associated Press poll in 1936, and did so again in 1940. His résumé lacked high-profile bowl appearances because the Big Ten in those days prohibited participation in post-season games, but the college football universe still marveled at Bierman's consistent excellence, wondering how his Gophers could possibly rule the college football landscape from the center of the country with a statewide population base of fewer than three million people. The sport had arguably not seen a dynasty so fierce since the late Knute Rockne led Notre Dame to five undefeated seasons between 1918 and 1930. "Bierman," esteemed journalist Gordon Gammack wrote in the *Des*

Moines Tribune before the 1941 season, "is one of the most successful coaches in the United States."[13]

Bierman would need to draw on these accomplishments to navigate his team through the tumultuous autumn of 1941, as Selective Service and an international emergency threatened his program's reign. Seeking a fifth "mythical" national title, as determined by subjective pollsters like the Associated Press in the absence of a playoff system, Bierman wanted to prove to the world that his team could withstand the turmoil and produce another undefeated season. He was the right man to do it. Bierman's entire life to that point—his birth on a farm in Springfield, Minnesota, his frightening medical condition as a boy, his own stellar football career at Minnesota from 1912 to 1915, his service in a previous world war, and his nomadic path of a half-dozen coaching jobs in a

Head coach Bernie Bierman (center) and athletic director Frank McCormick (second from right) meet with high school coaches from Ortonville, Minnesota. Bierman's success at the University of Minnesota drew wide admiration across the state. *Big Stone County Historical Society*

decade and a half—had prepared him for the adversity he was about to
face in 1941.

* * *

Bernard W. Bierman, born March 11, 1894, spent his childhood on the
move. Due to his father's business career as a merchant, the family
relocated at least five times before Bierman's fifteenth birthday, bouncing between the rural Minnesota communities of Springfield, Waseca,
Paynesville, and Litchfield, with a brief out-of-state stop in Oklahoma
and another short stint in Minneapolis. Bierman attended eighth grade
in the state's largest city, before the family ultimately drifted back to
Litchfield, a small town about sixty miles west of the Twin Cities.[14]
During these various moves, young Bierman's athletic career started
slowly because of a serious bone condition, possibly osteomyelitis,[15] that
relegated him to crutches and sometimes left him confined to bed
altogether. He rarely, if ever, spoke publicly about the disease in his
later life, but it must have irritated him as he developed an early love
for sports during grade school.

    After a series of serious operations, Bierman overcame his physical
ailments by the time he reached adolescence, transforming from a sick-
ly young boy into a speedy and nimble teenager. Starting in 1908 at
Litchfield High School, he played halfback, fullback, and quarterback
for an enthusiastic young coach named Archibald Robertson, a former
collegiate track star with the Gophers. Robertson modeled his high
school offensive system after the one championed by fabled University
of Minnesota head football coach Dr. Henry L. Williams, whose success
since the turn of the century had earned his program the nickname
"Giants of the North." Williams, a serious-natured medical doctor who
once tutored at Yale under the "Father of American Football" Walter
Camp, established a powerhouse in Minneapolis with multiple Western
Conference titles and left an indelible legacy on the sport with his
various innovations.[16] His invention of the "Minnesota shift," where
players changed formations moments before the center snapped the
ball, proved revolutionary as one variation of a now-basic football ma-
neuver, and he also served as one of the most prominent voices in the
Midwest to call for the legalization of the forward pass.[17]

Having already learned Williams' "Minnesota shift" under Archibald Robertson at Litchfield High, Bierman grew enamored with the idea of one day playing football for his state university. "In those days, Minnesota had a national reputation in football," Bierman later said. "Dr. Williams had turned out several champions and to make the grade on one of the Gopher elevens under this famous coach was the ambition of every youngster who played high school football in our state."[18]

Without hesitation, Bierman left for Minneapolis in the fall of 1912 to join the freshman football team at the University of Minnesota, where his older brother, Al, had already played for two years. After adding some weight to his weakly 160-pound frame, Bierman landed a spot on "Doc" Williams' varsity team the next year as a nineteen-year-old sophomore and finally carved out a role for himself at the end position during the 1913 season. Following Al's graduation, Williams slid Bierman into his brother's halfback spot, where he grew into a regular starter on a one-loss team in 1914 before emerging as an All-American for the "Giants of the North" during his senior year, which saw the Gophers finish undefeated with only one tie. Newspapers splashed Bierman's face across the state throughout the fall of 1915, including the *Minneapolis Sunday Tribune,* which featured a black-and-white photograph of Bierman on the front page in October after he scored one of the Gophers' six touchdowns against North Dakota. "Bernie Bierman Looked Mighty Good Yesterday,"[19] the accompanying headline read, as Bierman sported a wide smile from ear to ear while crouched in a two-point stance. His teammates named him a captain by the end of the month, dubbing him "Bashful Bierman" because of his reserved nature.[20]

During his four years at the University of Minnesota, the most consequential moment for Bierman happened away from the football field. At some point, he met a Kappa Alpha Theta sorority member named Clara McKenzie, a native of Havre, Montana, and the perfect foil to his stoic personality. It was the beginning of their lifelong love story, one that would influence the Minnesota football program for decades to come.[21] "The old Minnesota players are absolutely unanimous in their love for Clara Bierman," wrote James P. Quirk in his 1984 book, *The Golden Years.* "She was everything that Bernie was not—open, bubbly, emotional, verbal—the one who remembered every player by name."[22]

After receiving his diploma in 1916, Bierman accepted a job as a teacher and coach at Butte High School in Clara's home state of Montana, capturing a state championship in his first season. Then, in April 1917, America's entrance into World War I interrupted his budding coaching career. "Like any youngster," Bierman said, "I couldn't get into a uniform fast enough."[23] He dropped his whole life in Butte and reported to an officers' training camp in Quantico, Virginia, where he rose to the rank of captain in July 1918 before heading to Cuba with a fleet of more than two thousand other United States Marines. Bierman did not see any combat in Cuba, but he managed to find some time to play pickup football on the base as he continued to keep an eye on the future. Impressed by his state championship at Butte High School, the University of Montana wrote letters to Bierman after the war ended in November 1918 to gauge his interest in a college-level job. "If the position was to be offered to me tonight," Bierman responded in May 1919, "I would accept."[24] A month later, Bierman signed a contract worth $2,000 annually.

Over the next three years, Bierman's football teams at Montana experienced a range of successes and failures, winning eight games, losing ten, and tying three times. "He was without a doubt a competent coach—probably the best we ever had," school president Charles H. Clapp later wrote. "Although quiet and almost retiring, he was forceful and certainly a leader—perhaps somewhat of a martinet. I know that some of his players thought he drove them too hard. My only real complaint was that he seemed gloomy."[25]

President Clapp must have sensed his head coach's unhappiness. Newly married to Clara and making the modern equivalent of roughly $30,000 a year adjusted for inflation, Bierman craved stability and higher earning potential as he prepared to start a family. After three years at Montana, Bierman informed his supervisor that he would resign as head coach, so that he could return home to Minnesota as a municipal bond salesman. That new lifestyle took an immediate toll. Responsible for a northwest sales territory, he traveled on the road constantly with a schedule even more demanding than college football—much to Clara's dismay. She thought her husband should return to coaching the sport he loved so dearly. In 1923, he accepted a part-time job as an assistant at Tulane University in New Orleans, where a former Gopher teammate named Clark Shaughnessy served as head coach. That opportunity led Bierman to another head coaching job at Mississippi A&M (now Mississippi State) in 1925, before he returned to New Orleans in 1927 as the head coach at Tulane, where he would spend "five of the happiest years of my life."[26]

Bierman's subsequent tenure with the Green Wave, though wildly successful by the end, did not run so smoothly in the beginning. Shortly before the start of his second season, Bierman blasted Tulane leadership for what he perceived as misplaced priorities. "Studies," he said, "should not be sacrificed for athletics." Bierman then made a bold threat to the administration. "Unless those in control of Tulane, and particular[ly] in control of her athletics, thinks as I do and will cooperate with the purpose of putting athletics on the above basis," Bierman wrote, "I wish to be relieved from the obligations of my contract; such release to take effect at the end of the college year."[27]

The threat must have worked. Bierman never resigned and instead led Tulane to a winning season in 1928, followed by the finest season of Bierman's career to date in 1929—an undefeated campaign that caught the attention of his alma mater Minnesota, which needed a head coach after the departure of Clarence Spears to Oregon. Ultimately, the administration declined to pursue Bierman and settled on Herbert "Fritz" Crisler, an assistant at the University of Chicago, to lead the Minnesota football program in 1930. If Bierman himself felt stung, he did not show it. Regrouping for a fourth season with the Green Wave, his team lost just one game in 1930 and shut out six of nine opponents.

Weeks later, in the thick of winter in December 1930, Bierman's old college coach Henry L. Williams fell gravely ill back home in Minneapolis. Doctors admitted the sixty-one-year-old that month to Swedish Hospital, a facility in the Elliot Park neighborhood, after he showed signs of heart disease. One day, while resting in his hospital room, Williams received a visit from his former fullback Clark Shaughnessy, at that point about two decades removed from his playing days with the Gophers. According to an account written by Shaughnessy for the Associated Press and published in several U.S. newspapers, the two discussed football for two hours that day in Williams' hospital room, at which point the conversation inevitably turned to the current state of the Minnesota program. Following Williams' departure a decade earlier, the university had cycled through three head football coaches, including the most recent hire, Fritz Crisler. A losing record in his first season in 1930 did not help Crisler's cause at all—not with alumni, not with fans, and not with Doc Williams. As he sat in that hospital bed in Minneapolis, shortly after the 1930 season, Williams reportedly made a bold plea: "Minnesota should get Bernie Bierman," he told Clark Shaughnessy, "and put him in charge of football. Until they do, they will never win a championship."[28] It was one of the Doc's final requests, prior to his death in June 1931.

His words may have held some influence. Months later, after Bierman led Tulane to an outstanding 1931 campaign and earned a Rose Bowl invitation, the University of Minnesota formally announced that the former Gopher captain would replace Fritz Crisler as the head football coach for the 1932 season. "I am making no predictions," Bierman said at a testimonial dinner before a crowd of six hundred at the Nicollet Hotel in January 1932, "but I will attempt to build football teams on the foundations already laid so well by Dr. H. L. Williams and Fritz Crisler."[29]

✿ ✿ ✿

Doc Williams did not live long enough to see his cherished pupil lead the football program at Minnesota, but he would have been immeasurably proud of Bernie Bierman's accomplishments over the next nine years. He also surely would have smiled at the coaching staff Bierman assembled, since it consisted almost entirely of Williams' favorite understudies. Ends coach Bert Baston captained his 1916 team, line coach George Hauser served in the same capacity in 1917, and longtime scout Sig Harris played quarterback for Williams in the early 1900s.

By 1941, Bierman and these trusted assistants had firmly reestablished the culture of success that Williams first created from scratch at the turn of the twentieth century—which is precisely why the coaches were so shocked to see sloppy effort during spring practices in April and May of 1941. The miserable performance in the spring scrimmage on May 10 was totally uncharacteristic for a program that had dominated the previous decade of college football with four mythical national championships. "It pleases veteran followers of Minnesota's gridiron affairs immensely to see the recognition given their alma mater since Bernie Bierman took over the coaching reins in 1932," *Minneapolis Tribune* sports editor George Barton wrote after Bierman's coaching staff brought home another title in 1940. "My, how times have changed under Bierman!"[30]

The Silver Fox never lost sight of his roots. During the height of his program's success in the 1930s, he even dedicated his co-authored book, *Winning Football,* to Williams, describing his late coach as a "brilliant student of football, a great teacher and a fine gentleman."[31] Drawing on the Doc's lessons, Bierman installed an adaptation of his mentor's "Minnesota shift" out of the single-wing formation—the same scheme he had been running since the first day of practice at Butte High School in 1916—and labeled it the "Minnesota system." Forging his own identity as a coach, Bierman created a list of twelve "fundamental rules"[32] for his new generation of Gophers to follow, which emphasized teamwork over star power and an unapologetic commitment to basic fundamentals like blocking and tackling.

Although Bierman incorporated some special passing plays, he designed his single-wing offense primarily to run the football. Minnesota's version of the single-wing, a popular formation that traced back to the great Pop Warner in the early 1900s, featured an unbalanced line that usually added extra manpower to the right of the center. Under this structure, the center would snap the ball several yards into the backfield to either a halfback or fullback, giving him the option to run or pass as he set the rest of the play in motion. The quarterback served purely as a blocking back in this run-heavy system, while "ends" blocked outside the tackles and ran passing routes. A modern fan might draw comparisons between the single-wing and the "Wildcat" offense, since both use some form of deception to keep defenses guessing as to who might handle the football. "My boys at Minnesota, once they acquired the knack," Bierman later said, "loved to block mostly and they fit in perfectly with my scheme of things."[33] His tenacious tackles, guards, and centers played the most important roles in the whole machine, by opening paths for the ball carriers on offense and stuffing opposing tailbacks on defense. Although weight estimates were inexact, Minnesota's linemen often ranked among the heaviest in college football on an annual basis.

Bierman's ferocious ground attack and intimidating style of play became the envy of every program in America, leaving an unforgettable mark on the fans fortunate enough to witness the Gophers with their own eyes. "Minnesota football teams have always been known for their brawn," Vice President Hubert H. Humphrey said in a speech before a College All-Star game in 1965, "especially during their golden years of Bernie Bierman when I was going to school."[34] During this so-called "golden" period, the Gophers produced several All-Americans—including future College Hall of Fame inductees Pug Lund and Ed Widseth—and churned out some of the nation's most dynamic offensive and defensive stars. All of them played both ways during this era of college football, although their defensive positions were much less defined and coaches did not regularly make use of terms like "safety," "cornerback," or "linebacker." On offense, the concept of a "wide receiver" was also in its infancy.

Remarkably, Bierman built his program without the ability to offer athletic scholarships. The Big Ten Conference, in stark contrast to the looser policies of other leagues, strictly prohibited such practices, although it did allow schools to help players find legitimate paid employment as a form of financial assistance.[35] Bierman was never cited for any violations while coaching at Minnesota, helping him avoid the major scandals that occurred even in those days, like bombshell revelations in 1940 that unearthed widespread corruption and illegal recruiting in the Pacific Coast Conference.[36] Many in the coaching community, including Bierman, publicly condemned such cheating and fought hard against the growing corporatization and exploitation of the game. The University of Chicago took the most drastic measure in 1939 when it dropped football altogether in protest of corruption, before formally departing the Big Ten athletic league seven years later. (Despite dropping the league's total number of football teams to nine starting in 1940, it was still popularly known as the "Big Ten" among fans, coaches, and journalists.)[37]

"Here is the truth and the whole truth, so help me," Bierman said in a speech before the 1941 season. "The Gophers have managed to hit the championship heights pretty consistently in the last decade with squads that were never recruited or subsidized. We've done it without the benefit of football scholarships, loans, well-heeled alumni or other commonly effective methods."[38] Unlike some of his abrasive old-school peers, who instilled a tyrannical, win-at-all-costs mentality, Bierman took a more measured approach and genuinely enjoyed teaching the game to young players. But they didn't always find him very approachable. "Bierman is not the coach to walk over to a discouraged or bewildered boy, put his arm around his shoulder and work out a problem with words. Minnesota football players have often admitted that they never could get 'real close' to Bierman," *Esquire* observed. "Instead, they have more or less feared him because of his strictness; they have respected him for his knowledge of the game and his fairness."[39]

Despite his distant personality, Bierman earned a reputation as a no-nonsense winner and enjoyed wide name recognition as one of the titans of his profession. From an exposure standpoint, his program benefited tremendously from the invention of radio, something that would have seemed unfathomable during the days of Doc Williams. The emergence of this state-of-the-art technology in the 1920s created a whole new base of followers over the next few decades and pumped college football—oftentimes spotlighting games featuring Minnesota—into millions of American homes, through NBC, CBS, and Mutual Broadcasting System network coverage as well as local stations. The new mass medium brought the sport to life on an unprecedented scale and familiarized fans with stars like Michigan's Tom Harmon and TCU's Davey O'Brien. In December 1939, radio affiliates across the nation carried the broadcast of a rivalry game between two undefeated teams, USC and UCLA, played before more than 100,000 people at the Los Angeles Memorial Coliseum. The contest ended in a scoreless tie, but the large crowd and national radio publicity helped introduce an American audience to a young UCLA halfback, Jackie Robinson, about eight years before he would break Major League Baseball's color barrier. "Robinson has it, running wide!" an announcer boasted, the fans roaring as Robinson scrambled for a first down.[40] Despite the lack of scoring, the *California Eagle*, an African American newspaper in Los Angeles, called the game "one of the best and most thrilling" of the year.[41]

In the Upper Midwest, youngsters idolized Minnesota's football team and felt a special connection to the squad through local radio broadcasts heard as far away as the Dakotas. Many players on the 1941 Minnesota team, in fact, said they developed an early love for the Gophers by listening to games on the radio in their childhood bedrooms, kitchens, and living rooms. It was even a Twin Cities radio announcer, the legendary Halsey Hall, who so famously started calling Minnesota the "Golden" Gophers during the 1930s while vividly describing the players' all-gold uniforms.

With a national brand firmly established, the Golden Gophers' season opener in 1941, against the University of Washington in Seattle, would be featured on NBC Radio as network executives clamored to broadcast one of America's premiere college football programs. "Exclusive NBC Blue broadcast of the Game of the Week," alerted one radio listing in a Utah newspaper. "Minnesota, undefeated national champion last year."[42]

Bierman's program had reclaimed its position atop the college football universe in 1940 with that undefeated record, bouncing back from a rare 3–4–1 mark in 1939—the first losing year Bierman and his coaches had ever endured at Minnesota. The Gophers treated fans to an exhilarating 1940 season, filled with a number of wild comebacks and narrow victories. They mounted rallies to defeat Washington, Northwestern, and Wisconsin, handed Nebraska its only regular-season loss outside of the Rose Bowl, and beat Ohio State on the road in Columbus in front of sixty-three thousand people. Still, there was no bigger moment than the one that came on the disgusting, rainy afternoon of November 9, 1940, during the sixth game of the 1940 campaign. Minnesota, gunning for a national title and ranked second in the Associated Press poll, trailed 6–0 against third-ranked Michigan at Memorial Stadium. With everything hanging in the balance, the Gophers opted to call a reverse out of the single-wing in the second quarter, placing the fate of the 1940 season in the hands of a junior named Bruce Smith. His next move—hailed to this day as one of the most famous plays in school history—guaranteed his status as an all-time Minnesota legend and set him on a path for even greater accomplishments in 1941.

2

FARIBAULT FLASH

America could not stop talking about that play, the one where Bruce Smith defied logic and made a fool of eleven Michigan Wolverines after a torrential downpour in Minneapolis. With more than sixty thousand fans cowering nervously in the stands of Memorial Stadium and thousands more listening with curiosity on NBC and CBS national radio, Smith took the reverse handoff from All-American George "Sonny" Franck, charged to his left through a gaping hole provided by his blockers, and broke free for an eighty-yard touchdown. The extra point gave Minnesota a 7–6 lead in the second quarter that it would never relinquish, clearing a path for the Gophers to finish undefeated in 1940 and claim the national and Big Ten championships. Michigan senior Tom Harmon won the Heisman Trophy that year, but he remained winless against Minnesota during his career and later called it the regret of a lifetime.

With Harmon's collegiate playing days over, the nation's focus shifted to Bruce Smith in 1941 as he returned for his senior season. The heroic touchdown-in-the-mud, heard by listeners that afternoon on multiple radio stations in every U.S. market, made him a household name among college football fans. "Bruce Smith of Minnesota," Grantland Rice wrote in September 1941, "is almost sure to be one of the great backs of the year."[1] Writers in Big Ten country, like Bert McGrane of *The Des Moines Register*, agreed wholeheartedly. "With a thunderbolt halfback like Bruce Smith who already has proved himself one of the greatest in the game," McGrane said, "observers can't see just who is going to ambush these unchecked Gophers."[2] The press fawned over him. The fans adored him. His teammates voted him captain.

Yet nobody loved Bruce Smith like the city of Faribault did. "This town is Bruce Smith conscious," the *Faribault Journal*'s Johnny Kerr wrote during the summer of 1941. "Bruce, a Faribault lad, is captain of the Golden Gophers for 1941 and all his fellow townsmen want to attend the home games."[3]

Smith felt that love. Instead of remaining on campus that summer, he found a job at the local highway department in Faribault and trained twice a day during the scorching months of June, July, and August. None of this was surprising to anyone who knew him. Smith adored his hometown and valued his time with family and friends, so much that after every football game in the fall he liked to go back to Faribault for the remainder of the weekend to lounge on the couch and eat his favorite apple pie with cheese topping. He felt more comfortable there than anywhere else in the world, and his neighbors buzzed at the presence of a celebrity whose name and face had been plastered on newspapers across the country. When the *Journal*'s Johnny Kerr conducted an informal poll of the most prominent citizens in Faribault that summer, almost everyone in town responded with the same answer: Bruce Smith.

❀ ❀ ❀

The roughly fifteen thousand folks living in this historic riverfront trade post, situated about fifty miles south of the Twin Cities, must not have been totally surprised that a Smith kid made a name for himself. Bruce's grandfather, a force in Republican politics named George L. Smith, served as Faribault's mayor from 1907 to 1910. Bruce's father, Lucius, practiced law and worked as the city and county attorney after playing football for Dr. Henry L. Williams at the University of Minnesota. And when Bruce came along in the winter of 1920, his birth announcement made the front page of the *Faribault Journal*. "Smith," the blurb read simply and to the point. "To Mr. and Mrs. Lucius Smith, on Sunday, Feb. 8, a son."[4]

Lucius and Emma's five kids—George, Olive, Bruce, Wayne, and June—grew up in a quaint two-story home on Division Street in Fari-

Bruce Smith, a senior captain from Minnesota, entered the 1941 season as one of the top halfbacks in college football. *Rice County Historical Society Collection, Faribault, Minnesota.*

bault, not far from the Cannon and Straight Rivers that cut through the heart of town. Nestled on top of a grassy hill with a porch overlooking the neighborhood, the property was not overly lavish, but it provided just enough space for a bustling family of seven.

As a child, Bruce impressed his parents with a "sunny disposition," according to his father. "I can never remember him having a temper tantrum," Lucius noted, "nor can I remember a time when he showed serious anger. He was the most relaxed person I have ever known."[5] Bruce could play the piano by ear without any formal training, and he also displayed some quirky interests, including an obsession with bird watching. "He had a thing about pigeons. He loved pigeons," youngest sister June recalled during an interview at her suburban Twin Cities home in August 2019. "He had a whole flock of pigeons that he managed in the backyard."[6] One time, June said, Bruce wanted so badly to fly like the birds that he tried to do so himself, leading him to fall flat on the family's front porch as he learned a valuable lesson about the limitations of human flight. Soon enough, he would gravitate to sports, which was a way of life in the Smith household. It buzzed constantly with athletic activities, ranging from makeshift football and basketball games in the living room to shot put competitions in the backyard. Bruce and his siblings could only hope they might play college sports one day like their father.[7]

A decade before Bruce's birth, Lucius Smith spent one year at Carleton College in Northfield before transferring to the University of Minnesota, where he performed a versatile role at guard and end for some very good teams under Doc Williams in 1910 and 1911 (coinciding with Bernie Bierman's older brother Al, but just barely missing Bernie's arrival by one semester). In December 1911, local newspapers described the son of the Faribault mayor as "one of the best all [a]round athletes this city has ever turned out."[8] An accompanying picture on the front page of the *Faribault Journal* showed a youthful Lucius barely breaking a smile, arms crossed, with his flowing blond hair and facial features bearing a striking resemblance to his future son.

Although he developed into a steady football player, Lucius originally caught Doc Williams' attention through another sport. Williams, a former world-class hurdler himself at Yale, scoured the Minnesota track team in 1910 for football talent as he looked to compete for a fifth Western Conference championship since the turn of the century. He identified Lucius as a strong candidate for the gridiron, even though the young Faribault native had never played a down of football in his life. It did not matter. With Lucius contributing at two positions, the Gophers held their first six opponents scoreless in 1910. It set up a seventh and final game in Ann Arbor against Michigan—a season finale that Minnesota football fans would reference for generations to come.

Lucius found himself out of place that day because Doc Williams asked him to replace an injured teammate at right tackle, an unfamiliar position that he had not practiced. Minnesota lost 6–0 to the Wolverines—with the only touchdown coming right through Lucius' side on defense. "I felt responsible for the loss and devoutly wished for the chance to play Michigan again," Lucius later remembered in *The Game Breaker*, a 1977 book about his son's life. "That chance never came. My last year of football was 1911 and we did not play Michigan that year."[9] Over the years, a folk tale emerged, claiming that young Lucius vowed from that day forward to have a son who could avenge his loss to Michigan. The story was somewhat of an exaggeration. Although Lucius certainly felt extra motivation for Bruce to play well against Michigan due to his own personal defeat, he maintained he never made an actual vow of any sort before his son was born.

Lucius did, however, instill the principles of Gopher football into Bruce at a very young age. One of Bruce's earliest memories at Memorial Stadium came with his older brother, George, just a few years after the stadium opened. During a game in the late 1920s, a wide-eyed Bruce and George seized the opportunity—seemingly once-in-a-lifetime at that point—to tour the field after a game that featured a miserable rainstorm. They did not care about the condition of the field—not when they were walking on the same grass as their heroes. One of the boys noticed a cleat mark in the mud and carved it out with a knife. Lucius seemed puzzled. "Why Dad," George and Bruce explained, "that might be Nagurski's."[10] They were referring to the giant foot of Minnesota's Bronko Nagurski, a larger-than-life superstar who excelled for the Gophers from 1927 to 1929 and later enjoyed a Hall of Fame professional career with the Chicago Bears. Eager to savor the memory of their beloved idol, Bruce and George preserved the cleat mark and brought it back to Faribault as a keepsake. It remained in the Smith home for decades.

Young Bruce Smith, nicknamed "Boo" by his family, came of age as a Gopher football fan in the mid-1920s and early 1930s during the Clarence Spears and Fritz Crisler eras—both future Hall of Fame coaches—but his fondest years as a fan came when the school hired Bernie Bierman for the 1932 season. Smith would have been about twelve years old at the time, and he loved Bierman's early teams at Minnesota almost as much as he loved big Bronko Nagurski. Smith also had a football role model in his own household: George Smith, his charismatic older brother and the namesake of his grandfather. George played at Faribault High School for a well-known coach named Win Brockmeyer, a former Gopher halfback himself and coincidentally an old teammate of Nagurski (Bronko was a "pillar of concrete," Brockmeyer remembered).[11] When Bruce joined the varsity team in eighth grade, it gave him the unique opportunity to play in the same backfield as George for the next two years. In 1935, George followed in father Lucius' footsteps and joined Bernie Bierman's football program at Minnesota, leaving Bruce alone as the next star of the Faribault Falcons.

Bruce blossomed into a tremendous football player at the age of sixteen, and his extra playing experience dating back to eighth grade gave him an advantage. By his junior year in 1936, he was dominant on both sides of the ball for Faribault. Although no official statistics survived from that era of high school football, Brockmeyer would later say that Smith carried most of the load on offense, tallied at least ten tackles a game on defense, and usually nabbed a few interceptions, too. "He was as close to a perfect football player," Brockmeyer said, "as I have had or seen in the high school ranks."[12] The Falcons nearly won the conference, known as the Big Eight, during Smith's junior year, narrowly missing out only because of a 7–7 tie with Rochester in the middle of the fall.

Brockmeyer left Faribault after the 1936 season to take another high school coaching job in Wausau, Wisconsin, where he would remain for the next three and a half decades. Faribault replaced him with Mal Eiken, another former Gopher football star who had emerged as one of Bernie Bierman's top offensive threats during the undefeated 1935 season.[13] Expectations for the young Eiken were sky-high at Faribault High School in his first season heading into the fall of 1937, mostly because football experts around the state recognized that he had a first-rate talent on his squad. Growing into a 185-pound stalwart, Bruce

Smith could overpower tacklers with his size or evade them with his agility, boasting a lethal combination that few high school football players in the state of Minnesota could match. The *Minneapolis Tribune* predicted Smith would probably enroll at his father's alma mater to play with his brother after his high school career ended. "He is rated one of the finest halfbacks in the state," the paper told readers in the Twin Cities, "by game officials and Big Eight conference mentors in addition to his own coach."[14]

During his senior year, Smith did not disappoint. Playing in front of packed crowds on Friday evenings under the lights at Teepee Tonka Park in Faribault, he battled through injuries to lead his Falcons to a 6–0 start as one of only thirty-two undefeated teams remaining in the state. Despite a loss in late October to Northfield, the press described Smith as "brilliant"—and he proved worthy of that label by helping the Falcons win their final two games against Waseca and Mankato.[15] June Smith, who was about six years younger than Bruce, attended most of her brother's games in high school and admired his athleticism. "He was just really good," said June, who was a stellar athlete herself. "Just like when we were playing basketball. He could make you miss."[16] Smith's peers recognized him nearly unanimously as an All–Big Eight halfback, and his classmates at home dubbed him the "Perfect Specimen" in his high school yearbook.[17] The nickname referred to his football talents, sure, but also his movie-star looks and easygoing personality. "He was, of course, everybody's idol," said Millie Bowers Johnson, who graduated from Faribault High School a year behind Smith. "He was just a really neat guy and everybody thought he was, you know, the 'cat's meow,' so to speak." Johnson recalled the thrill of riding home in the same car as Smith after a football game at Teepee Tonka Park. "I've got that in my diary, written down," she said.[18] It was an experience she would remember for the rest of her life.

✽ ✽ ✽

Due to Big Ten Conference regulations, Bernie Bierman likely would not have actively recruited Bruce Smith, nor would other programs have necessarily courted him—if they were following the rules. Regardless, it does not appear that Smith ever considered any options other than Minnesota. His father and both of his high school coaches had all played there. His brother George currently played there, although a knee injury would soon cut his career short. And as one of the top prep players in the state of Minnesota, Smith could easily find a spot at his flagship university if he desired.

With Faribault spreading stories of his athletic prowess far and wide, Smith stepped on campus in the fall of 1938 as one of the most celebrated freshman players the Gophers had seen in a long time. In the September 27, 1938 edition of the *Minneapolis Tribune*, a photograph of Smith in punt formation appeared on Page Fourteen. "At the left above is the Faribault Flash, Bruce Smith," the newspaper wrote, "who is regarded as an unusual college prospect."[19] Even with more than one hundred players vying for attention, Smith stood out among them all on Dallas Ward's freshman team in 1938, both physically and mentally. Coaches described him as Big Ten ready, and it appeared he would contribute immediately to the varsity once eligible as a sophomore. Smith wasted no time. At the ripe age of nineteen, he found himself fielding the opening kickoff of the 1939 season against the University of Arizona, returning the kick for a modest four yards in his Memorial Stadium debut. He now shared the same field as his heroes, on the same grass that Bronko Nagurski once roamed. "Just realizing that I was at last to play for Minnesota," Smith would later remember, "did something to me I can't explain."[20] The Gophers blitzed Arizona 62–0 that day behind a strong performance from the Faribault Flash. "Bruce Smith, heralded sophomore back, lived up to his advance notice," the AP wrote, "scoring twice, running elusively in end sweeps and passing in one touchdown drive."[21]

Smith seemed to get better with every passing week. By the end of the 1939 season, he placed as the third-leading rusher on the team and second-leading pass catcher, helping him earn honorable mention honors on the Associated Press All-American team. Smith had played a key role in the backfield in all three of Minnesota's wins, including a 23–6 victory over Wisconsin. In that game, the sophomore halfback scored the final touchdown of the 1939 season on an eleven-yard burst through the Badger secondary. Smith's late-season surge carried him into a fabulous junior season in 1940, when he led the national champions in both rushing and passing yards—though still somewhat in the shadow of All-American Sonny Franck, who finished third in Heisman Trophy voting.

Now Franck had graduated and joined the New York Giants. Minnesota would be Bruce Smith's team in 1941, and outsiders would accept no less than an All-American season from Smith and another national championship for his Gophers. In *Look* magazine, George Kirksey of the United Press proclaimed Smith the preseason Back of the Year.

Smith remained unaffected by the glowing reviews. "Yes, I know what they're saying," he told the *St. Paul Pioneer Press*. "But I hope I'm sensible enough to realize that those fellows have a job to do. They have to write up someone. There's no use thinking about it."[22] Smith did not want his individual accolades to define the 1941 Golden Gophers. This was no one-man team.

3

THE SUPPORTING CAST

Even if he refused to acknowledge it, Bruce Smith entered 1941 as the face of the Minnesota program. No doubt about it. He was the team's lone captain and unquestioned senior leader, after all. But, in the exaggerated words of one Ohio sports columnist, the Golden Gophers seemed to have "50 other potential All-Americans" on the roster, too.[1] Indeed, at the tackle position, they already boasted a reigning All-American: Urban Leroy Odson.

With his massive six-foot-three, 247-pound frame, Odson needed no introduction to the national experts. The tough farm kid from South Dakota terrorized the Big Ten as a junior and captured both All-Conference and All-American honors on the 1940 national championship team. The accolades brought great pride to Odson's hometown of Clark, a tiny agricultural community about eighty miles from the Minnesota border, where the Chamber of Commerce threw Odson a celebratory banquet at the high school auditorium in January 1941. Halfback Joe Mernik and fullback Bob Sweiger traveled all the way from Minneapolis to express public gratitude for their favorite blocker. "One of the best-liked fellows on the team,"[2] they told the audience of more than two hundred people, which included Odson's cheerful parents, Edward and Gladys.

Had fate charted a different course, Odson may have found himself thousands of miles away from the family farm in Clark, instead in the Deep South, playing college football for the University of Mississippi. A doctor in South Dakota, recruiting on behalf of the school thanks to lax

Southeastern Conference policies, worked aggressively to convince Odson that Oxford, Mississippi, was the right fit for him. The doctor did
not know that Odson had an uncle from Amboy, Minnesota, a little
town just twenty-five miles south of Mankato, who turned out to be a
much better recruiter. At his uncle's urging, Odson ignored the doctor's
pleas to enroll at Mississippi and instead signed up to play freshman
football for Minnesota in September 1937, along with 128 other first-
year hopefuls under freshman coach Dallas Ward.[3]

Odson, one of a handful of players hailing from the Dakotas, spent
his first day of practice listening to Ward teach fundamentals but soon
drew the attention of the varsity staff. The coaches heard tales from his
days in South Dakota, and there was no way they could miss a big fellow
who loomed so high over his teammates. "Urban," Bob Beebe of the
Star wrote before the 1938 season, "is a very large young man."[4] Odson
had always been big for his age. Naturally, he played both ways at tackle
for the Clark Comets in high school and earned a combined ten letters
in football, basketball, and track. By the time he entered college, the
Minnesota coaches admired his size; rarely had they ever seen a tackle
like him. Odson reportedly wore the largest shoulder pads in school
history, described by equipment manager Oscar Munson as "size extra-
extra large."[5]

He quickly developed a nickname on campus, though it had nothing
to do with his stature. Odson's teammates called him "Fireman," because he lived on the second floor of the aging Fire Station 19 across
the street from Memorial Stadium. It wasn't a fancy arrangement.
Alarm bells probably rang at all hours of the morning and night inside
that cramped, nineteenth-century brick house, and it would have been
remarkable if Odson ever managed to catch a good night of sleep.
Crammed into a military-style dorm with little to no privacy, the chaos
of the firehouse and city life often drove the towering South Dakotan to
the edge. Seeking peace and quiet, Odson sometimes liked to hop on
the streetcar and head for the Minnesota farmlands, where he could
complete his football training regimen in solitude. In the end, though,
he always returned to charming Fire Station 19. For all of its faults,
living at a firehouse carried some perks. The firefighters, for example,
gave Odson free meals—and didn't even make him fight fires to pay for
them. Any extra spending power would help, since the Fireman's upbringing on a farm during the Depression years left him with very little

Bruce Smith kneels front and center in a practice uniform, joined by teammates from the 1941 Minnesota squad. Other players include Bob Sweiger (first in line on the left behind Smith), Butch Levy (first in line on the right behind Smith), Dick Wildung (second in line on the left), and Urban Odson (second from back, on the right). *Courtesy of University of Minnesota Archives, University of Minnesota–Twin Cities*

disposable income. He was likely one of the poorer players on the Minnesota football team. To support himself through college, Odson worked on and off at a Coca-Cola plant.[6]

On the field for the Gophers, Odson did not appear in any games in 1938 (preserving a year of future eligibility through a redshirt), but he made his presence known as a sophomore in 1939. "It also might be mentioned," wrote Bob Beebe in another praising article after the third game of the season, "that big Urban Odson came in late in the game and rudely tossed the Purdue backs for a few losses. He too may be on his way."[7]

He certainly was. As a junior in 1940, Odson started every game at right tackle and played almost sixty minutes both ways the entire season, save for a few short breaks. Odson developed into a mainstay for the national champions. His size and skill set helped Minnesota execute the single-wing, run-heavy offense to perfection, and on defense, Odson routinely found himself charging through opposing backfields to bring runners down for huge losses. In the Michigan game, Odson played a key role in containing soon-to-be Heisman Trophy winner Tom Harmon.

Standing out both offensively and defensively, Odson was selected as an All-American tackle after the 1940 season by at least three publications: *Newsweek*, *Liberty*, and the International News Service, enough to qualify Odson as a "consensus" choice. On the INS team, Odson and Frankie Albert of Stanford were the only juniors. The rest were seniors, including Minnesota's Sonny Franck. Seniors simply dominated college football in those days due to their physical maturity, so it was quite notable that Odson earned so many accolades as a junior. Coincidentally, Urban Odson had an even younger friend and teammate on the other side of the line: sophomore Dick Wildung, a blossoming star from southwestern Minnesota.

✿ ✿ ✿

Dick Wildung spent his teenage years in Luverne, Minnesota, a town of about three thousand people only thirty miles from Sioux Falls, South Dakota. The second-oldest of five siblings, Dick spent most of his time either obsessively running sprints on the high school football field or helping his parents, Adahlia and Harold, run their dry goods store on Main Street. Adahlia, known as "Dale" by her family, handled the majority of the work due to her husband's deteriorating health. Harold Wildung had fought in France as an army sergeant during the First World War, and he suffered long-running effects from exposure to mustard gas at the hands of the German soldiers. His series of strokes began in the mid-1930s, around the time his son Dick started high school.[8]

Norbert Manion, the head football coach of the Luverne Cardinals, vividly remembered his first encounter with Dick Wildung as a high school freshman in 1935. Describing him as a "short little guy and pretty heavy," Manion tossed the fourteen-year-old Wildung into a scrimmage against the high school varsity squad to gauge his skills. "I saw a couple of the bigger boys roughing him up pretty much, but I noticed Dick just grinned that shy smile of his—and on the next play set the boys back on their heels," Manion said. "I figured right then he'd play an awful lot of football some day."[9] After the powerhouse Cardinals finished undefeated in 1935 and 1936, Wildung led the team in tackles as a junior in 1937 and then captained the team in 1938 as a guard, tackle, and even fullback at times. During his senior year, he earned "All-Outstate"[10] honors from the Twin Cities press, prompting Norbert Manion to remark that Wildung was easily the best lineman he had ever witnessed at the prep level. The competitive, dark-haired Wildung also excelled under Manion on the basketball court, and had in fact crossed paths with Faribault's Bruce Smith at the state tournament in Minneapolis during the spring of 1938. But football was the game he truly loved.

After graduating from Luverne High School as salutatorian in May 1939, Wildung briefly considered attending junior college in nearby Worthington, but he changed his mind after the coaching staff at the University of Minnesota expressed alarm. "Knowing the set up here as we do," freshman coach Dallas Ward wrote in a letter to Wildung a month after his high school graduation, "we all agreed that in the long run you would be much better off to attend the University of Minnesota starting next fall."[11]

Dick Wildung would never forget one of his earliest interactions with the incomparable Bernie Bierman. "Okay now," the head coach explained to young Dick during his freshman year. "I want you to go over and hit that blocking dummy, two hundred times in the right shoulder, and two hundred times in the left shoulder. *As hard as you can hit it.*"[12] The stern coaching might have intimidated some freshmen, but not Wildung. Instead of wilting under Bierman's demanding style, Wildung thrived. Norbert Manion had taught him well at Luverne High School. "After Dick was out for practice two weeks, I found that I was unable to tell him anything about the tackle position he didn't already know," Dallas Ward said. "From then on, I let him develop himself."[13]

Wildung soon won the attention of the varsity coaching staff for reasons much different than Urban Odson. Although he stood a sturdy six feet tall and weighed two hundred pounds, built with a compact frame and strong lower body, he played more of a speed and agility game with off-the-charts athleticism. In a letter that year to Wildung's mother, Dale, Bernie Bierman wrote that Dick was the only football player he had *ever* coached at Minnesota who was ready to start as a freshman, if only the Big Ten had allowed it. In a separate letter to Dick himself, Bierman commended him on his strong grades in the classroom and wrote that he was "looking forward to seeing you have a big year in football next fall."

True to Bierman's personality, however, he offered some constructive criticism for the young tackle to consider. "I do believe you have to learn to play from a little lower position and get to charge in a little deeper," Bierman wrote. "You still are growing and the lapse in keeping in shape may have a tendency to soften you up. I merely want to caution you to keep in shape at all times during the summer and be ready to come back and play a lot of tough hard and smart football next fall."[14]

Bierman's letters arrived at a time of great tragedy for the Wildung family. During the second semester of Dick's freshman year, in April 1940, his father died at the age of forty-four, finally succumbing at the veterans' hospital in Minneapolis after years of decline from mustard gas exposure in France. Overnight, Dale became the sole breadwinner for five children. Determined to keep the family's finances afloat and not totally happy with the dry goods business, Dale pivoted to a slightly different line of work. She opened Luverne Style Shop, a women's dress store, and quickly built it into a profitable business by working long, hard hours, including many weekends. With an unbreakable, determined spirit, Dale even managed to rebuild the store twice, after multiple fires in the early years. Luverne Style Shop would remain in the Wildung family for three generations.

Dale's incredible work ethic in the face of tragedy left a lasting impression on her children. "Day by day I grow stronger, and do more of what is right, because she's with me longer, and has helped me in my fight," Dick wrote years earlier for a high school English class. "I am often weakened, as I go along the way, yet I'm just a little better, because she's with me day by day."[15] Five months after his father's death, Dick Wildung returned to the University of Minnesota for his sophomore season in 1940 and made his mother prouder than she ever knew possible. He started most of the year for Bernie Bierman at left tackle, opposite All-American Urban Odson, and established himself as a force on the finest team in college football. During busy Saturdays at Luverne Style Shop, Dale placed a radio at the counter and fed the

WCCO radio broadcast of her son's Gopher football games to custom-ers, allowing them to listen as they searched for dresses.

It was unusual for a first-year varsity player like Wildung to make such an impact. Renowned experts, like Steve Snider of the United Press, commented on the rarity of Bierman using a sophomore at the first-team tackle position. Clearly, there could be exceptions. "He is our only sophomore lineman as yet," Bierman said, "who could step into a Big Ten lineup without noticeably weakening the team."[16]

The gushing praise for Wildung reverberated across Luverne. "Un-like most athletes, who have the idea the world owes them a living, Dick works for what he gets," Al McIntosh of the *Rock County Star* wrote. During the summer, the locals became accustomed to seeing Wildung run sprints at the old Luverne High School track, and they often spot-ted him performing manual labor in his temporary seasonal job with the highway department. Wildung had become the toast of the town after the 1940 season. "Most summer nights," McIntosh wrote, "you can find Dick sitting on the steps of the Methodist church surrounded by a bunch of hero worshipping youngsters."[17]

✿ ✿ ✿

Indeed, Luverne hailed Dick Wildung in the same way that Faribault hailed Bruce Smith, just as Clark, South Dakota, hailed Urban Odson. During a time in history when a significant portion of Americans lived outside of large urban centers, these small communities shaped many of the key contributors on the 1941 Minnesota football team and played a direct role in the program's success. At the same time, Bierman also benefited significantly from the University of Minnesota's prime loca-tion in the Twin Cities, with a population approaching a combined one million people in the immediate Minneapolis–St. Paul metropolitan area.[18] Rail transportation also made Duluth, St. Cloud, Winona, and Rochester easily accessible on a daily basis. In 1941, about two-thirds of the Minnesota football roster came from the state's largest urban cores—with an especially heavy emphasis on Minneapolis, home to roughly twenty-five of the players on the varsity team and at least a half-dozen prospective starters. Dick Gordon of the *Star* later wrote that he wouldn't see another Gopher team with as much Minneapolis flavor until the late 1950s under Murray Warmath.[19]

Eight high schools played one another annually for the city championship: Central, North, South, Edison, Washburn, Roosevelt, Marshall, and West. For whatever reason, that last school, West, seemed to produce more future Gophers than any other school in town—including one curious character with an unforgettable nickname. That was "Butch" Levy, even though his real name was far less exotic. "Name is Leonard . . . Who woulduv thunk it?" Bill Carlson of the *Star* wrote when describing the lineman on West High School's 1937 football team. "Big Butch Levy's name is Leonard."[20]

The nickname's origins trace back to Leonard Levy's childhood days on Humboldt Avenue in Minneapolis, when he needed a playful moniker to hide his Jewish faith. A group of Catholic kids from the neighborhood wanted him to join their baseball team, but young Leonard knew that name would blow his Jewish cover. So he invented an alias: "Butch O'Malley." The last name never caught on; the first name stuck for the rest of his life.[21]

The story of "Butch," though rather innocuous, offers a subtle hint into what it was like for Levy to grow up in Minneapolis before the war. It was an infamous and ugly chapter in the city's history. "One might even say, with a measure of justification, that Minneapolis is the capitol of anti-Semitism in the United States," journalist Carey McWilliams wrote in a groundbreaking 1946 article for the magazine *Common Ground*. "In almost every walk of life, 'an iron curtain' separates Jews from non-Jews in Minneapolis."[22]

As early as 1934, the fascist Silver Legion of America, known as the "Silver Shirts," had a presence in Minneapolis and on the University of Minnesota's campus. Led by William Dudley Pelley, the anti-Semitic and white supremacist organization mirrored the rhetoric of Nazi Germany and lured thousands of followers across the United States during the mid-1930s, including a self-reported six thousand members in Minnesota. A *Minneapolis Journal* investigation by a twenty-three-year-old reporter named Arnold Eric Sevareid, later a renowned journalist at CBS under Edward R. Murrow, brought the activity of the Silver Shirts in the Twin Cities into the public consciousness. With alarm bells already ringing, Jewish leaders banded together to form the Anti-Defamation Council of Minnesota in 1936, fighting against local fascist groups as well as the structural discrimination that Jews faced in employment, housing, and social circles during this era. "Though Jews had

been living in Minnesota since the mid-nineteenth century," Sarah Atwood wrote in the Minnesota Historical Society's *Minnesota History*
magazine in the Winter 2018–2019 edition, "the end of World War I
marked the beginning of a decades-long period which Jews faced discrimination and exclusion from both formal and informal cultural and
economic networks."[23]

The Automobile Club in Minneapolis denied them entry, for example, and Jews also "experienced considerable difficulty in buying residential property," Carey McWilliams observed. "The most striking as-
pect of anti-Semitism in Minneapolis, however, consists in the lack of
significant Jewish participation in the dominant economic activities of
the city."[24] Many employers simply refused to hire Jews, and they publicized these policies widely. Newspaper advertisements routinely
showed disdain for Jewish job candidates by expressing a preference for
"gentiles." In May 1937, an ad in one local publication sought an executive who was "native born 37 yr. young healthy Minneapolitan, gentile,
married, own home."[25] And in 1938: "Must be gentile," a grocery store
owner wrote in the Business Opportunities section while looking to sell
to a new party.[26]

Wary of the stifling anti-Semitism across the city, many Jews in Minneapolis—largely recent Eastern European immigrants—clustered on
the North Side. Butch Levy's family, however, lived in a different area
of South Minneapolis, within walking distance of West High School. In
September of 1937, at the start of his senior year, Levy appeared at the
Oak Grove Hotel in Minneapolis to accept the Mercury Club's prestigious award for Outstanding Jewish Athlete in the city. As a varsity athlete since the age of fourteen, Levy excelled in many sports beyond
football—everything from baseball to hockey to boxing to wrestling.
But especially wrestling. He won two heavyweight high school titles in
that sport.

Levy's Jewish faith was a significant part of his story: he met his
future wife, Loretta "Lucky" Bellson, in college, shortly after her family
escaped Nazi Germany. The Bellson family had survived the notorious
Kristallnacht in November 1938, a two-day pogrom supported by the
Nazis and an event that historians would later view as a precursor to the
Holocaust. During Kristallnacht, or "The Night of Broken Glass,"
crowds set fire to synagogues, smashed windows of thousands of Jewish-
owned businesses, and devastated thriving Jewish communities in cities

like Berlin, where the Bellsons lived.[27] Lucky Bellson was a teenager in 1938 and, years later, remembered having to evacuate her home during the frightening chaos of Kristallnacht. It was her father's decision to leave. "He thought you would be better off anywhere," she said, "than in your house."[28] After waiting years to gain a visa into the United States, the Bellsons finally found refuge from the terror in Holland. Then, in late August of 1939, Loretta and her parents boarded a ship for Ellis Island, met up with American resettlement agencies, and were told to move either to Kansas City or Minneapolis. They chose the latter, and it would soon lead Lucky on a blind date with Butch Levy.

The first time they met, Lucky remembered seeing the hulking Butch strolling down the sidewalk in his "M" sweater. *Here's this big lummox*," she thought to herself, as the five-foot-ten, 238-pound lineman approached.[29] Despite his size, Lucky may have felt at ease with the big-hearted Butch, whose welcoming, clean-shaven face and short, dark hairstyle belied his muscular physical characteristics.

The football team had grown accustomed to this sight. During his freshman and sophomore years in 1938 and 1939, Levy worked at both guard and tackle and immediately drew praise for his strength. As an early enthusiast of weight training in its primitive form, Levy could bench press five hundred pounds and squat massive amounts. In March 1939, Bernie Bierman wrote the freshman Levy a letter—partly informative, partly motivational. Bierman addressed the correspondence, *"Dear Butch."*[30]

"You appear to have the interest and are willing to apply the energy to football. However, it will take a lot of work to coordinate all these facts," Bierman told Levy. "You can begin your sophomore year if you want to badly enough." Months later, shortly before reporting to his first varsity practice, Levy then received another letter from his line coach, George Hauser, imploring him not to waste any time preparing for the start of September workouts. Coach Hauser addressed the correspondence *"Dear Leonard."*

"You have everything to make a great football player, but the determination will have to come from yourself," Hauser wrote. "So don't leave anything undone as far as being ready."[31]

With five other West High School alumni on the 1939 Minnesota team—Win Pedersen, Jim Shearer, Fred Van't Hull, Bob Smith, and Judd Ringer—Levy logged a total of sixty-seven minutes of playing

Leonard "Butch" Levy (far right) spends an evening with his future wife Loretta "Lucky" Bellson (center) and her brother, Peter Bellson (far left). Lucky's family escaped Nazi Germany in 1939. *Upper Midwest Jewish Archives, University of Minnesota*

time, the fourth-most among fellow tackles. Although other sophomores like Central High star Bob Sweiger and Faribault's Bruce Smith saw more immediate playing time, Levy gained valuable experience in 1939. After the football season, he made an even bigger mark in wrestling under coach Dave Bartelma. "I can see a big change in Butch during his short stay with the wrestlers," Bartelma said. "You football fans will see the improvement in him next fall as a result of his activity in this sport. He already is developing a fire and spark that will be invaluable to him on the gridiron. He'll be much better physically. In fact, I think wrestling will be the making of him."[32]

As a junior on the 1940 football team, Levy's physicality impressed the local sportswriters—and his reputation only improved after he won the NCAA heavyweight wrestling title in March 1941. His victory in the finals brought unbridled joy to his family back in South Minneapolis. "Dear folks/I did it/You have a champ in the family," Levy said in a telegram to his parents, just hours after capturing the NCAA crown in Bethlehem, Pennsylvania. "Get the convertible ready/Love Leonard."[33]

Looking ahead to Levy's senior football season, Charles Johnson of the *Star Journal* identified Butch Levy as a strong fit at guard rather than tackle, writing: "You saw Butch Levy as a guard coming up to the high standards that [Bill] Kuusisto, [Helge] Pukema and [Gordon] Paschka have been setting for game after game."[34] With Urban Odson and Dick Wildung holding down the tackle positions, Levy's best bet for playing time in fall 1941 would most certainly come at guard. Johnson might have been on to something.

* * *

Butch Levy had dealt with position changes before and thrived. Back in high school, his senior yearbook mentioned the following: "Statistics don't show . . . that 'Butch' Levy stepped into an entirely unfamiliar center position in mid-season and performed like a veteran."[35] Manning a new spot on the line, Levy's West team fared well enough in 1937 to remain in contention for the city championship in late October. The Cowboys just needed to defeat future Gopher standout Bob Sweiger and Central High School. "And now," the *Star* wrote a day before the game, "comes the biggest high school football [game] natural Minneapolis has ever had."[36] With a reported crowd of at least eight thousand, West led 7–6 in the final minute of the game—behind the strength of another future Gopher Bob Smith's touchdown—but lost in heartbreaking fashion on a long touchdown pass from Central's Don Schneider to Ira Ilsham. Levy and his West teammates sulked as Central fans poured onto the field in celebration during a mob scene that lasted an entire fifteen minutes.

Bob Sweiger, as it turned out, played a small role in the win: his fumble recovery set up Central's first touchdown. Although he may not have provided the heroics in the game-of-the-century against West High School, he still established himself by the end of the season as the top fullback in Minneapolis prep football. With six touchdowns and two extra points against city competition, Sweiger captured the scoring title and led his team to an undefeated conference season. Central's only loss came in the final game on the calendar, in a rivalry duel between the champions of Minneapolis and St. Paul. Sweiger still scored both touchdowns in a 14–12 loss to Washington High School before a crowd of nearly twelve thousand. "Sweiger," Bill Carlson of the *Star* wrote, "was perhaps the most outstanding player on the field."[37]

Growing up in the old Central High neighborhood about three miles south of downtown, Sweiger and his eight other siblings quickly learned how to function independently when their mother died in 1930. After their father remarried, the Sweiger kids had a tumultuous relationship with a not-so-friendly stepmother, so rocky at points that Bob often stayed elsewhere instead of coming home. Coupled with the fact that he was the youngest boy in the family, Bob developed a resilient spirit that surely helped lead him to stardom in basketball, baseball, and football at Central. "A mighty hero on the grid," his yearbook recounted, "but modest as to what he did."[38] The yearbook raved for him, even if he wouldn't. "Bob Sweiger, all-city fullback," it said, "excelled in line-smashing and strong defensive play."[39] His performance helped Central win the city championship for the first time in a decade.

Carrying a strong reputation from his Minneapolis prep school days, Sweiger transitioned smoothly from high school to the college game at Minnesota. In his varsity debut against Arizona in 1939—when fellow sophomore Bruce Smith started at halfback and returned the opening kickoff four yards—Sweiger burst into action off the bench at fullback. He quickly announced his arrival by grabbing two interceptions in the first quarter, the second of which he returned twenty-three yards for a touchdown. As a starter at fullback in three of eight games, Sweiger totaled more than two hundred yards on the ground in 1939 and found the end zone three times, including a seven-yard scamper against Wisconsin in the season finale. The gregarious Sweiger, a natural leader and the type of people-person to never forget a name, packed a serious punch as he grew to roughly six feet and two hundred pounds. By 1940, however, a healthy competition for his fullback position began to develop, when a newcomer by the name of Bill Daley arrived on campus.

✦ ✦ ✦

"The battle for the fullback post," the *St. Cloud Times* wrote before the 1940 season, "should be doubly interesting to fans in this city inasmuch as Bob Sweiger and Bill Daley have definite connections with St. Cloud."[40] Sweiger's extended family lived in St. Cloud and five of his older siblings were born there, but Daley actually grew up in the area himself. The son of a railroad engineer, Daley hailed from nearby Melrose and idolized the Gophers like so many other children across Minnesota. He would later recount traveling to Minneapolis to see his first game at Memorial Stadium in November 1934, when Bernie Bierman's first national championship team thrashed the University of Chicago behind the strength of the electric Pug Lund from Rice Lake, Wisconsin. Lund intercepted future Heisman Trophy winner Jay Berwanger's pass in the first quarter and later scored the first touchdown of the game in a 35–7 route. "I saw my hero," Daley said.[41]

After developing into a star himself in high school, Daley pursued a brief pit stop in Chicago, where he boxed and played football at DePaul before the university eliminated the latter sport. In 1940, he desired a return to his roots, so he connected with former DePaul basketball coach Jim Kelly, by that point a track coach and close confidant of

Melrose native Bill Daley landed at the University of Minnesota after a brief stop in Chicago out of high school. He donated this autographed photo to the Melrose Area Museum. *Melrose Area Museum*

Bernie Bierman at the University of Minnesota. That link brought Daley home. He stepped foot on campus later that fall and saw Bierman for the first time at the Cooke Hall athletic building. "I didn't know whether I should kiss his ring as we used to do to the bishop, or salute him," Daley said. "I was just in awe."[42]

In his first year of eligibility, Daley started one game at fullback, yielding to the more experienced Sweiger in the other seven contests. Even so, they finished with nearly identical statistics, combining for more than five hundred yards rushing and five touchdowns between the two. A few inches taller than Sweiger but roughly the same weight, Daley offered a different blend of speed, athleticism, and mobility at the fullback spot. Looking ahead to his second year of varsity football, Daley vowed to improve his blocking and physicality. "Take that business of smacking the line for those short gains," Daley said. "That's supposed to be Sweiger's specialty on this team. I aim to make it mine, too."[43] In 1941, it seemed backfield coach Sheldon Beise would have a decision to make: he had two outstanding fullbacks but only one starting fullback position to fill. Luckily for the coaching staff, a rule change by the NCAA would make that decision much less stressful.

✿ ✿ ✿

Under the NCAA's groundbreaking policy, approved in January 1941, players could now *freely substitute* for each other during games. It marked a major shift from the previous rules, which required players to sit out the rest of the quarter if they were replaced. In another momentous change, the rules committee lifted a ban on communication during substitutions, making it easier for coaches to share play-calls with their players on the field. The loosened restrictions paved the way for platoon-type systems, allowing coaches to mix and match their lineups as often as they pleased and dig deep into their reserve strength. "1941 football," George Kirksey of the United Press wrote, "will feature all-out blitz attacks."[44]

Designed to spruce up the game and prevent injuries by allowing for more rest opportunities, the free substitution rule offered a natural solution to Minnesota's competitive position battles. Bob Sweiger and Bill Daley, for example, could now take turns at fullback without having

to sit out a whole quarter, or they could play multiple positions and slide
to halfback if needed. The coaching staff saw endless possibilities.

It was also a thrilling development at quarterback, the position responsible for calling plays and serving mostly as a blocking back under
Bierman's single-wing system. The Gophers looked to two strong candidates for the starting gig: senior Warren Plunkett and varsity newcomer
Bill Garnaas. Plunkett, a battle-tested veteran and standout in the boxing ring, brought steady leadership, toughness, and reliability to the
position. In March 1941, the six-foot, 195-pounder had shocked the
whole campus by defeating gridiron teammate Bill Daley in the University of Minnesota intramural heavyweight boxing championship, reportedly the first defeat suffered by Daley in twenty-three tries. "Surprising
Warren Plunkett of Austin, who pulled a heap of surprising quarterback
plays for Bernie Bierman last fall," the *Tribune* remarked in a photo
caption, "grimaced as he simultaneously let one fly and backed away
from a Bill Daley punch."[45] The former St. Augustine High School prep
star from southern Minnesota, a son of an attorney just like Bruce
Smith, hoped to finish his college football career on a high note entering the fall of 1941 as the likely starting quarterback.

The sophomore Garnaas, however, had also worked his tail off during the off-season, displaying an acute sense of football intelligence and
a newfound aura of maturity by the start of fall practice. Garnaas was a
late arrival to Minneapolis. Originally born in North Dakota, he spent
most of his early years in Northfield, Minnesota. Garnaas had no memories of his father, who died of pneumonia when he was only two years
old after catching a cold while trying to push a car out of a snowdrift.
His mother never remarried and raised five children as a single mom
before moving the family to Minneapolis, where Garnaas promptly enrolled at Marshall High—a school famous for producing the likes of
Gopher legends Andy Uram, George Svendsen, and Babe LeVoir. He
wasted no time making his own impression on the football field. "Bill
came up unheralded from Northfield at the beginning of the year," his
senior yearbook said, "but before the season ended he established himself as the best fullback in the city. He won unanimous All-City recognition."[46]

When Garnaas moved a few blocks from Marshall High School to
the University of Minnesota, freshman coach Dallas Ward placed him
at quarterback and found immediate results. "I think he will become

one of the best quarterbacks Minnesota has had since Bierman took over the coaching reins," Ward told George Barton of the *Tribune* in November 1939.[47] Garnaas craved the varsity coach's attention and often liked to tell a story about an interaction that occurred during his freshman year. After a grueling afternoon practice, young Bill rushed home to his mother to share some important news. "Mom," he said, "Bernie Bierman yelled at me!" Mom was concerned, until Bill explained that the tongue-lashing from Bierman was actually a good sign. "He knows my name!"[48] Entering his second year on campus, the U of M's news service described Garnaas as a "good punter" and "competent ball carrier."[49]

Garnaas, however, struggled in 1940, languishing on the bench as a member of the reserve "Bomber" team. "He never got into any of the games and he never went on any of the trips. It was disappointing all right and Bill thought about dropping football many a time," according to a press release from the University of Minnesota news service. "But somehow he stuck it out."[50] Bernie Bierman was glad he did. Flaunting the skills that made him an All-City performer at Marshall High, Garnaas stunned the coaching staff with his off-season progress and had shaped himself into a viable candidate for the starting quarterback position in 1941. Thanks to the free substitution rule, he and Warren Plunkett could share playing time, rather than fight for sole possession of the job.

At the start of the season, Minnesota listed more than sixty names on the 1941 fall roster. Half of them would not travel for road games and might not even play a down of varsity football. Still, the free substitution patterns must have been welcome news for those who wanted more playing time. At end, talented blockers and pass-catchers like Judd Ringer (Minneapolis), Cliff Anderson (Minneapolis), Herb Hein (Billings, Montana), and Joe Hirscher (Shakopee, Minnesota) would push the probable starters Bob Fitch (St. Louis Park, Minnesota) and Bill Baumgartner (Duluth) for snaps. At tackle, strong backups like Ed Lechner of North Dakota, Jim Lushine of Minnesota's Iron Range, and Paul Mitchell of Minneapolis might be able to crack the lineup behind Urban Odson and Dick Wildung. A deep group of experienced guards, ranging from Butch Levy to Helge Pukema (Duluth) to Gordon Paschka (Watertown, Minnesota) to John Billman (Minneapolis) to Bob Smith (Minneapolis), could all share duties. Gene Flick (Minneapolis),

Don Nolander (Minneapolis), and Vic Kulbitski (Red Wing, Minnesota) could rotate at center, tasked with snapping the ball into the backfield in the single-wing.

That backfield worried Bierman. Despite the reliable presence of veterans like Bruce Smith, Bob Sweiger, and Bill Daley, his team had lost more than seven hundred yards of combined rushing with the departure of All-American Sonny Franck and other seniors from the 1940 team. "Tell me who is going to carry the ball for those lost yards this season," Bierman said, "and I'll feel a lot easier about how we are going to finish in November."[51] He would need his reserve depth to mature quickly. Bud Higgins, an energetic sophomore from Washburn High School in Minneapolis, possessed a stellar combination of explosiveness and agility but probably needed to bulk up from his tiny 150-pound frame. Fellow sophomore Herman Frickey of Billings, Montana, showed promise but arrived on campus as an unproven commodity. It was the same story for juniors Gene Bierhaus of Brainerd, Mike Welch of St. James, and Joe Lauterbach of Redwood Falls, three rural Minnesota prep stars aiming for their first college breakthrough in 1941. They could only hope that unlimited substitutions would create more opportunities.

Bierman viewed all of these backups as wild cards, and he wondered how they might hold up against a brutal 1941 schedule. Four of Minnesota's eight opponents—Washington, Michigan, Northwestern, and Nebraska—had finished in the Top Ten of the Associated Press rankings the year before. "I don't think we'll be on top in the conference," Bierman told a group of Iowa high school coaches during an August 1941 speaking engagement.[52]

The Silver Fox, known to some members of the local press as a hopeless pessimist, harbored fears about his lack of proven depth and scheduling difficulties. He also continued to monitor the war situation and Selective Service. In that respect, Bierman was no curmudgeon. Since the implementation of the nation's first-ever peacetime military draft in October 1940, a growing list of college football players had left school to enlist, leading Bierman to make some of those worried remarks prior to his team's spring scrimmage in May 1941 about how the draft would "probably affect us some." The first year of Selective Service had not devastated the sport by any means, but the lingering anxiety led the Associated Press to echo some of Bierman's concerns. The

AP's journalists published a series in the summer of 1941 about the "likely effects of the National emergency on 1941 college football," examining the impact to schools on a region-by-region basis. The final article in the series expressed a cautiously optimistic tone. "This country's college football coaches are going into the 1941 campaign with their fingers crossed," the AP wrote, "and with a manifest tendency to concentrate only on the business at hand and let the future take care of itself."[53]

4

"FOOTBALL IS ONLY A GAME"

As Americans fretted over whether they would be able to watch football during the upcoming fall of 1941, their counterparts across the Atlantic Ocean hid in bomb shelters with no such leisure time to ponder inconsequential matters like sporting events. Tens of thousands of soldiers had already died in the European war, with the year 1940 bringing the most despair as Hitler took frightening steps in the wrong direction. Nazi Germany seized the likes of Norway, Denmark, France, Luxembourg, the Netherlands, and Belgium, accelerated a violent bombing campaign against the British, and formed the Axis powers with Japan and Italy, fortifying an enemy now easily identifiable by a divided American public.[1]

After initially opposing U.S. involvement in overwhelming numbers at the start of the war in 1939, some people began to reconsider their feelings after seeing the dramatic fall of France and other painful images of Nazi conquest in May and June of 1940. Bill Amyotte, a young Native American man from the far northeastern corner of Minnesota, enlisted in the Army a month later in July 1940 because "it was about the time France was falling and I figured that it won't be long and we'll be in it."[2] If Hitler could crush the French and march through Paris, many feared he might overrun the British next and control the Atlantic. And where would that leave the United States? Public polling reflected heightened concerns among the general public and a greater willingness to lend military aid to the Allies. During the second half of 1940, for example, the number of Americans in support of helping the British "even at the risk of getting into the war" nearly doubled from 35 percent to 60 percent.[3]

At the same time, a separate faction of anti-war isolationists continued to insist that the United States had no business interfering in the newest overseas debacle. This particular ideology resonated with a substantial number of Americans, who felt they had been manipulated into supporting the First World War at the cost of more than one hundred thousand deaths of U.S. service members (both from combat and the influenza pandemic).[4] Playing to these anxieties, the America First Committee, founded by Yale students and later aided by high-profile spokesperson Charles Lindbergh, first emerged in the fall of 1940 to lead an anti-war crusade that would last for another year and a half.

The isolationist feeling was quite strong in Lindbergh's home state of Minnesota, evidenced by the fact that twelve thousand people—more than double the audience of the Golden Gophers' spring football game on the same day—attended his America First rally at the Minneapolis Auditorium in May 1941. As a mid-sized state in the Upper Midwest, Minnesota sometimes felt a universe away from both the war itself and the horrors of Nazi Germany. "Every once in a while something would crop up that would be kind of alarming, but I'm afraid people didn't take it seriously. They just didn't think that sort of thing was really happening," said Wayne Hanson, a high school student at the time in Benson, Minnesota, about sixty miles from Bernie Bierman's hometown of Litchfield. Within a matter of years, Hanson would help liberate the Dachau concentration camp with the 42nd Rainbow Division. He never forgot the attitude of his peers before the war. "They heard it and dismissed it," Hanson later said. "I guess probably because it wasn't at their back door or something."[5]

The anti-intervention folks, in Minnesota or elsewhere, did not fit neatly into just one political category. Some merely felt terrified about the idea of another deadly world war and remained fatigued and soured from the first one that ended just two decades earlier. Some were opposition Republicans from the Midwest or West Coast; others were Democrats from the president's own party, or even Communists on the far left of the political spectrum. Some were outright sympathizers with the Nazi regime and held vicious anti-Semitic beliefs, or at least trafficked harmful stereotypes about American Jews that falsely accused them of holding excessive influence over the decision to go to war. "The years just prior to World War II," the historian Edward S. Shapiro has argued, "were the highwater period for American anti-Semitism in Congress and in the country at large."[6]

Regardless of their various motivations for opposing the conflict, the isolationists all found themselves fundamentally at odds with FDR, who forged slowly ahead with military preparations in anticipation of what he increasingly viewed as an inevitable war. Most notably, the president pushed for a revision to the Neutrality Act in 1939 to lift a ban on selling arms to nations at war, sent old U.S. Navy destroyers to the British in exchange for military bases, and eventually supported a politically risky Selective Service program that would subject young American men to military conscription. "Because of the millions of citizens involved in the conduct of defense," Roosevelt said while accepting his party's nomination for re-election in July 1940, "most right thinking persons are agreed that some form of selection by draft is as necessary and fair today as it was in 1917 and 1918."[7]

As Roosevelt continued to seek an extraordinary third term against spirited Republican challenger Wendell Willkie, Congress approved a historic peacetime draft measure in September 1940. Under the Selective Training and Service Act, males between the ages of twenty-one and thirty-five would need to register for conscription. The move to implement Selective Service *before* a declaration of war had no precedent in American history. "Your boys are not going to be sent into any foreign wars," Roosevelt told a crowd of twenty-three thousand at the Boston Garden on the campaign trail in late October. "They are going into training to form a force so strong that, by its very existence, it will keep the threat of war away from our shores. The purpose of our defense is defense."[8]

❖ ❖ ❖

Sixteen million young American men signed up for Selective Service on October 16, 1940, including some of the most recognizable celebrities in American sports. Bob Feller of the Cleveland Indians kept a shotgun in his car as he arrived at his registration office. Joe DiMaggio reportedly didn't know how to answer the local draft board when officials asked him where he worked. "American League baseball club of New York," he finally told them.[9] The thirty-four-year-old manager of the Boston

Red Sox, Joe Cronin, registered gleefully at his suburban office. "I'm glad of the chance," he said. "Any country that can let a kid like me make a lot of dough is worth throwing a few punches for."[10]

In college football, two of Minnesota's chief Big Ten rivals saw their best players register for Selective Service: Michigan's Tom Harmon and Northwestern's Bill DeCorrevont. "I sure would rather be dodging tacklers than bullets," DeCorrevont told the United Press, "but if worse comes to worst, we'll all be in there pitching hand grenades."[11] On Minnesota's 1940 team, senior halfbacks Sonny Franck and Bob Paffrath, as well as co-captain linemen Bill Johnson and Bob Bjorklund, would have all fit the compulsory draft age of twenty-one.

The Gophers' top upperclassmen returning for the 1941 season—high-profile names like Bruce Smith, Urban Odson, Bill Daley, Bob Sweiger, and others—also filled out draft registration cards with their local boards and might have privately hoped for college deferments. Listing their occupations as some form of "Student—University of Minnesota," the young men handwrote their home addresses, dates of birth, heights and weights, and emergency contacts. Smith designated his father, Lucius, on the "Person Who Will Always Know Your Address" section of the card.[12] "Permit Bierman to keep this squad intact next fall and no one will have to do much apologizing for the class of the 1941 Minnesota team," Charles Johnson of the *Minneapolis Star Journal* wrote, "unless the war drains the ranks of some of the eligible aces."[13]

As the Gophers slogged through rainy spring practices at Northrop Field in April and May 1941—culminating in that poor scrimmage performance at Memorial Stadium on May 10 just hours before the Lindbergh appearance across the Mississippi River—the long-term future of college football began to look especially hazy, given the rapidly changing landscape of the international crisis. "The summer of 1941 will undoubtedly prove a very decisive period in the world conflict," Edgar M. Jaeger, the Minneapolis chapter president of the Committee to Defend America by Aiding the Allies, wrote to potential financial donors in a direct rebuke to Lindbergh and the America First supporters. "It is necessary for the Committee to conduct a never-ceasing effort in the matter of meetings and publicity to develop public information and opinion backing the government's effort to build up our defense and aid the embattled democracies."[14]

The headlines turned dreadful that summer, perhaps as bad as 1940. Before dawn on Sunday, June 22, 1941, three million Nazi troops barged through the Russian border in an unexpected invasion of the Soviet Union, shattering a previous non-aggression pact between the two countries and forcing a still-neutral United States to forge an uncomfortable alliance with Joseph Stalin's brutally repressive regime. Weeks later, President Roosevelt dispatched one of his closest advisors, Harry Hopkins, to Moscow. The fifty-year-old envoy, a former basketball star at Iowa's Grinnell College now in poor health following a cancer diagnosis, met with Stalin to discuss extending military resources to the Soviets under Roosevelt's Lend-Lease Act, which had just passed Congress in March 1941 despite objections from the Charles Lindbergh isolationist types. "No man could forget the picture of the dictator of Russia as he stood watching me leave," Hopkins later said about Stalin. "He's built close to the ground, like a football coach's dream of a tackle."[15] A month after Hitler's invasion of the Soviet Union, German ally Japan continued its aggressive imperialism in Asia by occupying southern French Indochina, a move that angered the United States because it threatened Allied territories like Singapore, the Philippines, and the Dutch East Indies. Roosevelt promptly froze Japan's assets and saddled the country with crippling sanctions, cutting off an oil supply that Japan depended on so heavily. The move set the stage for months of anxious peace negotiations between the Americans and the Japanese.

Although the war had not yet reached the United States, the escalating tensions and ongoing Selective Service requirements decimated colleges and universities across the country. At the University of Minnesota, President Guy Stanton Ford's administration estimated an enrollment decrease of at least 10 percent for the upcoming fall semester due to the military draft, which was likely to result in a staggering loss of tuition revenue. President Ford, in one of his final actions before retiring in June 1941, asked the Committee on Fees to study a potential tuition increase in order to raise an extra $100,000.

Bidding farewell to the Class of 1941 at the end of the spring semester, Ford's final cap-and-gown speech as university president underscored the grave reality these graduates were about to face. "None of us can know the extent of the immediate effort and sacrifice involved," Ford told the students, "but he is blind indeed who would not willingly make it to end the danger of Hitlerism rather than cower under its shadow through years devoted to military preparations that would sap our resources, undermine our democratic institutions and destroy our ideals of individual liberty."[16]

❀ ❀ ❀

Some of Minnesota's football players spent their summers in the expanding U.S. defense industry, working in plants and assisting with the shipping of supplies to Allies overseas under the Lend-Lease Act. "They are getting the necessary manual labor to maintain top physical condition," the university's news service reported in July 1941, "and at the same time they are doing their share in the nation's vast defense program."[17] The school reported that Bob Sweiger and end Bob Fitch had been working in a plant "with large defense contracts," while Butch Levy found work in a steel plant with a few other teammates. College football players all over the country toiled away in similar factory jobs. In fact, Marquette University head coach Tom Stidham joked that the jobs were so lucrative that some of them might not even bother to return to school in the fall.[18]

But most coaches that summer viewed the military situation, specifically the draft that endangered the status of most college seniors, as a serious matter. Iowa's staff worried about captain Bill Diehl because his deferment only lasted until July. Temple University in Philadelphia lost its starting quarterback to the military, Penn's fullback reported to an air base in Georgia, the University of Florida braced for the departure of eight first-string players, and Georgia Tech coach Bill Alexander resigned himself to the fact that he might need to play his sophomores next fall.[19] "Football?" Alexander said. "It'll be wild as a turkey!"[20] Writing for the *Daily Times* in Davenport, Iowa, Leo Kautz suggested that coaches across the country were struggling to prepare for the 1941 season. "They know not what to expect," he said, before adding: "Football is only a game. And there will be other years."[21]

At Minnesota, the military exodus began with Fred Van't Hull, a promising would-be senior tackle who played a major role for the Gophers on both sides of the ball in 1939 and 1940 and certainly could have competed for a starting position in 1941. Instead, Van't Hull announced over the summer of 1941 that he would skip his final season of college football to join the U.S. Navy. After passing an entrance exam,

Van't Hull would report to the U.S. Naval Academy in Annapolis, Maryland, on June 24. "I'm tickled to death about it," Van't Hull said. "I'll miss playing my last year with Minnesota, of course, but going to Annapolis is a great privilege."[22] After pouring his heart and soul into football for the better part of the past decade, the West High School graduate would leave behind his hometown of Minneapolis—and the game of football—to serve his country. His former West teammates, including Butch Levy, must have been crushed. So were others. "We lost him," backup tackle Ed Lechner, a close friend and fraternity brother of Van't Hull, later wrote in his memoir, "which was tough for me. Some players were hard to replace."[23]

The Gophers lost a second player just one month later, this time due to Selective Service rather than voluntarily enlistment. "First definite draft loss to the 1941 Minnesota football team was revealed," the *Minneapolis Tribune* reported in late July, "when Bernie Bierman said that Ralph Lundeen, promising six-foot, 185-pound end from Minneapolis, would be lugging a gun instead of a pigskin this fall."[24] The press speculated that more players would soon depart. In his *Star Journal* column that summer, Charles Johnson predicted the draft would steal at least five or six players from the Minnesota roster as other writers began to spread unconfirmed chatter.[25] A few months before fall practice began, a report emerged—later proven erroneous—that Bruce Smith was listed third on his home draft list in Faribault. The revelation, despite not being true, left writers in Faribault and Minneapolis frenzied. "It was regarded as an outside chance," Bernard Swanson wrote in the *Tribune*, "but the danger was there."[26]

In all, Minnesota lost roughly a half-dozen players to the military before the 1941 season.[27] In addition to Van't Hull and Lundeen, Bierman reported in August that a few unnamed third and fourth-stringers also left the program; by September, the *Star Journal* then reported that backup quarterback Jim Shearer "was among the missing" due to "defense work."[28] He did not play in 1941, nor did Joe Mernik, a hero of the previous season due to his game-winning extra-point kicks against Northwestern and Michigan. After eligibility issues, Mernik ultimately wound up in the service playing for a Fort Snelling football team in the fall.

Despite the uncertainty, the bulk of Minnesota's 1941 roster ultimately remained untouched by the military—temporarily, at least. With fans anticipating another stellar squad, demand surged for season tick-ets ahead of the fall schedule:

at Washington, Sept. 27
vs. Illinois, Oct. 11
vs. Pittsburgh, Oct. 18
at Michigan, Oct. 25
vs. Northwestern, Nov. 1
vs. Nebraska, Nov. 8
at Iowa, Nov. 15
vs. Wisconsin, Nov. 22

The University of Minnesota received twenty-five thousand mailed ap-plications by June 1941 alone and saw overall ticket reservations jump by 33 percent compared to the previous year. Tickets for all five home games, including postage costs, ran almost fourteen dollars. "War or no war," the *Minneapolis Star Journal* wrote, "Minnesota football fans haven't lost interest in their Gophers."[29]

5

"WASHINGTON FIRST"

As the University of Minnesota opened fall practice in September 1941 on the hunt for another national championship, a nineteen-year-old United States Marine named Aubrey Dunkum restlessly awaited updates from his dilapidated steel barracks outside of Reykjavik, Iceland. The South Minneapolis native and rabid Gopher football fan would miss every single game in 1941, following his deployment to the North Atlantic Ocean with the First Provisional Marine Brigade. Serving alongside four thousand fellow Americans, Dunkum spent his leisure time learning Icelandic, exploring remote villages in the mountains, playing pickup football games against British soldiers evacuated the previous year from Dunkirk, and pondering day and night whether his beloved Golden Gophers could live up to the hype and finish undefeated for the second season in a row. The young marine craved news from the gridiron. "Dunkum's parents—Mr. and Mrs. Aubrey R. Dunkum—have been sending him the *Sunday Tribune* and *Star Journal* each week," the *Minneapolis Star Journal* proudly noted in a feature piece about the U.S. forces in Iceland, "together with clippings about the Minnesota football team."[1]

These warm letters from home sustained Dunkum and his companions during their anxious days in Iceland, an island first occupied by the British in 1940 before the Americans arrived with reinforcements during the summer of 1941. Although the United States remained technically neutral in the war, the Roosevelt administration's strategic decision to send troops to Iceland placed more American service members in the thick of the precarious Battle of the Atlantic with Germany. The ongoing conflicts at sea had already seen British merchant ships decimated by roving Nazi U-boats, as the two sides fought for control of vital shipping lanes.

On the morning of September 4, 1941, twenty-three days before the start of the college football season, an American ship got a taste of the chaos. The USS *Greer* was traveling toward Reykjavik carrying cargo, passengers, and mail (perhaps those Gopher football clippings for Dunkum) when a messy situation unfolded about 175 miles southwest of Iceland. A British plane had detected an oncoming German U-boat about ten miles away and warned the *Greer* of the danger. As the *Greer* followed and kept a close eye with underwater sound technology, the British aircraft attempted to strike the U-boat, prompting the German submarine to fire errant torpedoes at the *Greer*. The American ship, suddenly entangled in a skirmish, dropped a total of nineteen depth charges toward the Nazi U-boat during an encounter that lasted more than three hours. All of the depth charges missed, but a milestone occurred: the Americans had fired some of their first shots of World War II, three months before officially entering the conflict.[2]

President Roosevelt issued a blistering response to the Germans. "We have sought no shooting war with Hitler. We do not seek it now," FDR said in a fireside chat exactly one week later. "But neither do we want peace so much, that we are willing to pay for it by permitting him to attack our naval and merchant ships while they are on legitimate business." In that same national radio address on September 11, 1941, the president outlined a landmark "shoot-on-sight" policy against any Axis ship that swarmed inside designated American patrol zones. Roosevelt also clarified a change in protocol allowing U.S. ships to fully escort and protect British carriers to and from Iceland, and he offered unmistakably forceful words for the isolationists. In his mind, these opponents still failed to grasp how Britain's dire position left the U.S. exceedingly vulnerable. "It is time for all Americans, Americans of all the Americas," he said, "to stop being deluded by the romantic notion that the Americas can go on living happily and peacefully in a Nazi-dominated world."[3]

Over the next several hours, the White House proceeded to trade punches again with nemesis Charles Lindbergh. The *Greer* incident had done nothing to change his mind about the conflict. Four months after his Minneapolis Auditorium appearance, the America First spokesperson turned his attention to Iowa on the evening of September 11, telling an animated crowd of eight thousand people at the Des Moines Coliseum that the "British, the Jewish and the Roosevelt administration" were pushing the nation into war. Though Lindbergh said it was "not difficult to understand why Jewish people desire the overthrow of Nazi Germany," he accused American Jews of cheerleading for the war. "Their greatest danger to this country," Lindbergh said in his most inflammatory line, "lies in their large ownership and influence in our motion pictures, our press, our radio and our government."[4] After Lindbergh departed Des Moines on a train headed for Chicago, a spokesperson for President Roosevelt admonished the speech for its "striking similarity" to Nazi propaganda.[5]

Lindbergh's rhetoric, already troubling to some when he spoke in Minneapolis the previous May, had now evolved into blatant anti-Semitism with the infamous Des Moines speech. His support collapsed even among some of the staunchest isolationists. And now German U-boats were clashing with U.S. ships in the North Atlantic. Although not the consensus opinion by any means, the public had slowly started to come around to the idea of U.S. involvement. A Gallup poll taken just a few weeks after the *Greer* debacle showed that 64 percent of Americans now favored helping the British "even at the risk of getting into the war," representing a modest 4-percent increase compared to November 1940.[6]

Whatever one thought of Roosevelt's foreign policy strategy, the third-term chief executive used mass media and the power of radio to command the nation's attention like no other president before him. His fireside chat on September 11, the one about the *Greer* and the shoot-on-sight policy, reportedly reached forty million Americans—the second-largest radio audience in history at that time. Cities and towns shut down during the late-night speech, which began at 10:00 p.m. on the East Coast. "Virtually everybody in the Philadelphia area heard President Roosevelt's address last night," the *Inquirer* reported. "Bartenders and waitresses joined with taproom and restaurant customers in a period of complete inaction while radios [blared] forth the history-making pronouncement."[7]

Speaking in his familiar, deliberate tone, Roosevelt's words reverberated across the country, in living rooms, restaurants, theaters, and

apparently even dorm rooms on the campus of the University of Minnesota. With his ears perked to the radio that evening at Pioneer Hall,
hearing tales of North Atlantic shooting wars and German aggression,
Bruce Smith could not help but ponder his future beyond college football. "From listening to the President talk the other night," the All-
American hopeful said during the first week of fall practice, "there's not
much doubt where I'll be—in the Army."[8]

* * *

When practice began at rickety Northrop Field in the second week of
September, roughly half of the players on Minnesota's 1941 roster had
already registered for Selective Service.[9] Bernie Bierman, the Marine
Corps reservist and First World War veteran who gave up coaching in
1917 and 1918 to serve in Cuba, could likely relate to their stress but
still refused to accept any excuses. In a letter to all of his players in late
August, Bierman made no mention of the draft and implored them to
arrive on campus in tip-top physical shape. Extra conditioning would be
particularly important this year, Bierman told them, because the long
train ride to Seattle for the season opener against the University of
Washington on September 27 would steal at least three days of practice
from the Gophers. "Be ready physically for a hard 60-minute football
game by September 10," Bierman wrote, "then you will be ready for a
proper start in what can become a great season."[10] In his own letter to
teammates dated August 23, 1941, captain Bruce Smith made similar
pleas and, with the tone of his writing, clearly established himself in a
new leadership role. "We have got to know our plays so we can start out
with our routine practices," Smith wrote, using an underline for emphasis. "Bernie likes us to line up in the fall and tell us to go through a few
plays just to see who hasn't learned them—and you know what happens
then!"[11]

   The players heeded their captain's advice as they trickled back to
campus in strong playing shape—especially the tackles. Dick Wildung
looked svelte at 207 pounds, and Urban Odson had dropped about
twenty pounds after reportedly ballooning to 270 during the off-season.
"This will be my best year," Odson said. "I'm ready for them. Watch me
go."[12] Unfortunately, Odson's senior season started on an unlucky note.
In the early days of fall practice, he tweaked his knee while making a

quick cut, according to trainer Lloyd Stein. It was not a good development. Although the coaching staff hoped the injury was only minor, Stein reported that Odson might not be able to participate in any preseason scrimmages. "I want it to heal up perfectly," Stein said, "so we don't have to worry about it through most of the season."[13] Bob Fitch, an outstanding multi-sport discus thrower and the likely starter at left end, also hurt his leg in an early scrimmage. His injury was not as serious. The suburban Twin Cities native, whose father ran a veterinary practice in St. Louis Park, returned after missing just a few days of practice and alternated snaps at end with a sophomore Montana native named Herb Hein.

Fortunately, the other practice developments were more encouraging, helping to brighten Bierman's spirits after such a disappointing

The 1941 team, seen here in full with each member of the varsity and coaching staff, faced a stiff challenge as it traveled to Seattle for the season opener against the University of Washington. *Courtesy of University of Minnesota Archives, University of Minnesota–Twin Cities*

spring scrimmage four months earlier. Bruce Smith, for instance, looked even more fantastic than expected, as it appeared his two-a-day workouts in Faribault over the summer had greatly improved his passing ability. During a scrimmage against the reserves on September 13, Smith wowed the coaching staff with an eighty-yard toss to Bob Sweiger on the very first play. If he could add a lethal aerial attack to his already-strong running, blocking, and tackling abilities, there was no telling what kind of senior season the Minnesota captain might have. Outside of Smith, Bierman continued to toy with his backfield during the early fall sessions, at one point even surprising the local press by inserting sophomore Herman Frickey of Billings, Montana, into the starting line-up at right halfback. The hard-charging Melrose native Bill Daley, fresh off a haircut that left him unrecognizable to his teammates, excelled as an open-field runner and seemed ready to contribute at any of the halfback or fullback positions in the single-wing. Sweiger, according to reports, appeared a step faster. And up front? "It should be a good line," assistant coach Dr. George Hauser reported.[14] Butch Levy earned the unofficial honor as "most improved," starting at first-team right guard in every single drill. "He is unusually active for such a bulky fellow," George Barton of the *Minneapolis Tribune* wrote, "his agility and sense of balance being due to his wrestling skill."[15]

Mixing scrimmages, "chalk talk" study sessions, and individual drills, the Gophers completed eleven two-a-day practices that month as they prepared for a two-thousand-mile train ride to Seattle for a non-conference opener. Writers across the country would monitor the game with great interest and curiosity, since many considered the Huskies a potential challenger in the Pacific Coast Conference. They had only lost two games in 1940, both to undefeated teams: Minnesota and Stanford, the latter of which qualified for the Rose Bowl and claimed a share of the national title despite losing out in the AP poll. The Huskies would return even stronger in 1941. "We all know just what brand of ball Washington plays," Bruce Smith wrote in that letter to teammates over the summer. "This year, a good start can easily mean the difference between a good season and a poor one. It might even mean the difference between a national championship and no championship at all."[16]

✳ ✳ ✳

"WASHINGTON FIRST." The simple two-word sign was hard to miss in the Minnesota locker room during fall practice. The trainer, Lloyd Stein, put it there as a reminder that nothing mattered beyond Week One at this critical moment. Illinois didn't matter. Pittsburgh didn't matter. Michigan didn't matter. Northwestern, Nebraska, Iowa, and Wisconsin didn't matter. Only Washington mattered.

After finishing tenth in the Associated Press poll the previous year, Washington returned mostly the same starting lineup that gave the Gophers serious trouble in the 1940 opener. Minnesota won a hard-fought, come-from-behind game that afternoon by the score of 19–14 at Memorial Stadium, and the Huskies hadn't forgotten the heartbreak. They felt they had missed an opportunity. Washington coach Jimmy Phelan and his players, including potential All-American end Earl Younglove, wanted to flip the script against the Gophers in this 1941 rematch in Seattle. Phelan's program had lost three straight games to Minnesota, not only in 1940 but also in 1938 and 1936. That worried Bierman. "Sure, we aim to make it four in a row over Washington," he said. "[But] we know from experience that Phelan teams are tough."[17]

Even so, the Huskies felt their own pressure to set the tone for a Pacific Coast championship run. "Where Washington winds up," the Associated Press wrote, "depends chiefly on what happens in the Minnesota opener." Phelan, known for his bombastic Irish personality, refused to allow the Gopher hype to unsettle him. "Nobody's going to shove our forwards around," Phelan said, in response to predictions that Minnesota had one of the most feared lines in the country.[18] Formerly the head coach at Missouri and then Purdue, Phelan was not intimidated by powerful Midwestern-style football. He boasted his own crew of twenty-four returning lettermen and nearly a dozen returning reserves from a team that had finished second in the Pacific Coast Conference, including Younglove, halfback Ernie Steele, and fullback Jack Stackpool, although do-it-all backfield star Dean McAdams had graduated after a stellar 1940 season. The Huskies' left guard, Ray Frankowski, earned specific praise from Bierman, who called him the best "submarining" guard he'd ever seen.[19]

Washington, it was clear, could match the Gophers from a pure talent standpoint. Phelan's crew also enjoyed a built-in advantage as the home team, which afforded them a few extra days of practice on campus. Minnesota didn't have that luxury. The Gophers needed to leave town on Tuesday, September 23—almost five full days ahead of Saturday's game and only nineteen days after the USS *Greer* incident—just to make it to Seattle in time. After finishing a grueling practice that Tuesday at Northrop Field, the players and coaches arrived at the Milwaukee Depot station in downtown Minneapolis around 5:30 p.m., where three thousand boisterous students, alumni, and fans greeted them to bid good luck and farewell. It was a sight to behold, described by some as the largest send-off in years for a Minnesota football team. Although the university band couldn't attend, the local Roosevelt High School band stood in as a replacement to roll the drums as the Gophers boarded the train and departed at 6:00 p.m. Friends, girlfriends, family members, cheerleaders, and even complete strangers pressed themselves against the windows and waved goodbye as the train left the station. *"Beat Those Huskies!"* they chanted repeatedly. It was a scene so enthralling, so encouraging and full of pure happiness and joy, it was as though all the troubles in the world had vanished temporarily. As the train began to inch away, a newspaper reporter for the *Pioneer Press* caught up with a reflective fan enjoying the moment. The unnamed fan thought the 1941 season could be the best in school history. "And may war never interrupt such a fine sporting event as this meeting of teams," he said, "divided by half a nation."[20]

* * *

The forty-one players selected for Minnesota's travel team rode on a special nine-car train, equipped with a dining car carrying more than six hundred combined pounds of prime rib, steak, spring chicken, fish, and ham, on top of two hundred whole potatoes and an assortment of spinach, beans, and eggs. Dr. George Hauser, the dietician as well as the team's line coach, coordinated the meal planning and ensured his players would be well fed for the week. The players occupied three entire train cars themselves, while the coaching staff, sportswriters, and special guests like Lucius Smith rode in the others. Trainer Lloyd Stein and assistant trainer Lloyd Boyce converted another car into a "training room on wheels," where they could access heat lamps and a diathermy machine to treat the players. Oscar Munson, the equipment manager, reserved his own space on the train for uniforms, helmets, and footballs.[21] Leaving at dusk, the team hustled out of the Twin Cities metro area, into the vast rural plains of Minnesota, for about fifty miles before stopping in Glencoe and then Montevideo, where another jubilant crowd of about five thousand people encircled the train with four musical bands. "*WE WANT SMITH*," they yelled.[22]

Emboldened by the support, the Gophers hopped back on the Milwaukee Road tracks and continued to head west. Passing the time with fiercely competitive card games like bridge, the team cruised through the dark prairie and entered South Dakota by 10:00 p.m. As the coaches and players slept, the train then slogged through Aberdeen and crossed the Missouri River in Mobridge, South Dakota, as the Gophers zoomed toward the Mountain Time Zone. "Just north of Mobridge Lewis and Clark camped on Ashley Island, October 8, 1804," a team official wrote in a pamphlet, recording the team's exact location. "Before breakfast time our train will pass through some very interesting sections of 'bad lands' between Ives and Marmath, N.D. The Little Missouri is crossed at Marmath. North of here, along the Little Missouri, Theodore Roosevelt spent many happy days on his ranch."[23] The train continued its overnight trek past Marmath and into Montana at the Yellowstone River, where the team finally came to a stop in Miles City around 8:15 a.m. The players, apparently well rested after sleeping on the train, tried on cowboy hats and toured historic stagecoaches before a 4:30 p.m. practice at the local high school.

The train left Miles City on Wednesday evening around 5:00 p.m. It traveled west through Montana for several hours, stretching from Cartersville through Harlowton, where the train replaced its engine, and then scooted through the Rockies in the middle of the night. Around 6:30 a.m., the players might have awoken to the spectacular view of luscious mountains dotted with evergreen trees as they passed through Missoula—home to the University of Montana, where Bierman had landed his first college coaching job after returning from the First World War. Following the Clark Fork River for many more miles, the train wound through an eight-thousand-foot tunnel at one point, crossed into Idaho and the Pacific Time Zone, and then came to a stop in Spokane, Washington, at 12:30 p.m. Thursday. After a walkthrough and another round of alumni events, the Gophers left Spokane around 10:30 p.m., twisting through Washington and "a very fine view of majestic Mt. Rainier"[24] before arriving in Seattle on Friday afternoon at 1:00 p.m. Minnesota would stay at the Olympic Hotel in downtown Seattle that night, which tackle Ed Lechner described as unusual in his memoir because Bierman never liked to stay in the middle of big cities. The players took advantage of the rare treat at one of the city's finest venues tailored to upper-class society, enjoying a "wonderful dinner at the hotel that night," followed up by a chalk talk from Bierman. "It felt good to stretch out in the big, comfortable bed that night, after our long train trip," Lechner later remembered. [25]

For months, the Minnesota Alumni Club of Seattle had been planning for this game under the direction of President Frank Gilman. He helped organize a banquet for four hundred alumni Friday evening at the Washington Athletic Club and welcomed as many as three thousand visiting Gopher fans to the Pacific Northwest. [26] They arrived in droves on cars and trains, including the Great Northern Railway, which offered an enticing two-cents-per-mile deal with reclining chairs, comfortable mattresses, and full-service meals prepared by top-notch chefs. Minneapolis mayor Marvin L. Kline, who in a few years would lose an election to a rising star named Hubert H. Humphrey, flew to see the Gophers face the Huskies. Seattle's mayor, Earl Millikin, met him at the hotel. [27] He must have been pleased to welcome even more out-of-town visitors to the Seattle metropolitan area, where the population had recently swelled with thousands of job-seekers—including many African Americans from the South—after the federal government made massive investments in defense contracts for the war effort. A full twenty thousand employees, for instance, worked for Boeing Airplane Company by September 1941—five times the number reported in September 1939. According to historian Quintard Taylor, the Puget Sound region also boasted eighty-eight military shipyards, one of which soon became occupied by a brand-new college football fan named Captain Douglas Fisher. [28]

Fisher commanded the *Warspite,* a British ship blasted by Nazi forces during the Battle of Crete back in May 1941. The *Warspite* had now come stateside seeking repairs from American crews at one of those naval yards in Bremerton, just across the bay from the University of Washington's campus. To provide a quintessential American experience during his temporary stay, Captain Fisher's new Seattle friends bought him and his fellow crewmembers tickets to the Minnesota–Washington football game. "My chief interest will lie in the crowd,"

Captain Fisher said. "I've heard so much about how American crowds behave and I'm eager to see one."[29]

Captain Fisher couldn't have chosen a better matchup for his first American football rendezvous. "That Minnesota–Washington game is the headliner of them all," rival Big Ten writer Henry J. McCormick wrote in the *Wisconsin State Journal*, "because it's conceivable that the winner may go on to win the national championship."[30] No game held higher stakes on the first Saturday of college football in 1941. A sellout crowd of at least forty thousand was expected at Husky Stadium, with such demand that ticket scalpers appeared in Seattle for perhaps the first time in history. Seats that should have cost fewer than three dollars suddenly tripled into the range of ten dollars.

The night before the game, winding down in the swanky Olympic Hotel, Bierman settled on his starting eleven. Since the players did not specialize in offense or defense—they played both, often in grueling fashion without much rest—Bierman would need to consider each side of the ball when picking his starters. He decided Bill Garnaas should make his first varsity start at quarterback instead of senior Warren Plunkett. And he decided he wanted Bruce Smith, Bob Sweiger, and Bill Daley to form a triple-threat trio in the backfield, making room for all of them by slotting Sweiger at right halfback and Daley at fullback. This backfield combination would catch Jimmy Phelan by surprise, but the rest of Bierman's prospective starting lineup looked about as expected. Dick Wildung and Urban Odson would hold down the tackle positions for Minnesota, Butch Levy and Helge Pukema would start at guard, and Bob Fitch and Bill Baumgartner would start at end (although sophomore Herb Hein would replace Fitch shortly before kickoff). Gene Flick was chosen as the starting center. The lineup was set.

✧ ✧ ✧

None of the players on the 1941 Minnesota team had ever traveled to Seattle, so the sight of Husky Stadium in all its glory must have left them speechless on the afternoon of September 27. Two decades earlier, the prominent Puget Sound Bridge and Dredging Company had constructed the U-shaped facility on the southern end of the University of Washington's campus with precise measurements, to ensure that the open end of the stadium faced away from the sun and straight east toward the calming blue waters of Union Bay and Lake Washington. Few venues in American sports enjoyed such prime real estate. Ahead of the 2:00 p.m. Seattle time kickoff, approximately forty-three thousand people clawed their way into the spectacular Husky Stadium.[31] The crowd included hundreds if not thousands of active duty soldiers from nearby Fort Lewis, who left the base at 9:00 a.m. Saturday with a military police escort.[32] This clearly would not be an easy season opener for the visiting Gophers. "Good luck," Butch Levy's parents and sister wrote in a telegram that arrived at the Husky Stadium locker room before the game. "Make your start a success/show us all you have the will to make good/everyone banking on you/From Mother Dad and Renee."[33]

Although they could not witness the iconic views of Lake Washington through their radios, listeners across the United States relied on veteran NBC play-by-play announcer Bill Stern to describe the scene— or, if they lived in the Twin Cities like the Levy family, they had their pick of WTCN, KSTP, WCCO, or WLOL. As the broadcasts opened, temperatures in the Pacific Northwest ran comfortably into the upper sixties and seventies on that Saturday afternoon, as the team captains marched toward midfield for the opening coin toss. The Gophers trotted out with their trademark all-gold look: gold pants, gold jerseys, and gold helmets, albeit with dark-colored cleats and white socks covering their feet and ankles. The pants were held together with a belt, carrying knee, thigh, and hip pads; the washed-out uniforms concealed the players' shoulder pads, with numbers printed on the front and back but no team or player names. The open-ended leather helmets blanketed the Gophers' eardrums, almost resembling the type of headgear a fighter pilot might wear. None of the players wore facemasks with their helmets—that was a novel technology at the time—leaving them exposed to the brutality of football. Washington, donning light-colored pants, purple jerseys, and white helmets with one purple streak through the middle, won the coin flip at the fifty-yard line. The Huskies elected to defend. Minnesota would receive the ball to open the 1941 season.

The kickoff promptly sailed out of bounds, meaning the Gophers would take over at their own thirty-five-yard line. On the first play of the game, Minnesota gave the ball to fullback Bill Daley, and he plunged his way forward for a two-yard gain. Then Bruce Smith's 1941 campaign began, as he took a handoff for another two yards before the play was called back due to an illegal motion. Smith carried the next two for eight yards, but he was stopped short on third down. Doubling as both a halfback and punter, the Minnesota captain booted the ball away to the Huskies on fourth down to end the Gophers' first offensive possession of the season.

Leaning on a powerful frontline, Daley and Smith carried the offense during the first several minutes of the game, at one point helping the Gophers advance to Washington's thirteen-yard line. A pass attempt from Smith to end Bob Fitch on fourth down very nearly gave the Gophers their first touchdown of the season, but Washington sophomore Bobby Erickson rushed over to knock the ball down before Fitch could grab it in the end zone. Backed deep in their own territory, the Huskies tried to pass their way out of trouble but could not convert. Odson blocked one of the pass attempts from the trenches. The Huskies placed their trust in young Erickson as a runner and passer, but they were unable to gain any traction against the insurmountable Minnesota line. The first quarter ended without any scoring. "It was a titanic struggle," George Edmond of the *St. Paul Pioneer Press* wrote from the press box, "between two brilliant lines."[34]

The Gophers finally broke through on the first drive of the second quarter. At the Minnesota forty-two-yard line, Bruce Smith showed off his newly improved passing skills with a beautiful toss to wide-open Herb Hein, a relatively unproven end out of Montana playing his first varsity game. Hein raced to the Washington twenty-one before Bobby Erickson shoved him violently out of bounds—possibly saving a touchdown. On the next play, Smith drove the Gophers deep into Husky territory with a twelve-yard charge, diving head-first toward the eight-yard line with his mouth wide open and the football cradled under his right armpit. A few downs later, the Faribault Flash finally punched in the first touchdown of the 1941 season, riding big Urban Odson on the right side of the line for a seven-yard score as he basically hurled himself into the end zone. Cuddling the football with both of his arms this time, Smith grimaced as he emerged from the pile with Washington's Ernie Steele draped over his left shoulder. Bill Garnaas, handling the extra point duties in addition to quarterbacking, kicked the ball through the uprights to give Minnesota a 7–0 lead. The score held through halftime.

Washington made life difficult in the second half. Erickson, continuing his outstanding coverage in the secondary, picked off one of Bruce Smith's passes early in the third quarter near the Husky thirty. Minnesota's defense immediately forced a punt; then Washington did the same. After Ernie Steele returned the ball to the Gopher seventeen-yard line, Bob Sweiger ended the danger with his own interception at the ten. Jimmy Phelan's crew could not figure out this defense.

Later in the third, Bill Garnaas nabbed another interception—and then fumbled the football near his own end zone to give Washington a new set of downs. In prime territory at the fourteen, Ernie Steele scrambled in the backfield but found himself in a quandary, surrounded by gold defenders. Passing was no longer a viable option. In a change of heart, Steele tucked the football under his arm and bolted for the left sideline, scampering into the end zone for a touchdown. In a crucial mishap, the center then botched the snap on the ensuing extra point attempt. Instead of tying the game, the Huskies trailed 7–6 heading into a make-or-break fourth quarter. "Washington's fire," the *Minneapolis Star Journal* wrote, "seemed to disappear after that tough break."[35]

Bill Daley nearly added to his team's narrow lead when he returned an interception to the Washington seven-yard line, but the Gophers waited until the next drive to deliver the final blow. In classic single-wing fashion, they fed Bob Sweiger, Bruce Smith, and sophomore Herman Frickey, the other Montana native who had surprised everybody after he got first-team reps on the first day of fall practice. Smith provided steady and consistent yardage in the open field, while Sweiger—excelling as a right halfback rather than his customary fullback position—"slammed his 206 pounds against the Huskies all afternoon until they were glad to see him leave town," as Perry Dotson of the *Pioneer Press* observed.[36] With the unlimited substitution rule in place for the very first time, Frickey received some carries in the final moments of the game, helping orchestrate a drive deep into the Husky zone and finally to the one-yard line. The Husky Stadium crowd chanted desperately. *Hold that line! Hold that line!* With two minutes remaining, the fans knew a goal line stand was the only shot their team had to stage a comeback. No doubt, Bruce Smith would get the ball here to seal the game. The Minnesota captain, receiving the snap about six yards in the backfield, rode left guard Butch Levy's tail for a one-yard score as Herb Hein signaled *"touchdown!"* with his arms. The Gopher contingent in

the crowd let out a collective rumble as the officials, with some hesitation, deemed the score good. "After the second touchdown," Bruce's
father Lucius later wrote, "he was so exhausted that when another Minnesota player lightly patted him on the back in congratulations, he fell
[flat] down on the ground and was helped up."[37] Bill Garnaas, capping
an impressive varsity debut, added his second extra point of the afternoon to extend the lead to 14–6. In a last-gasp attempt, Washington's
offensive attack stalled as time expired. The game was over. Minnesota
emerged victorious in perhaps the most important season opener in
recent memory. Bruce Smith scored both touchdowns.

※ ※ ※

"The boy they have been touting as an All-America candidate," the
Associated Press wrote, "lived up to advance notices today."[38] Minnesota dominated most of the offensive statistics, with Smith and Bill Daley
combining for almost two hundred yards on the ground. The Gophers
did all of it without a rushing gain larger than fourteen yards. "One of
the best defensive games I have ever seen in an opener," Bernie Bierman said, relieved that his team escaped Seattle with a victory.[39] Jimmy
Phelan did not believe it was a fluke. "Minnesota was farther advanced
for us than a year ago," Phelan said. "I hope we don't have to play
another team that good."[40] Although Smith scored two touchdowns
against his team, Phelan was most taken aback by the performance of
Bill Daley. "I think he did as much to beat us as Smith," Phelan said.[41]
    Bierman's new backfield combination had worked to perfection.
Bruce Smith led the way at left halfback, Bill Daley romped his way at
fullback, and Bob Sweiger slid nicely into the right halfback slot. At
quarterback, Garnaas and Warren Plunkett shared snaps and seemed to
work well in tandem. Bierman singled out Smith and Daley as two of
the offensive stars, but he was also extremely impressed with end Bob
Fitch, the St. Louis Park product, as well as Butch Levy, the starting left
guard. Levy had played an especially strong game. "That's the way to go
out there, pal! I heard the game and I could tell you were the best
lineman on the field," a friend wrote to Butch the next week. "I knew
you were the best goddamn lineman on the squad, and Saturday proved
it to me."[42] Levy's friend was among the tens of thousands of Minnesotans who listened to the game on the radio, before rushing to pick up

copies of the *Minneapolis Sunday Tribune and Star Journal* the next morning. In the famed "Peach Section," a special sports category near the back of the paper, fans could read eight whole pages devoted to the Gophers' thrilling victory and other college football results. "Minnesota Defeats Washington, 14–6: Complete Details of Game, Sidelights and Pictures in Enlarged Peach Sports Section," the front page teased. [43]

As Minnesota prepared to leave Seattle, trainer Lloyd Stein inspected the players for bumps and bruises. Urban Odson's knee, much to the training staff's delight, seemed to be in decent shape after some rough play in the trenches against the physical Huskies. Unfortunately, an injury to right end Bill Baumgartner during the game had become a worst-case scenario: X-rays confirmed he broke his leg and might miss up to six weeks. Otherwise, the Gophers had a lot to celebrate as they boarded their train back to Minneapolis. Embarking in the opposite direction now from west to east, they stopped in new locations on the way home—including Havre, Montana, hometown of Clara Bierman. [44] Relatives, friends, and more complete strangers greeted the Gophers during numerous other stops, including one 5:00 a.m. pause in New Rockford, North Dakota, about twenty miles east of second-string tackle Ed Lechner's hometown of Fessenden. *"Your mother and father are down there to meet you,"* a voice bellowed to Lechner. He did not expect it. "I got over my shock," Lechner later wrote, "quickly got myself dressed and went out to meet them." [45] His parents surprised him with an angel food cake and vanilla frosting—his favorite. Lechner shared the homemade delicacy with his teammates, likely causing a heavy sugar rush before sunrise. "We don't know just how many of the boys were out of bed at 5 a.m.," the *Wells County Free Press* wrote, "but one of Mrs. Lechner's angel food cakes ought to get anyone out any time any place." [46]

Playing card games again to pass the time, the players basked in the thrill of victory. "I can't decide whether that was the toughest game of my experience or not," Bob Sweiger said, telling a story about how he ran into big guard Ray Frankowski after the game and exchanged a nice moment. *Bob, you guys hit really hard*, Frankowski apparently told Sweiger during a handshake.

"That Frankowski," Urban Odson said, "was in my hair every time I made a move."

"Pretty stiff," Bruce Smith added. [47]

The Gophers all knew they had been lucky to get out of Seattle with a victory.

* * *

After returning from Seattle with a 1–0 record, the Gophers got a chance to catch their breath. Thanks to an early bye week, they would not play another football game for fourteen days, when Illinois was scheduled to come to Minneapolis for the home opener at Memorial Stadium on October 11. The break was so long that the New York Yankees and Brooklyn Dodgers played the entire World Series between Minnesota's first and second football contests; Joe DiMaggio and the Bronx Bombers took home the title in five games, beginning October 1 and ending October 6.

With classes starting at the University of Minnesota, Bernie Bierman transitioned from two-a-day practices to once-a-day sessions. The players welcomed the lightened load, but they returned to school with a cloud overhead. "Outwardly, at least, we are behaving as though noth-ing were amiss in the world," new acting university president Walter Coffey said in his opening address to students at Northrop Auditorium, "yet all of us know that the world is different."[48] Due to Selective Service and military enlistment, Coffey announced that student enroll-ment, as expected, had dropped 10 percent at the start of the 1941 fall semester. There were other signs of national defense at the university, too. The campus loaned lab space to the federal government for re-search purposes, the Civil Aeronautics Authority flight training program continued, and the physics department lost six members (and at least ten teaching assistants) to defense work. About ten miles away from campus in the rural fields of Ramsey County, the brand-new Twin Cities Ordnance Plant also grew at a furious pace. Construction on the sprawling facility had started just months earlier under the Army Ord-nance Department, and thousands of new employees—some flocking from other regions of the U.S. seeking defense jobs, just as they had in Seattle—signed up at the plant to help pump resources to the Allies under Lend-Lease.[49]

The ambitious employees included a young Lieutenant Joe Green, an engineer and operations officer for the federal government who once played college football for the University of Illinois. During the

week of the Minnesota–Illinois game, he returned to Memorial Stadium for the first time since 1924 and stood with Bruce Smith after a
practice, as an intrigued local press corps huddled nearby. With came-
ras flashing, the Gophers' captain offered Green a vintage football, with
the following score printed on it: *MINNESOTA 20, ILLINOIS 7, 1924.*
Green couldn't help but crack a smile. "Let me get my hands on that
ball again," he told Smith.[50] On that fateful day in 1924, Green had
played halfback for Illinois, replacing injured star Red Grange after
Minnesota knocked him out of the contest. With Grange on the sidelines, Green's team lost for the first time in 728 days. The upset echoed
across the country, and forever remained a stain on Illini football history. To make matters worse, they never had an opportunity for payback:
due to a bizarre Big Ten scheduling inconsistency after the 1924 season,
Illinois and Minnesota did not face each other for another seventeen
years. The rivalry would now be renewed in 1941.

6

RIVALRY RENEWED

That last game between Minnesota and Illinois, on November 15, 1924, marked the dedication for Memorial Stadium at the end of its inaugural season. Fueled by two million dollars in donations, which also included funds for Northrop Auditorium, the facility opened just six years after the First World War and owed its name to the 3,500 Minnesota natives who died while serving their country. The old Northrop Field, where the Gophers had played since the turn of the century, was no match for this new state-of-the-art building. With a permanent capacity of more than fifty thousand and one million pieces of brick holding the sturdy base together, the horseshoe structure of Memorial Stadium looked massive in comparison and even included brand-new dressing rooms, bathrooms, a press box, and a sparkling equipment room where trainers stuffed leather helmets into tiny lockers and draped the ceiling bars with football cleats. Towering above University Avenue, Memorial Stadium was large enough to cast shadows over the street pavement on a sunny afternoon.[1]

The time had simply come for the University of Minnesota to upgrade its facilities after the student population exploded to ten thousand in the early 1920s, roughly five times as large as the enrollment two decades prior. Ahead of the dedication on November 15 against the Illini, school president Lotus D. Coffman wrote optimistically in the game program about the impact of Memorial Stadium for generations to come. "The Stadium will make a tremendous contribution to University unity and spirit," Coffman wrote, "when it brings our thousands of students together at a moment when they are inspired by a common enthusiasm."[2]

It was precisely that enthusiasm that spurred Minnesota to a monumental upset on that afternoon in 1924. Most observers expected undefeated Illinois and folk legend Red Grange to roll the Gophers, but they clearly underestimated the power of a jazzed Memorial Stadium dedication crowd. Robert Zuppke of Illinois, at the time a heralded and highly successful collegiate head coach, was thoroughly humbled in the 20–7 defeat at the hands of the Gophers. "The Minnesota team, after playing mediocre football all season, found itself with a bang Saturday," young *Minneapolis Tribune* sportswriter George Barton recorded the next day, "and swept Bob Zuppke's football machine off its feet during the last three periods."[3] It was one of the most embarrassing losses of Zuppke's career.

Seventeen years later, Zuppke hadn't forgotten. Although well past his prime, the chisel-jawed, German-born Zuppke, whose accent was still noticeable despite his family moving from Berlin when he was two years old, was still plugging away in his twenty-ninth season at the University of Illinois. He was delighted to see Minnesota finally appear on his schedule again in 1941 after such a long hiatus. "Mr. Zuppke is

Fans pack Memorial Stadium in Minneapolis on a typical Saturday afternoon. The "Brickhouse" provided lasting memories for Gopher fans from 1924 through 1981. *Courtesy of University of Minnesota Archives, University of Minnesota–Twin Cities*

here for revenge," the *Minneapolis Daily Times* wrote. "Revenge for the tables that the Gophers turned on his 1924 team."[4]

This time around, most expected the Gophers to rout the Illini, who had not finished with a winning record in five seasons. Due to the slipping performance, the school canned athletic director Wendell Wilson during the off-season and informed Zuppke that he would be next if his team didn't shape up quickly. They told him the board would reconsider his status after the 1941 season, despite nearly three decades of contributions to the university. It was a difficult conversation for everyone involved. "Please be assured," university president Arthur Willard wrote to Zuppke in July 1941, "that I have in mind, not only the best interests of the University, which you have long served with conscientious and conspicuous distinction, but also that my friendship and high regard for you would naturally be an important factor in considering your own welfare and status."[5] Friendship or not, however, it still appeared 1941 was the last chance for the sixty-two-year-old to salvage his career.

If anyone could find a way to survive in such dire circumstances, it was probably Zuppke. That frightened Bernie Bierman. Despite a lack of talent across the board, Zuppke boasted a fast, hard-working group of players that had circled the Minnesota game on their October calendars for months. "Football fans," Eddie Jacquin of the *News-Gazette* in Champaign-Urbana wrote, "can look for a fine spirit on this squad."[6] Known for his trick plays and offensive innovation, there was no doubt that Zuppke would devise some type of master plan to keep the mighty Gophers on their heels.

Bernie Bierman made every minute of practice count during his team's bye week. He ran the varsity players through intense workouts and threw some of them against Dallas Ward's freshman team for the first time that fall. Bierman focused heavily on pass defense. If the Gophers had any weak spot, it was probably their secondary. It very nearly cost them a few games in 1940, and in this year's opener against Washington, Bierman was not pleased with how easily the Huskies were able to complete passes. Now facing an Illinois team quite fond of the aerial attack, defending the pass would be a surefire way to avoid an embarrassing and potentially season-derailing upset.

With his team idle during the weekend of October 4, Bierman took advantage of the free time. He caught a train to Champaign to personally scout the game between Illinois and Miami of Ohio, hoping to come away with a better sense of what the Gophers might face a week later. As rain fell persistently for four quarters in Champaign, Bierman saw the Illini blast Miami 45–0 before returning to Minneapolis with an intensive written scouting report. "It was positively the most versatile and perfected offense I have seen in a good many years," Bierman said about Illinois. "Their passing trickery prescribed by rather a light team was very impressive."[7]

Against Miami, Zuppke partially relied on the T formation to boost his offense, experimenting with a revitalized style of play that had taken the football universe by storm in 1940. Stanford, led by an old friend of Bierman's named Clark Shaughnessy, rode the T all the way to the Rose Bowl, and the formation helped coach George Halas and the Chicago Bears thump Washington 73–0 in the NFL Championship Game. Unlike the single-wing, the quarterback in a T formation lined up right behind center and handled each snap, typically with three backs positioned a few yards behind him. The T's emergence under Shaughnessy and Halas led to a seismic shift in offensive philosophy, as countless college football coaches took notice and began to implement the offense prior to the 1941 season. Although Minnesota largely resisted the temptation and remained committed to the single-wing, Bierman anticipated some T-related tricks from Zuppke the next weekend and vowed to prepare for every last one of them. "Seldom has a Minnesota practice been devoted to such intensive study of an opponent's probable intentions," Dick Cullum of the *Minneapolis Daily Times* wrote that week.[8]

Zuppke, meanwhile, could now turn his full attention to Minnesota after his team breezed through the opener against Miami. Instead of giving his players a rest day on Sunday, he ordered them to the football field for a light practice. By Tuesday, with more rain falling, the Illini began to ramp up the intensity of their practice sessions. They were energized and confident, walking with a hop in their step and ready to take on the world for their embattled head coach. Before the team left for Minneapolis, Zuppke named junior halfback Jimmy Smith, who missed the 1940 season with an injury, as an acting captain. He would play left halfback, teaming up in the backfield with another budding star named Don Griffin. George Edmond of the *St. Paul Dispatch* praised Griffin, a sophomore from Chicago, as one of the most underrated halfbacks in the Big Ten. In addition to those two, Zuppke appeared likely to lean on quarterback Liz Astroth to orchestrate the passing attack. The Illini felt their speed could make up for a lack of size. "Our team is better this year," Zuppke said that week. "We have more dangerous backs, but I don't know what to expect."[9]

The thirty-five members of the Illinois squad departed campus late Thursday afternoon, reaching Chicago for a one-night stay at the Palmer House before cruising into Minneapolis on Friday afternoon.[10] Soon, the team settled at the Curtis Hotel in the heart of downtown, where the players and coaches would stay the night before the game in one of the venue's dual towers. The Gophers, meanwhile, held a walkthrough at 5:30 p.m. at the stadium before the starters and immediate backups headed east on a Greyhound bus to Bayport, a small town in Washington County on the St. Croix River. Bierman liked to keep his team away from campus on the eve of home games, opting to bring his players and staff to the charming White Pine Inn about thirty miles away. The comfortable eighteen-room hotel, dotted with dark chimneys and four grand white columns on the front exterior, provided solace for the Gophers and eliminated distractions of the big city. At the White Pine Inn, the players slept two-to-a-room, ate sirloin steaks in the dining room, and listened to Bierman's chalk talks as they ran through mental preparations.

Bierman didn't plan to change his starting lineup much for the Illinois game, though he would need to replace the injured Bill Baumgartner with Judd Ringer at one of the end positions. Adding to his persistent concerns about backfield depth, 150-pound sophomore Bud Higgins had also cracked a rib in practice and remained questionable. Higgins, largely an unknown commodity entering his first varsity season, impressed the coaching staff during the bye week with a terrific scrimmage performance against the freshman team. He torched the outclassed freshmen for three touchdowns and proved to the varsity coaches that he deserved better than his third-string halfback slot.[11] If his rib healed quickly, Higgins might see carries against Illinois—especially if the game turned into a blowout as expected—but Bierman warned his team against overconfidence. "Anything can happen," he wrote in his weekly syndicated column that appeared in several regional newspapers and carried his byline.[12]

The pundits across America weren't listening. Practically all of them predicted an easy victory for Minnesota. From New York, Jack Guenther of the United Press joked that Zuppke "will wish he had taken that pension" after facing the Gophers.[13] Even in Decatur, Illinois, located about fifty miles from the U of I campus, the local newspaper wondered aloud: "Do we dare listen this afternoon to the radio broadcast of the Illinois–Minnesota football game?"[14]

❅ ❅ ❅

The roughly fifty thousand fans at Memorial Stadium on October 11, 1941, enjoyed pleasant fall weather to open the Big Ten football schedule, with high temperatures creeping into the upper fifties and only a few clouds scattered throughout the sky. Late ticket sales helped the Gophers tally a sellout. Prior to the 2:00 p.m. kickoff, the team arrived from Bayport on another Greyhound bus, enjoying a full police escort as adoring crowds cheered along their route. If either the players or the fans read the newspaper that morning, they might have seen a short write-up about their home opener on Page One of the *Minneapolis Tribune*, describing the game-day weather as "much to their liking" despite some wind.[15] The short, ninety-four-word football blurb appeared to the right of three syndicated stories about war topics, all from the Associated Press and all related to the situation in Russia. In summary, the U.S. House of Representatives had approved a new Lend-Lease bill that now increased the possibility of financial aid to the Soviet Union, as the Russian troops attempted to counterpunch advancing Nazi forces that had invaded their country over the summer.

The game-day atmosphere at Memorial Stadium, though primitive by today's standards, would look recognizable to a modern audience. The crowd took its cue from the University of Minnesota band, which sat field-level near the sidelines and blared the same fight song as it does today. There were also cheerleaders (although, in a sign of the times, they were all male), a public address announcer, and student sections. Among the most impressive features at Memorial Stadium was the electronic scoreboard—a rectangular structure situated on top of the athletic building Cooke Hall overlooking the end zone—that helped fans follow the time, score, and down. These were all revolutionary changes for the old-timers, who had fallen in love with the Gophers at prehistoric Northrop Field. Prince Wickersham, a manager for the team near the turn of the twentieth century, said that the new college football facilities of the 1920s, 1930s, and early 1940s were "enormous" and "magnificent," but he bemoaned the corporatization of the game as athletic departments began spending millions to feed their fans' obsessions. "Today the enthusiasm is so canned and manufactured," Wickersham wrote, "as to make me pause and wonder."[16]

Despite Wickersham's observations, there was absolutely no canned enthusiasm at the 1941 Memorial Stadium home opener—and the fans didn't have to wait long for something to cheer. After winning the toss, Minnesota elected to receive and Bruce Smith returned the opening kickoff to his own twenty-eight-yard line. As the starting eleven took the field, the gold-uniformed reserves and their well-dressed coaches—Bierman donned a fedora and trench coat—sat on rock-hard benches up against the wall of the bleachers, within an arm's reach of the fans in the first row. Within a matter of seconds, they would all prepare to explode with excitement.

On first-and-ten, the Gophers lined up as they normally did in single-wing formation and sent a back in motion to the right, before the snap went directly to Melrose native Bill Daley at fullback. With Garnaas and Smith serving as decoys, Daley darted through a hole created by Butch Levy and Dick Wildung, burst into the open secondary past a diving Don Griffin at the thirty-five, caught a block from Bruce Smith just before midfield, sped past two more desperate defenders, rode another block from Bob Sweiger at the twenty-five, and raced toward the end zone for a touchdown as the boisterous Memorial Stadium crowd let out an enormous roar. As Daley crossed the goal line, trailed by Judd Ringer, the official signaled *"touchdown"* with his arms raised straight into the air. The Minnesota band, without hesitation, rolled straight into the fight song. On the very first play from scrimmage, Daley had gone seventy-two yards for a score before the fans could even settle into their seats or process what on earth had just happened. Some of them, including a student writer for the *Minnesota Daily*, missed the touchdown as they fought their way through the congested Memorial Stadium concourse toward the bleachers. "I will take a parachute with me the next time and bail out," the *Daily* writer said. "It's as close to heaven as I'll ever get."[17]

Daley's touchdown set a strong tone, but Minnesota knew a one-score lead was not safe against a creative Bob Zuppke team. Bierman and backfield coach Sheldon Beise also must have cringed when they learned Sweiger injured himself throwing a block for Daley downfield on that first play. Herman Frickey, the Billings, Montana, sophomore who fared so well in the opener at Washington, replaced Sweiger only forty-nine seconds into the first quarter. Minutes later, the Gophers lost another senior starter when Urban Odson exited during a defensive stand. He had re-aggravated his knee. "The same old thing," trainer Lloyd Stein said in a discouraging tone.[18] Ed Lechner, arguably the best reserve tackle on the team, entered the game in Odson's place.

Even with its opponent down two starters, Illinois simply had no answer for the size of Minnesota's line or the power and speed of its backfield. It could not prevent the onslaught. On the third drive of the game, Daley capped a five-play drive with a seven-yard touchdown through the heart of the Illinois defense; 13–0. Later in the first, Bruce Smith followed Dick Wildung as they bullied their way through Illini tacklers for a five-yard touchdown; 20–0. At the beginning of the second quarter, with the backups now inserted into the lineup, little Bud Higgins built on his strong performance in practice and danced his way fourteen yards for a touchdown—the first of his varsity career; 27–0.

Zuppke's offense did itself no favors. With a heavy weight disadvantage on the line, Illinois failed to gain even a *single yard* in the first half. There was no semblance of a passing game. Receivers dropped balls and the center at one point misfired a snap. By halftime, Bierman had already taken full advantage of the new free substitution rule by emptying almost his entire bench; thirty-two reserves would see action by the time the game was over. Gene Bierhaus of Brainerd saw snaps in Bruce Smith's left halfback position. Mike Welch of St. James played some fullback. Garnaas ceded to Warren Plunkett, Paul Mitchell played tackle, and Bob Smith of West High School took over at guard for his old buddy Butch Levy. Fans became familiar with names like John Billman (guard), Joe Hirscher (end), Earl Eli (fullback), and Joe Lauterbach (right halfback).

Carrying a four-score lead out of the halftime break, Bernie Bierman cautiously reinserted his starters to ensure the 27–0 margin would not disappear. Only Sweiger and Odson remained missing from the original starting lineup due to injuries. After recovering a fumble deep in Illinois territory early in the third quarter, Ed Lechner opened running room at left tackle for Bruce Smith on first down, which the senior captain converted for twelve yards to the Illinois eleven-yard line. On the very next play, Bill Garnaas called a "delayed buck," handled the snap, and fed the ball again to Smith. He rushed into the end zone untouched for his fourth touchdown of the 1941 season; 34–0.

Bierman left the starters in the game through most of the third and fourth quarters, until it became apparent Illinois had no chance whatsoever for a comeback. Bruce Smith's final carry resulted in a fumble, giving Bob Zuppke's crew possession at its own forty-one with a chance to salvage at least one score. Facing a reserve defense, Zuppke's crew found a groove and needed only three plays to march to the Minnesota twelve-yard line. The Illini found the end zone through the air, on a connection from Don Griffin to Liz Astroth. The game ended with a final score of 34–6.

The visiting writers from Chicago summed up the affair with particularly harsh words, none harsher than Wilfrid Smith of the *Chicago Tribune*. "The truth about today's game, if it can be called that," Smith said, "is that Illinois was outweighed, outmanned and overmatched."[19] James Kearns of the *Chicago Daily News* called the performance "awe-inspiring."[20] Bob Zuppke, meanwhile, likened the contest to "sending boys against men."[21] The statistics told the whole story: Minnesota outgained Illinois 463 to 184 and forced nine punts, leading the Associated Press to observe that the Fighting Illini seemed "hopelessly outclassed."[22]

Bierman seemed mostly pleased with his team's performance through the first two games. He had grown especially impressed with his smallest player, halfback Bud Higgins. "I liked Bud Higgins' play from an offensive standpoint very much," Bierman said. "Despite his weight of 148 pounds, he has speed and follows his interference well."[23] Bierman would be calling the little man's name even more in the coming days as the Gophers shifted focus to the University of Pittsburgh, a once-dominant East Coast football power that sorely needed a victory.

7

THE LITTLE MAN

The Pittsburgh Panthers, at one time frequent visitors to the Rose Bowl, ranked among the most feared college football programs in America during the 1930s despite competing as an Independent with no conference affiliation. Bernie Bierman had a front-row seat to that bygone era. Early in his tenure at Minnesota, in 1933 and 1934, he scheduled a marquee home-and-home series with the Panthers and earned close victories both times—the only two games Pittsburgh lost in either season. The 1933 triumph at Memorial Stadium marked one of Bierman's early signature wins, while the victory in the 1934 return game helped transform Minnesota from a good program into a perennial national championship contender. Yet as things got better for the Golden Gophers, they seemed to just keep getting worse for the Panthers. After coach Jock Sutherland's departure in 1938, the program faded into mediocrity and now seemed to be veering toward its lowest point with two dreadful performances to start the 1941 season.

In the opener, Pittsburgh stumbled to a 6–0 defeat at home against Purdue. Then, the squad headed to Ann Arbor, where things spiraled completely out of control in a 40–0 shellacking at the hands of Michigan. It was "the most humiliating defeat ever stamped upon a Pitt grid team," according to Alex Zelenski, the sports editor of the student newspaper the *Pitt News*. "Captain Bob Westfall, Tommy Kuzma, and Co. ran rough-shod over a far inferior Panther team."[1] At 0–2, Pittsburgh was still looking for its first touchdown—no, first *point*—of the season. "That pasting [against Michigan] was the worst in modern Pitt football history," the *Morning Call* in Allentown wrote, "and there probably is more to come with Minnesota in the offing next Saturday."[2]

The narrative sounded almost eerily familiar to the Illinois game: a former football power, now downtrodden, would head to Memorial Stadium as a major underdog, looking to avenge losses from years earlier. Except there would be no Bob Zuppke roaming the sidelines this time. Pittsburgh's third-year head coach was Charley Bowser, a Pennsylvania native who had played football at Pitt under Pop Warner and later served as an assistant on Jock Sutherland's staff at his alma mater. With the odds stacked against him, Bowser decided to shake up his lineup to counter the Gophers' speed and power. "We're going to put 11 players in there against Minnesota who want to go," Bowser said.[3] With his opponent's frontline outweighing his own by an average of at least fifteen pounds, Bowser promoted George Allshouse to starting center and Matt Gebel to starting fullback. Both had previously spent time working with the third-team squad. Joe Connell would also get a shot at playing right halfback opposite Edgar "Special Delivery" Jones, the team's star senior and by far its most dangerous offensive threat when healthy. He would return to action against Minnesota after nursing an injury, providing a much-needed boost to the overmatched Panthers. "They may surprise a lot of folks," Bowser said optimistically, "and I can stand a few surprises."[4]

⁕ ⁕ ⁕

In the middle of the week, college football fans across the country picked up newspapers and read the results of the first Associated Press poll of 1941 (no pre-season rankings existed in those days, and the in-season polls did not begin until October). Unsurprisingly, Minnesota claimed the top spot by a healthy margin, followed by undefeated Texas in second place. Duke rose to third place after a torrid 3–0 start, which included an impressive 19–0 victory over dominant Southeastern Conference power Tennessee. In fourth place was Fordham, which was coming off a Cotton Bowl appearance. After that, the Big Ten earned representation with Northwestern (fifth place) and Michigan (sixth place), the two teams Minnesota would face back-to-back after Pittsburgh.

Determined to keep his team focused on Pitt, Bierman ran the varsity team through strenuous practices that week and scheduled a scrimmage against the freshman team to simulate game-like situations. The players also sat through agonizing blackboard study sessions to prepare for Charley Bowser's variation of the single-wing offense, which closely mirrored the formation utilized by his mentor Jock Sutherland and also largely resembled the principles instilled by Bierman at Minnesota. Unlike the bruising Pittsburgh teams of the 1930s, however, Bowser had added a few wrinkles to the single-wing and gave his players more freedom to attack opponents through the air. Considering Illinois had scored its only touchdown the previous week on a passing play, Bierman again concentrated heavily on pass defense in practice and tried to shore up hidden vulnerabilities. "Don't sell the Panthers short," Bierman told a group of students at Coffman Memorial Union four days before the game. "If Pittsburgh gets its share of gridiron breaks, their rugged, big eleven will give us a much closer game than the light Illini outfit."[5]

Thirty-four members of the Pittsburgh Panthers arrived by train in Minneapolis at 9:30 a.m. on Friday, October 17, heading first to Memorial Stadium for some passing and punting drills. "We just don't know what to expect tomorrow," Bowser said. "We'll have to wait until action starts to find out a thing or two about our boys as well as Minnesota."[6] Quietly, the Panthers then hurried over to the Curtis Hotel for the evening—the same place Illinois stayed—as Bierman shuffled his own team to Bayport again for some peace and quiet at the White Pine Inn. As he trekked east toward the St. Croix River for an overnight getaway, Bierman must have felt a surge of anxiety about his lineup. Urban Odson, still outfitted with a special knee brace and available only for limited snaps, would likely cede the starting tackle position to Ed Lechner, the pride and joy of Fessenden, North Dakota. And in the backfield, Bob Sweiger's spine injury—suffered while throwing a block during Bill Daley's seventy-two-yard touchdown on the first play against Illinois—threatened to keep him out of the Pittsburgh game entirely. Sophomore Herman Frickey planned to step into the right halfback position alongside Daley and Bruce Smith. Student writers at the *Minnesota Daily* also predicted that Bud Higgins of Washburn High School would see more carries in Sweiger's absence. The shifty 150-pound sophomore had loudly introduced himself to the Twin Cities with a touchdown in his varsity debut against Illinois. "Bierman tossed in a number of new faces in the Gopher secondary," the newspaper wrote after the game, "[including] a greased skyrocket—Little Bud Higgins—who will fit potently."[7]

☼ ☼ ☼

As the Gophers and Panthers prepared for their matchup in Minneapolis, the chief executive of Minnesota coincidentally found himself in Pittsburgh, of all places, for a scheduled event the night before the game. Governor Harold Stassen, appearing unofficially as a religious leader and as a member of the Northern Baptist convention, addressed one thousand Baptists in western Pennsylvania that Friday evening at the Schenley Hotel. "People are returning to the fundamentals these days," Stassen said. "They are taking the religious concept more seriously in times like these, and the church—every church—is adding strength."[8]

As the governor addressed the Northern Baptist crowd, concerning news reports began to roll in from the North Atlantic—once again involving a U.S. ship on patrol duty. The USS *Kearny*, a Navy destroyer weighing more than a thousand tons, had been attacked about 350 miles off the coast of Iceland, not all that far from where the USS *Greer* traded depth charges with a German U-boat about a month earlier. The *Greer* incident had been a near-mishap, a defining moment that helped shape Roosevelt's shoot-on-sight policy but avoided human casualties. The *Kearny*, however, appeared to be a full-fledged disaster. Although early press reports could not estimate the number of deaths, the American public would soon learn that eleven people had died aboard the *Kearny* after a German U-boat fired a torpedo at the watercraft. It was the first deadly attack on an American naval ship since the start of the conflict, spurring a variety of reactions from U.S. lawmakers. Democratic senator Claude Pepper of Florida said the Navy should respond with "two sinkings for each assault," while isolationist Republican senator Gerald Nye of North Dakota blamed Roosevelt's shoot-on-sight policy for the aggression and cautioned that he "wouldn't let this mean war, so far as I am concerned."[9]

From his getaway home in Hyde Park, New York, President Roosevelt defended the *Kearny*'s right to patrol the North Atlantic during a news conference held in his study room, but he referred journalists to the Navy Department for more details. Frustrated by the president's refusal to answer basic questions about the attack, White House correspondent Tom Reynolds pressed for answers. "Still on that same question, Mr. President," Reynolds started. "May we assume that the instructions you issued in the case of the *Greer*—to hunt down the marauder—apply in this case?" Roosevelt, the former assistant secretary of the Navy, attempted to deflect the important question with a dose of sarcasm. "Regular Navy orders. I don't know that I would say to hunt down the marauders. You ought to go into the Navy, Tom—really—honestly," Roosevelt responded. "Why, Lord—we'll get you to Annapolis and put you on the football team."[10]

The crisis involving Germany and the *Kearny* overshadowed another major development that week in Japan, where Prime Minister Fumimaro Konoe resigned and yielded power to War Minister Hideki Tojo. The leadership change had major consequences for relations with the United States, just months after the Roosevelt administration imposed sanctions in response to Japan's military occupation of southern French Indochina. Three U.S. senators, including Pepper, called for a "hard-fisted policy" toward the new cabinet in Japan on October 18 after learning that the U.S. Navy had called some American merchant ships back to port in the Eastern Hemisphere for "instruction." Senator George Norris of Nebraska stated his concerns directly: "We can't appease Japan any more than we can appease Hitler. If Japan wants to attack us, she'll attack. All she is waiting for is to try and feel certain she is on the winning side."[11]

It is unclear if Gov. Stassen knew yet of the incident involving the *Kearny* when he addressed the Northern Baptist convention on the Friday evening of October 17 in Pittsburgh; he certainly would not have had any knowledge of the pending cabinet upheaval in Japan. Regardless, it did not take long for him to shift from religion to discussion of the war. "Like everyone else," he said, "we hope that entrance into the war will not be necessary." Stassen, a Republican, then offered support for the White House: "The people of our region are fully behind the foreign policy of President Roosevelt." Only then did the conversation turn to football—specifically the big Minnesota–Pittsburgh game the following day. Stassen diagrammed plays for his Pittsburgh friends after the speech and spoke proudly of the mighty Gophers back in his home state. Lester Bumpus of the Pittsburgh Baptist Association admitted to the governor that he expected a blowout; Stassen thought it might be a closer game. "We haven't heard much about Pitt so far," he told Bumpus, "but we have a whale of a team and ought to have a margin of one or two touchdowns."[12]

* * *

Thanks to gloomy weather and a persistent drizzle, Memorial Stadium drew a lighter crowd for the 2:00 p.m. kickoff on Saturday, October 18, with a paid attendance of roughly thirty-five thousand. Bierman's starting lineup featured only one minor surprise, as Herb Hein slid into Judd Ringer's spot at right end. The other changes were expected: Ed Lechner started for Urban Odson, and Herman Frickey started for Bob Sweiger in light of his spine injury. The fans, likely paying closer attention so they wouldn't miss another seventy-two-yard touchdown on the first play, expected this lineup to dominate Pittsburgh from start to finish regardless of injuries. But it didn't exactly work out that way—at the beginning, at least.

After a touchback on the opening kickoff, Minnesota's first offensive drive of the game stalled. Bruce Smith carried three times in a row for only seven yards and then punted the ball away on fourth down. Joe Connell, the starting right halfback for Pitt, fumbled the return, which Ed Lechner recovered just past midfield in a major early break for the Gophers. It did not last. Connell immediately redeemed himself on the next snap, as he intercepted a Bruce Smith pass at his own seventeen to regain possession for Pitt.

The rest of the first quarter remained ugly and ended in a scoreless tie. Minnesota did not break through until the second drive of the second quarter, after Dick Wildung recovered a fumble by Edgar "Special Delivery" Jones at the Gopher thirty-five-yard line. First, Smith found Bill Garnaas for a fourteen-yard gain through the air. Then Smith added eight more himself on a rushing attempt as the Gophers rolled into Pitt territory. Daley marched forward for another first down, and then Smith took a reverse for an exhilarating thirty-seven yards to the Pittsburgh two-yard line. For the first time all afternoon, the crowd exploded. On the very next play, Daley smashed his way through for a touchdown, and the extra point by Garnaas gave Minnesota a 7–0 lead.

After forcing a punt, the Gophers took over on offense with strong field position near midfield. On first down, Smith again handled a reverse but instead of running, he abruptly launched a pass downfield, connecting with Garnaas for a twenty-two-yard gain. The officials spotted Minnesota at the Pitt thirty. After a six-yard run by Frickey, Smith barreled through several Pittsburgh players on second down, dragging them to the thirteen-yard line as a gang of tacklers crushed him. Officials called a roughing penalty while Smith, to the concern of the thirty-five thousand people in the stands, writhed in pain on the field after bruising his back. *Was it serious?* Memorial Stadium fell to a hush as trainers helped Smith off the field. Against a more formidable opponent, the All-American hopeful might have stayed in the ballgame, but the coaching staff did not want to risk anything against a team of Pittsburgh's caliber. Common sense prevailed. Bruce Smith's day was finished.

Smith's absence would change the entire complexion of the game—and the Panthers knew it. All of the players in dark blue jerseys "breathed a little easier" when they saw the Gophers' captain heading toward the Memorial Stadium locker room, according to *The Pitt News*. And they hardly paid any attention when "a little fellow by the name of Higgins"[13] came into the game to replace Smith. Perhaps they should have. Soon, they would know this backup's full name: Robert "Bud" Higgins. Described by his senior yearbook at Washburn High School as "football man, basketball man, last but not least, ladies' man," the confident halfback would soon make the Panthers regret their belittlement.[14]

❊ ❊ ❊

The roughing penalty against Pittsburgh, which came on the play that injured Bruce Smith and paved the way for Higgins to enter the game, gave Minnesota a first-and-goal from the one-yard line. On the very next play, Bill Daley converted the short-yardage carry for his second touchdown of the afternoon, extending the lead to 14–0. Despite his early success, he would not find the end zone again.

The final two and a half quarters belonged to Bud Higgins—starting with the very next offensive drive. On second down near midfield, the little man evaded a wave of Pittsburgh defenders, spurted through a hole on the left side of the line, outraced "Special Delivery" Jones, and faked out a defender at the goal line to cap a forty-seven-yard touchdown run. "Garnaas kicked goal to make it 21 to 0 and sent the rooters into a dither at half time as they sang his praises," the *Minneapolis Star Journal* observed. "That wasn't the last of Higgins."

Indeed it was not. Right out of the gate in the second half, Higgins ran back the opening kickoff seventy yards to the opposing twenty-one-yard line (although Warren Plunkett spoiled the opportunity by fumbling on first down) and added a forty-nine-yard punt return just minutes later. Hungry for another score, Higgins followed left end Bob Fitch's blocking on first down for a nineteen-yard gain, setting up his two-yard touchdown a few plays later to increase the lead to 27–0. In the fourth quarter, Higgins sprinted forty-two yards to the Pittsburgh thirteen-yard line after tricking the Panthers on a fake pass. The theatrics led to his third touchdown of the day, which came on a fourth-down conversion from five yards out. Adding in an interception returned for a touchdown by Bill Garnaas in the third quarter, the Gophers walked away with an easy 39–0 victory after scoring a total of six touchdowns. Higgins tallied half of them. "He was so sensational," the *Star Journal* wrote, "that every time the ball went to him the strictly Minnesota crowd of 35,000 rose in unison to get a better look."[15] Higgins finished with an absurd 157 rushing yards on just eleven carries, and he helped Minnesota outgain Pittsburgh 111 to 17 on punt return yardage.

Bud Higgins was the talk of the Twin Cities—and the talk of Pittsburgh, too, for that matter. *Pittsburgh Press* sports editor Charles Smith wrote that "Master Higgins" had exhausted Pittsburgh with his elusiveness and "runs like a jackrabbit."[16] Harry Keck of the *Pittsburgh Sun-Telegraph* could barely comprehend what he had just seen. "The Panthers might have kept the score down to a respectable margin with only Smith to contend with," he wrote, "but there ought to be a law against allowing little speed demons like Higgins to run loose."[17]

Even Bernie Bierman expressed some surprise. His little halfback who'd only recently graduated from the practice squad "really did some scampering," he wrote in his column.[18] Higgins, basking in his new stardom, hung out on his couch at home in Minneapolis the day after the game as he recuperated from his legendary performance. Staying humble, the five-foot-six wizard quickly credited his offensive line for offering such stout protection. "Maybe, too," Higgins said, "those Pitt guys couldn't see me behind all the interference."[19]

As a unit, Minnesota's line once again dominated the line of scrimmage, making it possible for Higgins to rip downfield repeatedly. The Gophers gained the vast majority of their yardage on the ground (286 yards) as well as through Higgins' punt and kickoff returns. Butch Levy and Helge Pukema led the way by pummeling the opposing guards, Ed Lechner stepped in admirably for the injured Odson at tackle, and Gene Flick held down the starting center spot for the third straight game. Still, no performance rose to the level of Luverne's Dick Wildung at tackle. The junior's speed and physicality—refined from those years of harsh workouts on his high school track in southwestern Minnesota—controlled the game, both offensively and defensively. "Dick Wildung," Bierman said, "had a lot to do with straightening out our line when the Panthers began rolling. You know Pittsburgh was a more rugged and powerful team than many believed in advance."[20] Captain Bruce Smith, watching from the sidelines after exiting with his back injury in the first half, came up with the same assessment. "My thrill in watching? Oh, that Higgins, sure," Smith said. "And did that Wildung play a game at tackle."[21]

Smith remained in decent spirits after the game. He did not break any bones and likely could have played if absolutely necessary, but the Gophers would need him and others to get healthy—quickly—with the two strongest opponents of the season soon approaching in Michigan and Northwestern.

✧ ✧ ✧

As Bud Higgins ran wild, Michigan and Northwestern slugged it out against each other in Evanston. In a vicious, physical battle between two of the other prime Big Ten contenders, UM sophomore Tom Kuzma tossed a go-ahead, forty-six-yard touchdown in the fourth quarter for a late 14–7 lead, stunning the partisan Dyche Stadium crowd. Rallying furiously, Wildcats' star Bill DeCorrevont orchestrated a downfield march inside the ten before a group of Wolverines sacked him on a desperate fourth-down scramble attempt. Michigan won the football game and remained undefeated, dealing a blow to Northwestern's Big Ten hopes and setting up yet another showdown with top-ranked Minnesota on October 25. "Next Saturday's clash at Ann Arbor between Michigan and Minnesota," Bill Boni of the Associated Press wrote, "should go a long way toward straightening out the national and the Big Ten alignment."[22]

The folks in Ann Arbor had been waiting an entire year for this rematch, ever since Bruce Smith's eighty-yard dash through the mud ruined their title hopes and spoiled an otherwise stellar 1940 season. That loss in Minneapolis crushed Tom Harmon, the Heisman Trophy winner who graduated without ever defeating the Gophers. It crushed the Wolverines' coaching staff, led by the former Minnesota man Fritz Crisler—the same Crisler whose hiring over Bierman caused an uproar back in 1930. And it crushed the Michigan fan base, which could not stand to lose possession of the "Little Brown Jug," the oldest trophy in college football that dated back to the early days of the rivalry. Indeed, the supporters in Maize and Blue spent all of 1941 gunning for revenge against Minnesota, buoyed by home-field advantage this time. Even before the Michigan–Northwestern game in Evanston, fans at home in Ann Arbor began buying tickets in bulk to prepare for the Gophers' arrival on October 25. "It may be," the *Michigan Daily* wrote, "the biggest gathering in Wolverine football history."[23]

8

LITTLE BROWN JUG ARMAGEDDON

Years before it was nicknamed "The Big House," the giant bowled structure on South Main Street in Ann Arbor was simply known by its official name: Michigan Stadium. Using the same engineering firm that designed Memorial Stadium in Minneapolis, famed University of Michigan coach Fielding Yost spearheaded efforts for a larger and grander football facility in the decade following World War I. The original configuration of Michigan Stadium in 1927 held more than seventy thousand permanent seats, but it could easily accommodate more than eighty thousand fans—making it one of the largest college football stadiums in the United States.[1]

Ann Arbor, population thirty thousand before the war, never had any trouble supporting Michigan football, but the explosion of the defense industry in southeast Michigan during the early 1940s only bolstered the local base of potential ticket-buyers. Already king of the automobile world, the Detroit metropolitan area had entered the beginning stages of a complete transformation, one that would make it into an unrivaled bastion of production for the war effort. Chrysler was manufacturing tanks in a massive million-square-foot facility in nearby Warren, and Ford Motor Company had recently started building the enormous Willow Run plant near Ypsilanti to produce B-24 bombers. Located just ten miles from Ann Arbor, the Willow Run Facility would eventually employ more than forty thousand workers; a large number, certainly, but one that would fill less than half the capacity of Michigan Stadium.[2]

There would be no empty seats on October 25, 1941, when third-ranked Michigan and top-ranked Minnesota would meet in a high-stakes, de facto championship game for the second year in a row. "The game of the week, maybe of the season," Herb Barker of the Associated Press wrote. "Both undefeated, both untied, both top-ranking outfits."[3] Much like the 1940 contest, the result would largely determine the trajectory of the season for both teams, leaving the winner soaring toward title status and the loser spiraling to a second-place finish in the Big Ten or worse.

Michigan did not fear big games nor big crowds. The program, winners of eight national championships, drew more than a half-million fans cumulatively during the years 1939 and 1940 alone. It had also topped 84,000 in single-game attendance four times since Michigan Stadium opened in 1927, including a paid crowd of 85,088 against Ohio State in 1929 that went unmatched for more than a decade. The contest with top-ranked Minnesota in 1941 would likely shatter that record, school officials now predicted, as ticket prices surged on the underground market. Almost a full week before the game, they were climbing as high as an astonishing $25 per seat, the modern equivalent of $437 adjusted for inflation. Police closely monitored the illegal ticket scalping practices and planned to scatter undercover officers throughout the crowd Saturday to find the perpetrators.[4]

Even with the game entirely sold out to the general public, fans continued to overwhelm ticket manager Harry Tillotson with desperate requests for seats that simply did not exist. Tillotson thought he could have sold another twenty-five thousand tickets, at least, if not for the limited space at Michigan Stadium. "We never have had such pressure for a game," he said.[5] Student tickets were no different. That Monday, hundreds of rowdy and sweaty college kids elbowed and shoved each other outside the University of Michigan administration building, all clamoring for a chance to attend the football game that would make or break their beloved Wolverines' season. The line for tickets began at sunrise and sprawled down the whole block, spilling into the streets of Ann Arbor in a spectacle so intense it shut down city traffic and required extra police officers to patrol the scene. Kathleen Roach, a Michigan freshman, reportedly fainted amid the chaos due to extreme exhaustion and needed friends to escort her to safety at a house across the street. Throughout the morning, afternoon, and early evening, the situation grew more and more out of control as the students damaged shrubbery and dented the doors of the ticket office. Senior George Cheffy managed to survive the brouhaha but still waited almost four hours to receive his tickets.

Tillotson, the ticket manager, found the whole thing ridiculous. Although the general public's portion of the tickets were sold out, Michigan Stadium still had plenty of room left to meet the demand of the student body. Any Michigan student who wanted seats could get them, Tillotson said, and the tickets would remain available for pickup the rest of the week. There was "no justification for such an unprecedented rush," Tillotson told the *Michigan Daily* student newspaper early in the week. Those kids just couldn't seem to help themselves.[6]

❊ ❊ ❊

After a heart-stopping victory over Northwestern the previous weekend, the third-ranked Wolverines had jumped to their highest Associated Press slot since November 1940—the week they lost to Minnesota for the seventh year in a row. Frankly, Michigan's success in 1941 came as somewhat of a surprise to the rest of the Big Ten and the college football universe. Most predicted the Wolverines would stumble after the departure of Heisman Trophy winner Tom Harmon, an icon and widely regarded as one of the greatest players in college football history. Coupled with the graduation of talented quarterback Forest Evashevski, it seemed likely Michigan would at least suffer some growing pains early in the 1941 season. That never happened. Undefeated at 4–0, the Wolverines reinvented themselves with a new crop of stars, including a dangerous backfield combination of Tom Kuzma and Bob Westfall. The two backs played with a strong, physical style, and together they could make life hell for opponents. Kuzma, a sophomore from Tom Harmon's hometown of Gary, Indiana, emerged as a fresh face in 1941 with his versatile offensive skills and tossed both touchdown passes in his team's win over Northwestern. "Michigan's new football hero," writer Harry Grayson announced.[7] The bruising Westfall, a fullback and team captain, brought experience and unrivaled toughness as a senior leader. "Once he gets rolling," the AP warned, "look out!"[8] On the line, Michigan would lack the weight advantage by an average of thirteen pounds, but it still boasted Chicago native Al Wistert—perhaps one of the best tackles in the Big Ten outside of Urban Odson and Dick Wildung.

Even with all that star power, Michigan did not have another Tom Harmon on the roster—that once-in-a-lifetime type of player who could define a program for decades to come. Only Minnesota had that. "Bruce Smith," Jack Guenther of the United Press wrote, "is perhaps the only back with a reputation now."[9] Through his first three games, it appeared Smith would coast to All-American status at halfback by the end of the year—as long as injuries, like the minor one he suffered against Pittsburgh, did not derail his course. The coaching staff fully expected Smith to play against Michigan, and even better, they fully expected Bob Sweiger and Urban Odson to return to the starting lineup after missing the Pitt game. Coming off an All-American season, Odson must have been frustrated by the knee injury that plagued him since the beginning of fall practice, but his special brace helped him fight through the pain. The training staff did have some mild concerns about Bill Daley, who missed repetitions in practice with a pesky toe injury and charley horse, but he appeared ready to play on Saturday. For the most part, the nation's top team would enter the most important game of the 1941 season at full strength.

Michigan's head coach, Herbert "Fritz" Crisler, knew he would need to devise a master plan to contain the Gophers' backfield and counterpunch their physical frontline. It would not be easy. "If you've never seen a Minnesota team," Crisler said, "you're in for a sight."[10] Crisler spoke from personal experience. He had not merely *seen* a Minnesota team; he had *coached* one himself in the not-too-distant past. In fact, while serving as the Gophers' head coach and athletic director, Crisler orchestrated the chain of events that brought Bernie Bierman back to his alma mater. The relationship between these two men ran deep, much deeper than a simple bond between opposing Big Ten coaches. If not for Fritz Crisler, the Bernie Bierman dynasty may never have materialized. And now they both roamed opposite sidelines, facing off against each other in another Big Ten showdown between Michigan and Minnesota. It was, by far, the most compelling coaching storyline of the 1941 season.

✩ ✩ ✩

More than a decade earlier, as a young assistant at the University of Chicago in 1930, Crisler received the opportunity of a lifetime when Minnesota offered him the position of head football coach to replace Clarence Spears. Crisler boasted strong credentials as both a player and assistant under Chicago's Amos Alonzo Stagg—the same coach who recommended Doc Williams for the Minnesota job in 1900—but the alumni and "M" Club much preferred another candidate. They wanted Bernie Bierman. Fresh off an undefeated season at Tulane in 1929, it seemed only natural the university would pursue their former halfback and captain for the head coaching vacancy. The press ran with the idea, and Bierman became the obvious front-runner for the job in early 1930. Then, in a stunning move, Minnesota stopped chasing Bierman and handed the job to Fritz Crisler for reasons unknown to alumni. The backlash was ugly. Two men on the university's Senate Committee re-signed their positions in protest of the hiring process and the school's perceived indifference to their input. "I characterize your conduct of the matter as being a grievous affront," committee member Russell B. Rathbun wrote to the administration, "and a severe slight to every man and woman who holds a diploma of the University of Minnesota."[11] Embattled from the start, Fritz Crisler assumed even more responsibil-ity when the school gave him the title of both head football coach and athletic director. The workload exhausted him, and the results showed on the field: Crisler's team stumbled to a 3–4–1 record in 1930, includ-ing shutout losses at Michigan and Wisconsin to finish the season. To fans in Minneapolis, the hapless efforts served as further proof that the Gophers made an enormous mistake hiring Crisler instead of Bernie Bierman.

Crisler must have sensed his unpopularity. After the disappointing 1930 season, he voluntarily agreed to give up his head coaching position to focus solely on running the athletic department. He immediately pursued Bernie Bierman as his coaching replacement. On April 27, 1931—about four months after Doc Williams supposedly expressed a dying wish for Bierman to return to his alma mater—Crisler addressed a personal letter to Bierman at his Joseph Street home in New Orleans, located a few blocks from Tulane University. "My dear Bernie," Crisler wrote, "I have been authorized to extend to you an invitation to become Head Football Coach at the University of Minnesota with an annual salary of $7750." Crisler informed Bierman the agreement would take effect at the start of 1932—after the next football season—and he wished to keep the matter away from the press and the alumni base. "If you accept I think it is unwise to make any public announcement of the connection until after the close of the football season," Crisler wrote. "It might work to the disadvantage of both institutions as well as present problems to both of us as coaches."[12] After some back-and-forth between Bierman and Crisler, featuring discussion of salary potential, moving expenses, and faculty duties, Bierman informed Minnesota in June 1931 that Tulane had granted him his resignation. "I am free to leave at any time after the football season is over," Bierman told Crisler.[13] Both sides agreed not to mention a word until then, and University of Minnesota president Lotus Coffman informed Crisler that the Board of Regents would approve Bierman's hiring in the fall. They would conduct all of this business behind closed doors in a confidential process shielded from public input.

The rumors leaked anyway. At the start of the 1931 season, the press began to report that Bierman would soon return to his alma mater as the head football coach and that Crisler would stay at Minnesota as the athletic director. The letters between Bierman and Crisler during the spring and summer of 1931 prove that these rumors were true, but all parties involved denied absolutely everything when reached for comment. "I don't know anything about it. The news is astonishing to me," President Coffman told the *Minneapolis Star Journal* in September 1931. Crisler admitted he once approached Bierman about an assistant coaching position but nothing more. "At no time did I approach Bierman with the idea of making him head football coach next year," Crisler said in a statement we now know was false. "I have enough to do right now not to be worrying about next season." From New Orleans, Bierman simply said: "It's news to me."[14] The two sides continued to deny, deny, deny.

Distractions aside, Crisler's Minnesota team made encouraging progress on the field in 1931. Despite three road losses, the Gophers finished undefeated at Memorial Stadium—including a win over Ohio State—and ended the year with a solid 7–3 mark. Down south in Tulane, Bierman's program reached new heights with yet another undefeated season and a Rose Bowl berth against USC on New Year's Day. Bierman, now the hottest name in coaching, finally admitted in December 1931 that he had been "wanting to go home," and that yes, the rumors were true.[15] He would return to Minnesota for the 1932 season as the head football coach, and Fritz Crisler would retain his position as athletic director. It seemed like a perfect match: Bierman was finally back where he belonged, and Crisler could shift his sole focus to overseeing the athletic department. Although not popular as a football coach, the student body and fans generally liked Crisler's energy, charisma, and people skills. They were pleased to know he would not be leaving the university.

Those good feelings would deflate within a matter of weeks, when more rumors began to leak—this time, connecting Fritz Crisler to open coaching positions at other universities. In late February 1932, the local press reported that Crisler would likely accept a job as the head football coach at Princeton University, a historic program that had recently fallen on hard times. Wisconsin had apparently courted Crisler, too. "Townsfolk and alumni were up in arms over the possibility of his departure," the *Chicago Tribune* wrote, "because the new combination of Crisler and Bierman was hailed as the start of a new era of athletics at Minnesota."[16] Dozens of student groups on campus overwhelmed Crisler's mailbox with letters demanding he stay at Minnesota as the athletic director. He received petitions from the School of Mines Society, Theta Sigma Phi, the Minnesota Chapter of the American Management Association, the Senior Committee, the cheerleading squad, the law school council, the Dental College, the All-University College, and others. "Dear Fritz," the school band wrote, "Minnesota NEEDS you!" Even the Minnesota Society of Aeronautical Engineers and the American Society of Civil Engineers begged Crisler to stay. "We feel that if you left," the civil engineers wrote to Crisler, "our loss would be irreplaceable, and that no successor to you would be able to foster either the intercollegiate or intramural sports as they should be fostered at Minnesota."[17]

Despite the pleas from students, Crisler announced in March 1932 he would leave his post as athletic director for the head football coaching position at Princeton. "I have a very deep feeling of regret in the termination of my service at the University of Minnesota," Crisler told President Coffman. "I have been very happy here in my friendships and work."[18]

❊ ❊ ❊

Bernie Bierman (right) meets with Fritz Crisler in December 1931, shortly after Minnesota announced that Bierman would replace Crisler as the head football coach. After remaining on campus as the athletic director, Crisler ultimately left for a coaching job at Princeton in 1932, which later led him to the University of Michigan. *AP Photo*

By all accounts, Fritz Crisler made the right decision for himself. In six seasons at Princeton, he won thirty-five games and led the Tigers to two undefeated seasons, helping him parlay the success into an even better coaching job at the University of Michigan in 1938. Upon his return to the Big Ten, Crisler maintained the storied tradition in Ann Arbor by losing only four games in his first three years. There was just one problem: entering 1941, Fritz Crisler had not yet won a Big Ten title at Michigan, and he remained winless against his former team, Minnesota, in three tries.

Crisler awaited his former program's arrival as the Gophers left Thursday from Minneapolis. It was their second road trip of the season, albeit a much shorter one than the western trek to Seattle back in late

September. And unlike that first train ride, when thousands of exuberant students and fans greeted the Gophers at the Milwaukee Road station to bid them good luck, the send-off for the Michigan game was somewhat underwhelming. The crowd numbered about five hundred people, and a police band played music instead of the university ensemble. The low turnout likely bugged Bernie Bierman and his staff. "An enthusiastic departure might have changed the Gophers' mood," Perry Dotson of the *Pioneer Press* wrote. "Something will have to change it." After four days of practice, the coaches had not been pleased with the team's attitude heading into the Michigan game, and they struggled to grasp how their players could seem so flat with such an important contest looming. "I never have seen a team with less spirit that is needed to win," Dotson observed. "The Gophers' indifference has dismayed everyone close to the team."[19]

With Bill Daley wearing a sandal to protect his injured toe, the Gophers departed east from the Great Northern depot around 6:15 p.m. on Thursday, headed for an overnight stopover in Jackson, Michigan, at the Hayes Hotel, a ten-story luxury brick structure with lavish ballroom and dining space. The Gophers apparently liked to travel in style, just weeks after splurging at the ritzy Olympic Hotel in downtown Seattle. They needed solid sleep so they could wake up bright and early Saturday morning, in time to catch a thirty-mile train ride from Jackson to Ann Arbor.

"In a few short hours," Hal Wilson of Michigan's student newspaper the *Michigan Daily* wrote on the morning of October 25, "Head Coach Fritz Crisler will again throw his grimly determined squad against the Giants of the North, rated by football experts as the greatest of Minnesota's invincible string of juggernauts which have virtually ruled the nation's gridirons for the past decade."[20] The heavyweight matchup would begin at 2:00 p.m. Ann Arbor time, broadcast nationally on NBC and CBS for the second straight year.

Even with explosive news coming from war zones that weekend—the Russians were fending off the Nazis near Moscow and had killed fifty Axis fighters in Odessa, the British were assaulting Germany through air attacks, and an American volunteer for Britain had been killed in the North Atlantic—the fervor in Ann Arbor remained electric. Michiganders had "forgotten the [world] war, the Moscow stand against the Nazi and the fight over the neutrality bill in Washington," Charles

Johnson of the *Star Journal* wrote, "as they concentrate on repeating in this thirty-second gridiron meeting between these two schools."[21] Ann Arbor's population basically tripled the day of the game, with two-dozen special trains and more than fifty special buses arriving in town shortly before kickoff. Every hotel within a one-hundred-mile radius had been sold out for days, while customers streamed into restaurants and downtown businesses in overwhelming numbers. Due to the crowds, Ann Arbor police chief S. H. Mortensen asked the Michigan State Police for reinforcements and received fifty-five additional troopers to bolster his force.[22] Ten minutes before kickoff, not a single empty seat could be found in Michigan Stadium; the announced total of 85,753 fans reportedly broke the school's all-time record, as expected.[23]

Huddling in the visiting locker room, the thirty-six Minnesota players in gold uniforms and leather helmets must have felt a mix of nervousness, anxiety, and excitement. Sensing a need for encouragement, Butch Levy's sister, Renee, wired a telegram to the dressing room that morning: *"Good luck hope you will do your best."*[24] Levy and his teammates had never lost to the Wolverines. Bruce Smith, the hero of the 1940 game, probably felt some pressure to extend that winning streak. He knew he had a special opportunity to finish undefeated against the program that frustrated his father, Lucius, three decades earlier and led to that mythical, slightly inaccurate tale that he always wanted a son to avenge his defeat from 1910.

This game meant more to Smith than perhaps anyone else in that locker room—except for Sig Harris, the Gopher assistant with the most seniority on staff. Nobody understood the venom between Michigan and Minnesota quite like that man, a longtime reserve coach and scout who had devoted himself to the Maroon and Gold for at least four decades. By 1941, Harris was the only person on Minnesota's staff who could vividly recall the famous "Little Brown Jug" game of 1903, an epic contest that would forever define the Minnesota–Michigan rivalry and led to the creation of a trophy that has been traded between the programs for more than a century.

The coaching staff felt the new generation of players could benefit from some context. They needed a history lesson. They needed to know why this all mattered, why beating Michigan was about something bigger than themselves, why there was a "Little Brown Jug" in the first place. Only Harris could explain that from a first-hand perspective. So, as he did before every Michigan game, Bernie Bierman yielded the locker room to his assistant for a pre-game motivational speech. Outside those closed doors, the Gophers could probably hear the 85,700-plus fans roaring in anticipation, or maybe even the booming voice of the public address announcer. They could probably hear the Michigan band playing the school fight song, *"The Victors,"* as the fans chanted along. Outside, there was bedlam; but inside that locker room, with the thirty-six members of the 1941 team just minutes away from the biggest game of their season, the air fell silent. Sig Harris, dark-haired and distinguished with the look of a man who could make a run for public office, had the floor.

The players gave Harris their undivided attention as he delivered a fiery, tearful address, recounting an afternoon thirty-eight years earlier that changed the dynamic of the Michigan–Minnesota series for eternity. Although no text of the speech exists, we can infer what Harris must have said because he was famous for telling the same story year after year.[25] Harris likely told the players about the time when he, as a spry twenty-year-old quarterback, faced coach Fielding Yost's explosive "point-a-minute" Michigan team on October 31, 1903, in front of a jam-packed Northrop Field crowd of twenty-five thousand fans. The Gophers tied the Wolverines 6–6 that afternoon on a touchdown by Egil Boeckmann in the final minutes, causing the crowd at Northrop to rush the field with such pandemonium that the team captains had to call the game early on account of darkness. For the first time in thirty tries, the University of Michigan had been denied a victory, and in the aftermath of the disappointing tie, Fielding Yost's team left behind a thirty-cent water jug. Although accounts vary widely depending on the source, both schools generally agree that Minnesota equipment manager Oscar Munson recovered the jug and helped paint the numbers 6–6 on it as a reminder of the dramatic final score on October 31, 1903. The two programs didn't play again for six years, partly because of Michigan's ongoing departure from the Western Conference, until 1909—when Minnesota athletic director L. J. Cooke told Fielding Yost he could have the "Little Brown Jug" back if Michigan won. The two teams started trading the trophy after every game from that point forward, with the Wolverines dominating most of the 1910s and 1920s before the Gophers stole back the jug for seven straight seasons starting in 1934.[26]

As an assistant and primary scout at Minnesota for nearly four decades, Sig Harris had seen the good, the bad, and the ugly between these two teams—and he often harkened back to that "Little Brown Jug" game as the pinnacle of the rivalry, just as he did again on October 25, 1941, in the close quarters of the locker room in Ann Arbor. His retelling of the "Little Brown Jug" story must have ignited those players as they stormed right through the doors and straight onto the field in front of the fiercest crowd Michigan Stadium had ever seen.

One can only imagine what those coaches and players felt as they trotted out before more than eighty-five thousand people, with the eyes of the nation's most influential sportswriters peering from the press box and the ears of American football fans listening to the NBC and CBS radio broadcasts from coast to coast. The atmosphere would have been stunning. According to eyewitness reports from Gopher fans visiting from St. Cloud, the "tension was greater than at any game they had ever

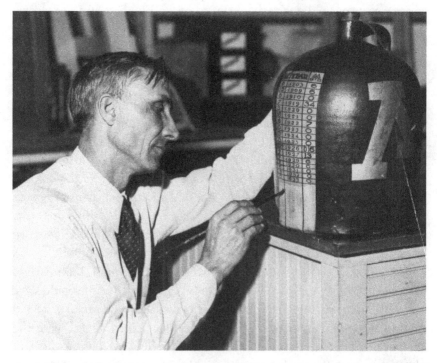

Oscar Munson paints another score on the "Little Brown Jug" early in the Bierman era. Munson was involved in the original recovery of the jug back in 1903.
Courtesy of University of Minnesota Archives, University of Minnesota–Twin Cities

attended."[27] The fans stood on their feet the entire game, starting with the opening coin toss. The ball would go to Minnesota first.

❀ ❀ ❀

Michigan's opening kickoff sailed out of bounds, so the Gophers began at their own thirty-five-yard line with a lineup mostly at full strength. Bob Sweiger returned to action at right halfback, opposite left halfback Bruce Smith and next to fullback Bill Daley. Bob Fitch and Judd Ringer started at end; Butch Levy and Helge Pukema at guard; and Dick Wildung and Ed Lechner at tackle, though Urban Odson expected to see a lot of playing time with his fitted knee brace. Bill Garnaas and Gene Flick started their fourth straight games at quarterback and center, respectively.

Bill Daley, undeterred by his sore toe and charley horse, carried the load with Bruce Smith on the opening drive. They alternated carries for three first downs in a row, helping Minnesota drive into enemy territory in the opening minutes. On first-and-long from the Michigan thirty-seven after a penalty, the Gophers saw an opening to strike first—and they took it. Bruce Smith hurled the football deep into the end zone, intended for end Judd Ringer, but the ball barely grazed his fingertips as Michigan's Tom Kuzma knocked it off course. Minnesota ended up punting a few downs later.

Taking over inside their own twenty, the Wolverines—wearing the iconic Maize and Blue striped helmets that Fritz Crisler implemented in 1938—put their own backfield punch on display. After fullback Bob Westfall chugged right for six yards, the sensational sophomore Tom Kuzma burst left on a sweep for a twenty-one-yard gain, electrifying the crowd as it witnessed the first big play of the afternoon (Michigan's senior end, Joe Rogers, was hurt on the play but remained on the field). Minnesota's defense was unrelenting during the rest of the possession. Kuzma broke a Garnaas tackle in the backfield on first down but only managed to gain two yards. Westfall found just one yard on second down after Butch Levy met him with force. And third down was no better when the Gophers bottled up Kuzma on a sweep to the left. Kuzma punted the ball away on fourth down—and only then did Michigan's Joe Rogers leave the game. Trainers realized he had hurt his spine and rushed him to the hospital, where Rogers soon learned he would never play college football again. The injury was too severe.

This was an extraordinarily physical football game. After a three-and-out on the next possession, Bill Daley raced downfield on the punt team and stopped Kuzma near midfield with a harsh collision. Urban Odson, who did not start because of that bad knee, saw his first action late in the first quarter. He played right tackle, opposite Wildung at left tackle. Almost immediately, the "Fireman" flaunted his South Dakota–born strength when he stopped Kuzma near the line of scrimmage for very little gain. On fourth-and-short, Bob Westfall faked a punt and instead scampered to the Minnesota thirty-eight for a first-down conversion. "The 3,000 Minnesota rooters got a little scared at this stage," the *Minneapolis Star Journal* observed, "as Michigan really looked the goods."[28] With Michigan driving, Dick Wildung put an end to the momentum with a big hit on Kuzma to stop him for a short gain. The first quarter ended in a scoreless tie, and this slugfest would not get any prettier in the second quarter as the teams continued to swap scoreless possessions.

Strangely enough, it was one of football's most mundane plays—a punt—that altered the course of the game in this second quarter. The punt, unsurprisingly, came from the right foot of senior captain Bruce Smith. By all accounts, Smith's kick was remarkable. Charles Johnson of the *Star Journal* called it the "most sensational effort of the afternoon."[29] The *Michigan Daily* called it "tremendous."[30] Bernie Bierman and Fritz Crisler both called it the turning point. Inside his own twenty, Smith booted the football high in the air, above the Michigan Stadium grandstands, sending it towering over return man Tom Kuzma as he gazed helplessly. The ball traveled three-quarters of the length of the field before dropping and rolling to the Michigan twelve-yard line. Officially, it was a sixty-nine-yard punt. Neither coaching staff had ever seen anything like it.

Beyond the sheer magnificence of the punt, it became a crucial play because of the ensuing sequence of events. Pinned at his own twelve, a rattled Kuzma fumbled on first down before recovering at the six. On second down, the Wolverines simply gave up and decided to punt the ball away. Kuzma could not re-create Smith's magic; his punt *only* went about forty yards as Minnesota took over near midfield. The Gophers felt a surge of confidence as they took over with strong field position.

After a Smith-to-Fitch pass fell incomplete on first down, Bill Garnaas entered the game to reclaim the quarterback position as Herman Frickey remained in the lineup at right halfback in place of Bob Sweiger. Bruce Smith took the snap on second down from the forty-eight. Hesitating for a moment behind his linemen, he looked like he might run. Then, to the surprise of every spectator inside Michigan Stadium, Smith lifted his rocket right arm and heaved the football down the right sideline in the direction of Herman Frickey. The Montana native leapt as high as he could, snagged the ball at the fifteen, and continued sprinting at full speed before Kuzma yanked his collar and knocked him out of bounds at the five-yard line. If Bruce Smith's sixty-nine-yard punt had been the most important play of the afternoon, his forty-three-yard pass to Frickey had certainly been the most thrilling. Bierman would later call it the "perfect play,"[31] among the greatest passes he ever saw thrown by a player wearing Maroon and Gold. Michigan knew it was in trouble now. It needed a goal line stand.

Sensing a precarious moment in the game, the anxious fans at Michigan Stadium revved up the intensity and screamed as loud as they could to give their defense a boost. It was first-and-goal from the five. Bruce Smith got the call. He plunged forward for one yard, into a mob of his own teammates, when suddenly a Michigan defender fell on his backside. It did not look good. Something was clearly wrong with his right knee. As Smith emerged shakily from the pile, his teammates rushed to his side and helped their captain off the field toward the sidelines. It would be his last play of the afternoon.

Unable to process the injury at first and unaware that Smith had torn cartilage, the Gophers knew they had three more plays to punch in their first touchdown of the game with the score still tied 0–0. With Smith out, Bierman decided to shift Frickey into his spot at left halfback and send Bob Sweiger back into the game at right halfback. On second down, Frickey took the ball in the backfield and surged into the line behind Ed Lechner at right tackle, gaining only a few yards. It would be third-and-goal from the two. The fans at Michigan Stadium again grew louder and louder, roaring as the Gophers approached the line of scrimmage. Bill Garnaas, at quarterback, took the snap and faked to Bill Daley before immediately handing the ball to Frickey. "Then with perfect precision and the vast power that has shot Minnesota to the pinnacle of the gridiron world," the *Michigan Daily* reported, "the Gopher backfield feinted right, then left, and the tailback, Herm Frickey, exploded directly over center for the score."[32] The sophomore had relied, smartly, on his big men on the left side of the line—Dick Wildung and Butch Levy—to score the first touchdown of the game. The Gopher contingent at Michigan Stadium, though heavily outnumbered, cheered wildly and made audible noise on the radio broadcasts back home in Minneapolis. After Garnaas kicked the extra point, Minnesota took a 7–0 lead with four minutes left in the first half.

Frustrated and motivated by the deficit, Michigan's Bob Westfall took the next kickoff near his own five and then charged ahead with a full head of steam, racing forty-two yards before Garnaas pushed him out of bounds. The Wolverines would not let one touchdown derail their championship hopes. Tom Kuzma, continuing his aerial assault, threw a thirty-three-yard pass to Paul White on the next play. Then came a nifty Kuzma-to-Westfall lateral for fifteen yards. Almost instantaneously, Michigan now had the ball at the five-yard line with two minutes to play in the first half. "Here was the big opportunity," the *Detroit Free Press* wrote.[33]

The Wolverines smelled touchdown and called a reverse, attempting to catch the Gophers by surprise just as Bruce Smith had done to them in 1940 on that epic eighty-yard touchdown. They completely botched the execution. The ball somehow ended up in Michigan fullback Bob Westfall's hands, but during the confusion, the senior fumbled for the first time in his three-year varsity career. Bob Sweiger recovered in a devastating turn of events for Michigan and a major sigh of relief for Minnesota. With only a minute left in the half, the Gophers played conservatively from their own eleven, handing the ball to Bill Daley for three straight carries to bleed the clock into halftime. The lead remained 7–0.

With Bruce Smith out of the game due to his knee injury, Minnesota struggled to gain momentum on the offensive side of the ball. The third quarter featured a combined six punts, zero touchdowns, and very little entertainment for a Michigan Stadium crowd that had paid good money for tickets. With Smith missing, the Gophers once again turned to Bud Higgins to re-create some of his magic from the week before. He replaced Herman Frickey on the final drive of the third quarter but could not find any running room, reportedly chastising his blockers in the huddle: "You guys have got to give me some protection!"

Bill Daley quickly offered Higgins a reality check, according to an account given to author James P. Quirk in 1984. "Look, kid, this isn't Pitt, this is Michigan," Daley told the young sophomore in the huddle, "and they're going to hurt you, protection or not."[34] Daley's words must have resonated. On the first play of the fourth quarter, Higgins finally displayed some flash when he returned a Kuzma punt for sixteen yards past midfield. Then he showed off his arm, tossing a pass to Garnaas for a twenty-six-yard gain to advance inside Michigan's twenty. With an air of desperation, the Wolverines' defense dug in their heels and denied the Gophers a chance to increase the lead to two possessions. They bottled up Higgins on two straight runs and then caught a break when Garnaas missed a thirty-three-yard field goal attempt. The ball sailed wide right.

Even after two more traded punts, Michigan still had a fighting chance. The score remained 7–0 with six minutes left in the game, and the end of the fourth quarter featured some tense moments, starting with a Bud Higgins fumble in his own territory that handed Michigan the football at the thirty-four-yard line. With good fortune finally on his side, Kuzma broke free from the Gophers' iron grip with a big play on first down. He connected through the air with George Ceithaml for a thirteen-yard gain, and if not for a heroic Bob Sweiger tackle, he might have found the end zone. First down at the twenty-one. Kuzma fired a pass intended for his receiver Al Thomas in the corner, but Garnaas swatted the ball away to continue his menacing coverage in the secondary. A play later, Westfall took the snap and gave the ball to Ceithaml, who then lateraled to Kuzma in the backfield. With the Gophers scrambling, Kuzma threw a perfect spiral to an end named Harlin Fraumann, re-creating an identical play that had apparently worked like magic a week earlier against Northwestern. This time, the magic ran out. With a chance to snag the ball at the three, Fraumann dropped the pass. After initially believing Fraumann caught the football, a reporter in the press box for the *Lansing State Journal* saw the ball squirt loose. "And that was that," he wrote.[35] There would be no touchdown this time. With one final chance on fourth down, Michigan again put its trust in Kuzma through the air—except this time Bill Garnaas intercepted the pass in the end zone and ran the ball out to the four-yard line. "And Michigan hopes," the *Daily* reported, "went up in smoke."[36]

After milking time with seven straight running plays, Minnesota left only fifty-three seconds on the clock when Bud Higgins punted to Bob Westfall at the Michigan thirty-five. Trailing 7–0, the Wolverines would need a miracle to drive the length of the field and possibly salvage a tie. To their credit, they did not quit. After gaining a first down at the Michigan forty-seven, Kuzma completed two passes in a row to put the Wolverines at the Minnesota thirty-nine. They had life. With hundreds of thousands of college football fans across the country listening intently to the voices of Bill Stern on NBC and Ted Husing on CBS, Tom Kuzma drifted into the backfield to attempt yet another pass. He locked eyes with end Rudy Smeja downfield, but the ball never got there. Bill Garnaas snagged it again for another interception. Minnesota took over at the thirty, handed the ball to Bill Daley for one final play, and cele-brated as the final horn sounded at Michigan Stadium; 7–0 was the final. "Magnificent things happened during my college football career," Bill Daley later said, "but [Michigan] was one of the greatest games. It was a beautiful day."[37]

As the Gophers sprinted toward the locker room inside the bowels of Michigan Stadium, riding high from the emotional victory, Sig Harris fought back tears. "Good Lord, man," he said. "It was just one long 60-minute highlight. Those kids." When he turned his head in the locker room, Harris must have lit into a smile at the sight of Dick Wildung, Bill Daley, and backup Bob Smith grabbing the Little Brown Jug. The trio posed proudly for a photograph with their favorite trophy, signifying yet another triumph over Michigan. Even the great Fielding Yost—the former athletic director and head coach of that 1903 Michigan team that lost the original Little Brown Jug—sought out his old buddy to tell Harris something he would never forget. "That Minnesota team," Yost said, "is the best Minnesota team I ever saw opposed to us."

Athletic Director Frank McCormick stormed through the crowd to find Bierman in the locker room. *"Congratulations, coach."* The two men shook hands. When reporters finally circled Bierman to ask his thoughts on the victory, the Silver Fox seemed pleased but not overly enthusiastic, true to form. "It appeared that we might wind up without a backfield the way the boys were getting hurt," he said, "but I'm happy everything came out the way it did."[38]

Understandably, the coaching staff expressed concern about Bruce Smith's knee injury. The training staff could not make a full assessment yet, but they remained hopeful he could heal with a few days of rest. Smith wasn't the only player shaking off an injury in the post-game dressing room. The other star of the day, Herman Frickey, was also having knee trouble. And Helge Pukema would need to spend the night at University Hospital in Ann Arbor after a hit to the kidney in the first half. "Winners on the scoreboard," the AP's William Weatherby wrote, "Minnesota's Golden Gophers were the losers from the standpoint of injuries."[39]

Despite a hard-fought victory over the nation's third-ranked team to improve to 4–0, some members of the press corps criticized the Gophers' style of play and lack of offensive punch. "Minnesota is a great football team," *New York Herald Tribune* writer Stanley Woodward wrote, "but not the kind that this department likes to watch. . . . It plays football so close to the chest that it gives anyone except a rabid supporter the horrors."[40]

And now Northwestern loomed.

9

THE TALKING PLAY

John J. Healy had never missed Homecoming Weekend at Memorial Stadium, tallying an impressive streak that dated back to his freshman year of college in 1924 when Minnesota fell 13–0 to Michigan. The loss did not deter his school spirit. For the next seventeen years—even after his graduation from the U of M in 1928—Healy sat in the bleachers for each and every homecoming game, no matter the weather and no matter the opponent. His Gophers treated him to triumphs, like six consecutive victories from 1931 to 1936, and disappointments, like a 27–6 loss to Northwestern in 1930 and a heartbreaking three-point defeat to Ohio State in 1939. Healy took the good with the bad each year for nearly two decades—until 1941. The night before Northwestern came to town, Healy abruptly canceled his homecoming plans when the United States Office of Personnel Management demanded he attend an emergency defense meeting in Chicago to discuss copper production for the war effort. "He left late Friday for Chicago," the *Minneapolis Tribune* reported, "uncertain as to whether he would even be able to hear the game by radio."[1] A frustrated Healy hoped he could at least fly back Saturday evening, so that he could entertain guests during the post-game dinner party he arranged at his home on Pillsbury Avenue.

The global crisis escalated on a number of fronts in the final days of October 1941. In snowy Russia, the brutal fighting for control of Moscow left thousands of Red Army and Nazi soldiers dead. In occupied France, the trio of Roosevelt, Winston Churchill, and Charles de Gaulle of the Free French condemned Hitler's cold-blooded execution of hostages, with Roosevelt calling the killings "acts of desperate men who know in their hearts they cannot win."[2] At home, the United States Senate prepared to vote on a revision to the Neutrality Act that would allow American merchant ships to arm themselves in defense of potential attacks. During a Navy Day speech on October 27, Roosevelt urged lawmakers to approve the measure as protection against the "rattlesnakes of the sea," like the ones he felt drew the USS *Kearny* into a shooting battle ten days earlier and resulted in the deaths of eleven American sailors. "We have wished to avoid shooting. But the shooting has started. And history has recorded who fired the first shot," Roosevelt said in an address heard by an estimated fifty million Americans, the fourth-largest audience in recorded history. "In the long run, however, all that will matter is who fired the last shot."[3] The *Hamburger Frendenblatt*, a German newspaper, called Roosevelt's speech "the last step to an undeclared shooting war against Germany and her allies."[4]

The month ended on a disastrous note, when yet another American ship found itself in a skirmish off the coast of Iceland on the morning of October 31. This time, it was the USS *Reuben James*, carrying 160 crew members on escort duty through the North Atlantic. A German U-boat fired upon the 1,190-ton Navy destroyer with a torpedo, causing a tremendous explosion that killed all ranking officers on board—including the ship's captain, a former Navy football player, Lieutenant Commander Heywood Lane Edwards. In all, only about forty-five members of the crew would survive the attack; more than one hundred had died. The *Reuben James* itself perished beyond salvation, dropping to the bottom of the ocean almost immediately upon impact.[5]

For the first time, the Axis forces had destroyed an American naval ship at sea. "The outrageous sinking of the *Reuben James* in our own defensive waters is another evidence of the murderous and defiant attitude of the Nazis," Senate Foreign Relations Committee Chairman Tom Connally said. "This dastardly act of aggression must be avenged."[6] The Germans accused the U.S. of the aggression, and then promptly began the month of November 1941 by storming oil fields near the Russian city of Rostov, described for American readers in the Associated Press as "about the size of New Orleans or Minneapolis."[7]

The *Reuben James* disaster surely came as a shock to the American public, but it did not completely reverse the tide of isolationism or singularly unite the country into an appetite for war. "The bereaved families mourned," wrote Roosevelt speechwriter Robert Sherwood, "but among the general public, there seemed to be more interest in the Army–Notre Dame football game."[8] Seventy-six thousand people at Yankee Stadium would watch that contest on November 1, 1941, as the sixth-ranked Irish looked to knock off the fourteenth-ranked Cadets. It was not, however, the only high-profile college football game of the weekend. In fact, the lone match-up featuring two top-ten teams would take place in Minneapolis, where Minnesota would square off against Northwestern in front of a crowd much larger than the permanent capacity of Memorial Stadium. In response to the demand, crews added temporary seating to Cooke Hall, the brick athletic building that provided a perfect view of the field from one of the end zones. Charles Johnson of the *Minneapolis Star Journal* came up with an even better idea to make room for more fans. "A new stadium," he suggested the morning of the game, before admitting the following: "That's out of the question now because of the defense situation."[9]

❖ ❖ ❖

Entering the final week of October, Minnesota remained atop the Associated Press poll. That was the good news. The bad? In a disappointing twist, the Gophers now shared the number one spot with the University of Texas. Coach Dana Bible's dazzling Longhorns had just routed in-state rival Rice 40–0, and apparently voters had grown quite fond of their explosive offensive attack compared to Bernie Bierman's plodding style. "If Minnesota and Texas, leaders in opposite parts of the country and exponents of contrasting types of football, were to meet today," the AP's Bill Boni wrote, "their game would end in a tie. That, at least, is the view of 127 of the country's gridiron experts."[10] Michigan slipped to seventh in the poll, behind Fordham, Duke, Texas A&M, and Notre Dame. Penn checked in at number eight.

Ninth place belonged to the Northwestern Wildcats, propelled by the strength of an impressive road victory at Ohio State. Despite a loss earlier in the month to Michigan, one-loss NU remained in contention for the Big Ten championship and could leap to the top of the standings with an upset in Minneapolis. "The game," Charles Dunkley of the AP wrote, "may decide the title."[11] Minnesota passed its first test with a road win in Ann Arbor, but the Gopher faithful refused to celebrate prematurely. They had known all season that the Wildcats would present the stiffest challenge of any visiting team at Memorial Stadium, and the coaching staff knew it, too. "They make me shiver in my boots," backfield coach Sheldon Beise told Bierman after scouting Northwestern. The head coach responded with the following statement: "Move over and I'll shiver with you."[12]

Coach Lynn "Pappy" Waldorf, now in his seventh season at Northwestern, had enjoyed modest success in Evanston since arriving in 1935—but his teams seemed to fare especially well when they played Minnesota. With a 3–3 mark, Waldorf owned the best head-to-head record in the conference against Bernie Bierman. His shining moment came in 1936, when the Gophers arrived in Evanston on Halloween carrying a twenty-one-game winning streak. Seemingly unstoppable at the time and building a dynasty unlike any other in college football, Bierman's team blew its chance for a third straight undefeated season that day by losing 6–0 on a rain-soaked field. The decisive touchdown came after a controversial officiating decision late in the third quarter, when referee John Getchell called Minnesota tackle Ed Widseth for unnecessary roughness against fullback Don Geyer. The penalty placed the football at Minnesota's one-yard line and set up the Wildcats' winning touchdown two plays later, infuriating Bierman and leaving the fan base inconsolable back in the Twin Cities. Northwestern won the conference in 1936, solely on the strength of that victory over the Gophers. The irony was that the official himself, John Getchell, was a Minneapolis native and a graduate of St. Thomas College in St. Paul. After reviewing film of the game, fans and critics became increasingly convinced that Widseth did not commit roughness and that Getchell's decision to charge a fifteen-yard penalty had cost Minnesota a league championship in 1936 (the AP still selected the Gophers as the national champions that year, despite the loss to Northwestern).

Getchell, a well-respected official in college and prep football circles, brushed off the criticism and continued to do his job. Five years after the controversial roughing call in Evanston, the Big Ten would again tap him for this November 1, 1941, rematch between the two teams at Memorial Stadium—except this time, his officiating crew would become the villains of Northwestern's story, not Minnesota's.

✻ ✻ ✻

The Wildcats' upset hopes in 1941 hinged largely on their two offensive stars, perhaps the best pair of left halfbacks in America. Both split time in Pappy Waldorf's single-wing backfield, thanks to the platoon system made possible by the NCAA's new substitution rules. One was an experienced senior named Bill DeCorrevont, a flashy product of the Chicago Public School League whose sixty-one-yard touchdown as a sophomore in 1939 lifted Northwestern over Minnesota in the final minutes of the game. The other was a budding sophomore named Otto Graham, the son of music teachers from Waukegan, Illinois, and the new darling of the Big Ten. Starting at left halfback in place of DeCorrevont, he threw both touchdowns in his team's 14–7 win over Ohio State the previous weekend, despite breaking his nose during the game. After a successful surgery, it appeared Graham would be able to play with the assistance of a nose guard installed by the Northwestern training staff.

Minnesota's injury situation was another matter. Bruce Smith's right knee seemed to improve by Monday, but his status remained questionable for the Northwestern game because of torn cartilage. Smith's father, Lucius, described himself as "thoroughly depressed and disheartened" about his son's condition.[13] Herman Frickey could hardly walk the day after the Michigan game due to a serious knee sprain of his own. And Helge Pukema, discharged from University Hospital in Ann Arbor after that vicious hit to the kidney, still needed some time to recover, even though Bob Sweiger attempted to convince his fellow senior that injuries were all about mind-over-matter. "What are you stalling for, Pukema," Sweiger asked as the two shared a training room tub after practice, hoping to raise his teammate's spirits. "We know you are just trying to get out of some work."[14]

With two starters and a vital backup in question, Bierman and line coach George Hauser paid closer attention than ever to a scrimmage between the reserves, known as the "Bombers," and Dallas Ward's freshman squad. Ward's players were no pushovers. He believed the 1941 freshman team was at least as good as in 1938, when Sweiger, Bruce Smith, and Butch Levy roamed the practice field as wide-eyed eighteen-year-olds. This time around, the 1941 freshman team carried a number of future Gopher stars, including left halfback Red Williams and right halfback Dick Luekemeyer. Assistant coach Bert Baston's son, Fred, impressed the staff at end, while Warren Plunkett's brother,

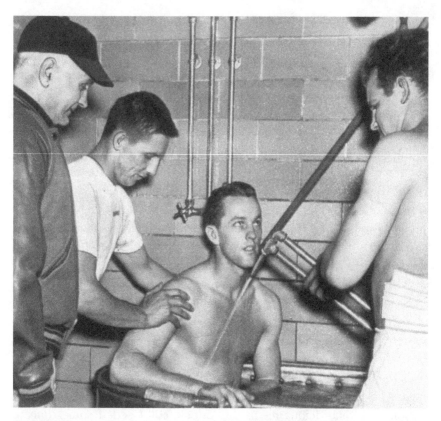

Bruce Smith looks apprehensive as he takes a spin in the hydrotherapy tub, with Bernie Bierman (far left), Herman Frickey (in white shirt), and Helge Pukema (far right) assisting. Smith missed the second half of the Michigan game with an injured right knee. *Courtesy of University of Minnesota Archives, University of Minnesota–Twin Cities*

Dick, had emerged as a top guard candidate. Jack Spewak and John Drake had proven themselves as the finest centers. They all did their best to hang with Sig Harris' varsity Bombers during a scrimmage that Tuesday, but the end result wasn't pretty: the Bombers blasted the freshmen 24–6, despite playing in frigid, rainy conditions at Northrop Field. Gene Bierhaus, the Brainerd native, rushed for one touchdown and scored another on a ninety-five-yard kickoff return. Fullback Mike Welch of St. James, Minnesota, added a third touchdown while Earl Eli scored a fourth by making a one-handed catch. Despite the strong efforts, Bierman walked away disappointed in his search for possible varsity reinforcements against Northwestern.[15] "We didn't find them,"

Bierman said plainly.[16] Speaking to a crowd of 1,200 students at the Union Ballroom the next day, the head coach spoke only the truth. "Toughest game of the year," Bierman said. "Injuries will force us to use a patched-up backfield."[17]

On an encouraging note, Bierman knew he could count on Bud Higgins, Bill Daley, and Bob Sweiger in the backfield, as all three appeared fully healthy for the first time in weeks. Even better, Urban Odson's sturdy knee brace seemed to be helping him immensely. There was no question about his status, nor was there ever any question about the status of fellow tackle Dick Wildung. He had managed to avoid the injury bug for the most part, but on Saturday he would face his greatest test of the season as he lined up against Northwestern All-American Alf Bauman. That would be a key matchup, almost as key as the Gophers' plans to contain Bill DeCorrevont and Otto Graham. The national press overwhelmingly chose the Gophers as the favorites, but not without slight hesitation. "Injuries to key figures, notably Bruce Smith and Helge Pukema, may cost Minnesota plenty both on offense and defense," Associated Press sports editor Herb Barker wrote. "Northwestern, with a great crop of backs, may turn out to be more than a handful, but in the meantime this old conservative picks Minnesota."[18]

❊ ❊ ❊

Following custom, Bierman sent his squad to Bayport on the Friday night before the game, hoping to avoid the lethal combination of homecoming *and* Halloween happening on a college campus at the very same time. They missed a party for the ages. With the slogan "Cage the 'Cats" hanging on decorations at every corner, the Mardi Gras–themed celebration kicked off Friday evening with an alumni dinner, a variety show at Northrop Auditorium, and the Class of 1904 law school reunion at the Raddison Hotel downtown. By Saturday morning, homecoming spirit raged across the Twin Cities. A two-mile parade, spanning from campus to downtown Minneapolis with more than one hundred floats, proceeded as scheduled despite a major snowfall. The combination of heavy snow and enormous crowds left the sidewalks near Memorial Stadium basically impassable. On the roads, traffic inched along slowly, worsened by the bad weather and poor visibility. Throughout the morning, the snow grew more and more intense, causing havoc across the state. As many as seventy phone lines in Minneapolis went down due to wet wires, and multiple traffic fatalities were reported in the metro area.

Despite the massive street crowd on campus, only a lucky 64,464 people would have tickets to see Minnesota play Northwestern inside Memorial Stadium at 2:00 p.m.—reported at the time as the largest crowd in school history, made possible only by the temporary seats arranged in front of Cooke Hall.[19] As the paid crowd filed into the building, the fans quickly spotted giant snow piles stacked behind both end zones. Across the country, NBC and Mutual Broadcasting System affiliates prepared to carry at least portions of the contest. WAKR in Akron, Ohio, dropped well-known singer Ray Kinney in favor of the game; WKAT in Miami interrupted an orchestra performance by Joseph Gallicchio. Football fans in every state wondered whether this might be the day the vaunted Golden Gophers finally stumbled. Their thirteen-game winning streak dating back to the end of 1939 was on the line.

✵ ✵ ✵

Bursting out of the locker rooms, the Northwestern and Minnesota players jogged onto the field, adrenaline pumping, and glanced up to see clear skies above them. The snow had finally stopped falling—just in time for kickoff. At that moment, in the Memorial Stadium press box, a baseball player named Ted Williams felt his stomach drop. He could relate to the pressure. Just weeks after posting a .406 batting average for the Boston Red Sox, Williams returned to the city where he had played his minor league baseball with the Minneapolis Millers, eager to watch two college football titans in action as they tussled for the Big Ten championship. "Those kids," Williams told sports journalist George Barton, "must be pretty nervous right now with so much at stake. Guess they're as nervous as I was the first time I went to the plate in the American League."[20]

Ted Williams and sixty-four thousand of his closest friends then fixed their eyes toward midfield, as the Northwestern kickoff team lined up in white jerseys and dark purple helmets following the coin toss. Don Clawson booted the football to Warren Plunkett, who returned it to the Minnesota twenty-seven. As the Gophers' offense trotted out, the fans immediately noticed that Bruce Smith was not starting. Bierman employed a slightly unorthodox backfield: Bill Daley at left half, Bob Sweiger at fullback, Bill Garnaas at right half, and Plunkett at quarterback. Ed Lechner got the starting nod at tackle over Urban Odson, but the "Fireman" expected to see plenty of action off the bench opposite Dick Wildung. John Billman started at right guard for Pukema. Bob Fitch and Judd Ringer started again at ends, while Butch Levy and Gene Flick remained in their spots at left guard and center, respectively.

A punting snooze-fest put the crowd to sleep during the first several drives of the game, but the Gophers finally found some running room late in the first quarter. Bill Daley followed Wildung and Levy for a ten-yard gain and a first down; then Daley handed to Garnaas on a reverse for eleven yards and another first down at the Wildcat twenty-eight. Waldorf called a timeout to regroup, allowing Bierman a chance to send big Urban Odson into the game with his knee wrapped in a brace. Although Northwestern's Alf Bauman caused major problems at the line of scrimmage, Minnesota managed yet another first down when Levy's blocking in the trenches helped Sweiger convert a third-and-short at the eighteen. A play later, Bill Daley took a direct snap and faded to his right for the first pass attempt of his career. A defender collided with him as he threw the ball, forcing it off course and into the hands of Northwestern fullback Don Clawson. He swiped the ball for an interception at his own ten before Bob Fitch rushed over to knock him out of bounds.

The interception, as it turned out, was a blessing in disguise. Just a play later, an errant snap by Northwestern center Don Johnson sailed past a frantic DeCorrevont, who immediately sprinted toward the football in the end zone in a determined effort to avoid a catastrophe. He grabbed the ball and tried to throw it away, but before he could do so, he apparently stepped out of the back of the end zone as his momentum carried him in the wrong direction. It was a safety. Minnesota had taken an early 2–0 lead and would now receive the ball on a free kick.

Two things happened in between the safety and the ensuing kickoff: Bud Higgins came into the game, and the public address announcer at Memorial Stadium urged fans not to throw snowballs onto the field. Higgins, doing his best Bruce Smith impression, sparked the offense for a first down on his very first carry as the Gophers again gained some traction into Northwestern territory. Their advances came to an abrupt end when Bauman wrapped up Higgins for a nine-yard loss, forcing an eventual punt that went into the end zone for a touchback. The next Minnesota drive resulted in another interception, this time on a pass attempt from Bud Higgins to Bob Sweiger. After the Wildcats took over at their own thirty-three, DeCorrevont rushed for a four-yard gain on first down—and then everything changed. Sophomore Otto Graham, fresh off his broken nose and two touchdowns against Ohio State, entered the lineup at left halfback. And for Minnesota, Bud Higgins left the game in exchange for Bruce Smith. It would be Smith's first action since the first half against Michigan.

The astute sophomore Graham, having paid close attention on the bench, felt he could expose Minnesota's secondary after noticing the backs were crowding the line of scrimmage. Midway through the second quarter, Graham put his plan into action. He faked a reverse, artfully evaded Minnesota defenders in the backfield, and then hurled the football fifty yards downfield to open receiver Bob Motl. Motl caught the ball in the end zone, having easily outraced a hobbling Bruce Smith to give the Wildcats an apparent lead. Head linesman Paul Goebel, however, waved off the touchdown by calling a fifteen-yard penalty, claiming that NU tackle Leon Cook had advanced past the line of scrimmage before Graham threw the pass downfield.

A few plays after the illegal touchdown, the Wildcats punted to Bruce Smith, who still did not look right as he returned the kick gingerly for a five-yard gain. Taking back his spot at left halfback, Smith's day only got worse. On the first set of downs, the Minnesota captain drifted back to pass and looked for Daley downfield. Incomplete. As the ball left his right hand, Bob Motl delivered a devastating blow that knocked Smith straight to the ground. It did not look good. "Spectators were in the position of one who sees two high speed trains approaching each other on the same track, powerless to avert tragedy," Gordon Gilmore of the *Pioneer Press* observed from the press box. "From the moment Smith got up from his first running play, limping slightly, there was a hovering sense of impending disaster. When it came, the crowd shuddered as one."[21] Trainers rushed a stretcher to the field, but Smith did not want their help. He did not want to leave this football game. Two of the trainers, however, managed to carry him off the field to safety as Warren Plunkett substituted into the backfield in his place. George Barton of the *Minneapolis Tribune*, the writer who had been sitting in the press box with Ted Williams before kickoff, scribbled a description of the injury on his blue notepad. *"Bruce Smith's bad right knee re-injured,"* he wrote. *"Smith carried off the field. A vicious tackle by Motl."*[22] With that, the chilly, winter-like air inside Memorial Stadium began to match the somber mood of the crowd itself, as the training staff placed Minnesota's captain on a stretcher and drove him to the hospital for observation. He had lasted only a dozen plays on this first Saturday of November.

The dejected Gophers punted the ball and turned to their defense to build some momentum. Dick Wildung, manhandling Bauman on defense all afternoon, worked with Judd Ringer to toss a Northwestern ball carrier for a loss on the first play, helping spur a three-and-out. Minnesota got the ball back but went barely anywhere—and then Northwestern blocked a Garnaas punt at the Gophers' thirty-eight-yard line. The comedy of errors continued on both sides when Graham heaved a pass toward the end zone on first down. Garnaas tipped the ball into the hands of Gene Flick for an interception at the Minnesota three-yard line before returning the ball to the twelve. In just one half alone, this game had already seen a barrage of punts, interceptions, and a safety. The Gophers were fortunate to even hold a 2–0 lead.

After another Minnesota punt, Northwestern took over in decent field position just before halftime. This was Otto Graham's moment to explode. He fired the ball in the flat to teammate Ike Kepford, who raced seventeen yards all the way to the Minnesota thirty-three—the very first Northwestern first down of the game. Bierman called a time-out with one minute remaining in the second quarter, giving Northwestern time to devise a big play. When the teams returned to the field for second down, the Wildcats went straight to the air again as right end Clarence Haase sprinted past Sweiger and Garnaas in the secondary. Graham, taking the snap from center, spotted him without hesitation. The sophomore halfback delivered a bullet right into Haase's hands in the end zone. Touchdown. The officials let this one stand. Minnesota was trailing in a football game for the first time in 1941.

Slight panic began to set in as Northwestern took a 7–2 lead into halftime. After Bob Motl's hit knocked Bruce Smith out of the game, the Gophers' offense looked utterly lost. How could they even manage a touchdown with their captain in the hospital? In the locker room, "Bierman was plenty disgusted," Bud Higgins later wrote. "He told us we were going to lose if we didn't snap out of it."[23] Bierman's pointed message was atypical for him; it was well-known that he openly disdained over-the-top halftime speeches and hardly ever delivered them, preferring to focus on strategy instead of appealing to pure emotions. "Rapidly sketched diagrams get across ideas much more vividly than do mere words," Bierman once said. "Teams coached by mentors who waste time on mere praise or condemnation between halves rarely make strong second-half comebacks."[24]

Luckily, Bierman knew he had something up his sleeve to draw up for the second half—something he had prepared to use against Michigan but never got the opportunity. It was a play that the Gophers had practiced extensively in the field house just one night before, during their walkthrough, knowing they might need a boost at some point against the rough-and-tumble Wildcats.

Northwestern never saw it coming.

＊ ＊ ＊

The first few seconds of "The Talking Play" have remained a mystery for eight decades, mostly because Minnesota team photographer Phil Brain missed the start of it and failed to capture visual evidence for later generations to review. In fact, not a single photographer in the stadium caught the beginning. It was *that* startling. To Brain's credit, once the incredible commotion began and it became apparent the ball was in play, he quickly recovered and successfully filmed the final ten seconds of the wildest and most peculiar play of the 1941 college football season.

It happened in the third quarter with nine minutes remaining, following three stagnant offensive drives to start the half. The Gophers, to put it mildly, looked hapless—until they caught a break on a poor punt by DeCorrevont following a mad rush from tackle Ed Lechner. The normally impeccable senior star for Northwestern had made yet another uncharacteristic mistake, as he struggled to make contact with the football thanks to mud left behind by the Minneapolis snowstorm. The punt sailed only eight yards, to the Northwestern forty-one, before landing out of bounds. Lechner then left the game as big Urban Odson and Paul Mitchell came in at the tackle spots. Still trailing 7–2, the Gophers took over with a chance to regain the lead. Bill Garnaas, the team's primary play-caller, recognized that Minnesota needed a spark—something, anything, to get his teammates going and take their minds off Bruce Smith's injury. *"TRICK PLAY!"* he yelled to his teammates in the huddle.

It was actually two plays. The first was entirely unremarkable: Bud Higgins handed the football to Bob Sweiger for an attempted reverse on first down, but Northwestern's line stuffed him for no gain. Referee John Getchell, like he did a hundred times every game, picked up the football and prepared to spot it back at the forty-one-yard line. Gene Flick watched Getchell closely as Sweiger started talking trash to his opponents, accusing Northwestern's line of rough treatment. *"Sweiger started argument with Alf Bauman,"*[25] George Barton recorded in his notes from the press box. It was all a decoy. As Sweiger and the Wildcats sparred, Flick shouted loudly to his teammate: *"Come on, Bob, let's go!"*[26] Then he waited for the moment Getchell would place the football on the ground.

The distraction worked as planned. Without huddling, six Gophers rushed to the line of scrimmage, aligning to the right of center, as Flick prepared for a quick snap. With the Northwestern defense still in shambles and not even remotely prepared for action, Flick fired the football back to Higgins before the Wildcats could return to the line. Earning every bit of his 150 pounds, the little guy raced furiously downfield—and totally unnoticed—with the football tucked under his arm. "This fooler," the *Chicago Tribune*'s Wilfrid Smith wrote, "caught the Wildcats flatfooted."[27]

Total chaos ensued. The fans had no idea how the play had started or how Higgins had ended up with the ball, but once they noticed him cutting down the sideline toward the end zone, they exploded into a roar so loud it was reportedly heard four miles away in St. Paul. The befuddled Wildcat defenders, caught in a daze and entirely out of position, realized in a panic that they had better go drag that Higgins down to the ground before he could score a touchdown. Six Northwestern players sprinted as fast as they could, including Bob Motl, but they were too far behind. He crossed the twenty, the fifteen, and then the ten. Higgins was on his way. Urban Odson and Judd Ringer, thanks to their enormous head start from the line of scrimmage, protected his front side like concrete. Near the five-yard line, Odson pulverized DeCorrevont and then knocked over Don Kruger before falling face-first onto the grass. Higgins, with a clear path to the end zone now, held steady on his feet and shuffled past the goal line for a touchdown as a desperate Northwestern defender dove toward his feet. John Billman, trailing on the play, rushed to Higgins' side as their momentum carried them toward the field goal post in celebration. A student manager on the sidelines couldn't believe his boys had really pulled it off. "Those Gophers practiced that play last night," he shouted. "It worked like they planned it in every detail."[28]

The crowd at Memorial Stadium whipped into such a frenzy that most probably didn't even realize the Gophers missed the extra point attempt after Higgins' touchdown. Who cared? All that mattered was that Minnesota regained the lead, 8–7. The rest of the game, though not necessarily uneventful, would remain a blur for the sixty-four thousand people in attendance—including Ted Williams. Sitting in awe at Memorial Stadium that afternoon, Williams said Bud Higgins' dash was the most thrilling moment he had ever experienced as a spectator other than the World Series. "The way the Gophers went to town with that play," Williams told George Barton in the press box, "was really something."[29]

Once the stadium settled down, there was still a quarter and a half of football left to play—and it remained a brash, bare-knuckled affair the rest of the way. Butch Levy, for one, apparently played the entire game with a bloody nose. Neither team threatened again offensively until Minnesota drove the ball inside the ten in the fourth quarter with a chance to seal the victory. Riding Bill Daley and Bud Higgins on three straight rushes for no gain, the Gophers turned the ball over on downs. Trailing by just one point, Northwestern took over at its own four-yard line with a chance—albeit a slim one—to win the football game. With DeCorrevont at left halfback, the Wildcats stumbled on their first two plays and faced a third-and-ten deep in their own territory. Under pressure, DeCorrevont scrambled out of trouble and managed a seventeen-yard gain to keep hope alive. With seconds ticking away, Waldorf sent his sophomore Otto Graham back into the game at halfback, hoping for a miracle.

There would be no such thing. On second down, Minnesota's Gordon Paschka intercepted Graham's toss at the Northwestern twenty-eight, effectively ending the ballgame. With only one timeout, the Wildcats were doomed. Three plays later, it was final: Minnesota 8, Northwestern 7. Bruce Smith learned of the result from a hospital bed down the street.

As the Golden Gophers skipped off to their locker room in euphoria, a distraught Northwestern squad tried to process what exactly had just happened. According to the *Pioneer Press*, Pappy Waldorf refused to allow the media into his locker room until all of his players had departed. Once they left, Waldorf did not hold back. "Our kids deserved to win that one," he said. Although careful to praise his own team's courageous performance and quick to credit Minnesota, the discussion inevitably always came back to that Bud Higgins scamper in the third quarter. "This ball game," Waldorf said, "will furnish a lot of coal for the hot stove league."[30]

Make no mistake: Northwestern believed the play was illegal, and the coaches would grow more vocal about that opinion in the coming days. Waldorf and his assistants claimed the Gopher linemen were in motion as the ball was snapped and that the rules required them to stop for at least one second before the center could put the ball in play. Just a few days later, speaking at a luncheon in Chicago with 1,500 people in the audience, Waldorf admitted he did not see the start of the play for himself but contended that "our press box observers were of the opinion that Minnesota's players did not come to a second's halt before the play started as the rules prescribe."[31] Waldorf, though still giving credit to Minnesota as a team, openly ripped the officials: "It was," he said, "as poorly officiated a game as I have ever seen."[32]

Bernie Bierman countered with his own response. He made no apologies for the play and felt Northwestern's staff was simply making excuses for not having its players prepared. "The story," he said, "is that the Northwestern team was caught napping." Nobody was in motion, according to Bierman, and he claimed all four officials would back him up on that opinion. John Getchell certainly did. He explained that the Gophers had warned the officiating crew that they would be attempting the trick play before it happened, and he said that when Gene Flick snapped the ball, Minnesota had the proper number of men on the line. Not one player was in motion, Getchell said. The play was legal. It would become forever known as "The Talking Play," an homage to Bob Sweiger's brilliant decoy.[33]

Most of the national writers lauded the Gophers' creativity on the trick play and gave them recognition for a hard-fought victory over a strong Northwestern team. "Looks like Bernie Bierman really put one over," Bob Brachman of the *San Francisco Examiner* wrote.[34] And in the Associated Press recap of the victory: "Minnesota's mighty mite—147-pound Bud Higgins—took the controls for one quick scoring drive Saturday to send the Golden Gophers express rolling along the Big Ten and national championship roadway."[35]

Minnesota, at 5–0, had now emerged from a two-game stretch against Michigan and Northwestern as the unquestioned favorite to win the Big Ten, but several teams in other leagues were still gunning for that top Associated Press ranking. Texas, already tied for first, looked like the most formidable challenger. For the sixth straight game, the Longhorns surpassed the thirty-point mark as they claimed victory over Southern Methodist for the first time in eight seasons. "The Longhorns definitely demonstrated that their team is one of the grandest ever to set foot on a Southwestern football field," Weldon Hart of the *Austin American-Statesman* wrote. "Their right to No. 1 ranking in the United States now can hardly be challenged."[36]

It made sense. From the outside, at least, Minnesota seemed in disrepair with Bruce Smith on crutches. Indeed, this team still had a lot to prove over the final three games of the season, starting the next week against Nebraska—a program coming off a Rose Bowl appearance. In a humorous development, freshman coach Dallas Ward relayed from his scouting report on Saturday that Kansas State had tried to use the same type of "Talking Play" against the Huskers, to no avail. Apparently, the play wasn't so uncommon after all. Missouri had tried it a few times under Don Faurot; even Bierman himself had already pulled it out once in an East–West All-Star game a few winters back. "Wouldn't it be funny if Nebraska should spring it on us on Saturday?" Bierman said, showing a rare moment of personality a few days after the Northwestern game. "Or would it?"[37]

10

"ONLY HUMAN"

The Nebraska team en route to Minneapolis in early November 1941 looked nothing like the one that narrowly lost to Stanford in the Rose Bowl, just ten months earlier, in front of ninety-two thousand fans in Pasadena. That 1940 squad had captured a Big Six title and suffered just one regular season defeat (to Minnesota, of course) before losing thirteen players to graduation, eight to the National Guard, and at least six to defense industries.[1] After winning their first two games of 1941 and cracking the top fifteen of the Associated Press poll, the newest crop of Cornhuskers quickly tumbled into a three-game losing streak. They dropped games to Indiana, Missouri, and, most recently, Kansas State, a 12–6 loss in Manhattan, Kansas, that plummeted Nebraska's winning percentage below .500 on the season. Coach Biff Jones, a West Point graduate and retired Army major, needed his team's fortunes to change quickly as he prepared for a second trip to Minneapolis in thirteen months.

Enter Lt. Col. Harold Browne. Formerly Jones' top football assistant, Browne had been instrumental as a defensive strategist and backfield coach for the Rose Bowl team in 1940. He left it all behind for military life. Over the winter, Browne joined Nebraska's 110th Quartermaster Regiment with the National Guard at Camp Robinson in the extreme northwest portion of the state, about five hundred miles from the University of Nebraska's campus, where his group of about eight hundred men provided logistics, transportation, food, and clothes for the 35th Infantry Division. It was a far cry from coaching football in

Lincoln. So, imagine how shocked the Huskers must have been on Tuesday, November 4, 1941, just days before one of the biggest games of the season, when their former assistant coach showed up to practice wearing a full suit, ready to coach again as though he had never left for Camp Robinson.[2]

Coach Browne was back. The military granted him a temporary ten-day leave from service—just enough time for the lieutenant colonel to help lead his Cornhuskers against the defending national champions. Wasting no time, he tutored the varsity ends during his first practice and seemed to not miss a beat. "Browne rolled up his sleeves, spat on his hands and is now engaged in helping what appears to everyone else as a lost cause," the Lincoln Journal Star observed. "It was Browne who used to fashion the defenses which Nebraska would use in all games. Maybe he can figure out how to stop the power and speed of the Gopher attack this year."[3]

Despite an undefeated record, that Gopher attack seemed somewhat vulnerable heading into the sixth game of the 1941 season. Minnesota could no longer proclaim itself the nation's top team, at least according to the unscientific Associated Press system. On the same morning Lt. Col. Browne arrived in Lincoln, the newest AP poll showed Minnesota sliding to the second spot in the rankings. Apparently wary of Bruce Smith's injury and perhaps unimpressed by the narrow victory over Northwestern, the voters instead chose Texas as their top team for the first week of November. Dana Bible, coincidentally the former head coach at Nebraska and predecessor to Biff Jones, seemed to be capturing the imagination of the national writers with his high-scoring offense. Led by halfback Jack Crain, the Longhorns shredded defenses left and right over six games as they averaged thirty-eight points a contest. After sitting dead even the week before, Texas now led Minnesota by a narrow but healthy margin in the AP poll, followed by undefeated Fordham, Duke, and Texas A&M.

The AP ranking—and to a lesser extent a few other polling systems—remained the barometer for a national championship in 1941 due to factors outside of Minnesota's control. First, college football had no true playoff system in sight, leaving a collection of independent experts and sportswriters to determine the mythical champion each year. Furthermore, the Big Ten Conference had outlawed teams from playing in bowl games for the previous two decades because of concerns about amateurism and financial corruption involving post-season contests. The ban prevented the Gophers from proving themselves against top non-conference competition at the end of the regular season and robbed them of several chances to play in the prestigious Rose Bowl. Bernie Bierman was on record as opposing the rule, saying as recently as 1937 that "I believe practically every Minnesota alumnus would like to see the team in the Rose Bowl in a championship year." He had tasted that success himself, having led Tulane to Pasadena on New Year's Day in 1932 before returning to his alma mater. However, Bierman also stressed the need for moderation. "This matter of 'bowl' games is getting beyond control," he said. "If it keeps up, there will be so many of them it will be a joke. One of these days football will wake up to find the public isn't taking it seriously anymore."[4]

With the Rose Bowl out of the question for Minnesota in 1941, it really must have stung to see Texas take hold of that top spot in the AP poll, especially so deep in the second half of the season. The Gophers had to face the facts: they would not be allowed to play in a bowl game because of Big Ten rules, and at this point in the season, they also did not have a strong claim to the mythical 1941 national championship. Still, with three games remaining, there was plenty of time for Minnesota to change the writers' minds.

✧ ✧ ✧

"ONLY THREE MORE!" That was the message posted on Minnesota's locker room bulletin board early in the week as the team prepped for the Cornhuskers. Bernie Bierman, fearing a letdown after two highly emotional Big Ten victories, ordered his players on several jogs around the field that week after they made mistakes during practice sessions.[5] As his teammates suffered the consequences, Bruce Smith watched from a distance on crutches, beyond flustered over the knee injury that kept him off the field for the second half against Michigan and almost the entire Northwestern game. "The situation is extremely dark where Smith is concerned," Maury Diamond of the *Minnesota Daily* wrote.[6] With time running out in his illustrious college football career, Smith desperately wanted to play against Nebraska and sought a miracle cure early in the week as he stretched under a training room heat lamp. By Thursday, the senior captain had ditched his crutches, but progress did

not come fast enough. His knee hadn't recovered in time for him to suit up against the Huskers on Saturday, meaning Smith would miss his final "Dad's Day" weekend with his father. It was a real disappointment, especially considering Lucius Smith was the guest of honor and a scheduled speaker for the Dad's Day dinner at Coffman Memorial Union following the game.

Gopher fans were heartbroken about Smith's injury and prayed they had not seen the last of him in a Minnesota uniform. Joe Ferguson, a university alumnus living in Portland, Oregon, sent a nervous telegram that week to *Minneapolis Tribune* writer Bernard Swanson. "Please wire collect condition of Bruce Smith, our captain," Ferguson asked Swanson, "and team's general condition for game with Nebraska Saturday."[7] To make up for his potential absence, Bierman and backfield coach Sheldon Beise did their best to develop depth during practice that week. Gene Bierhaus, Mike Welch, Joe Lauterbach, and a few others saw more repetitions on offense as their chances of playing increased. In addition to Smith's injury, it appeared Herman Frickey would also miss another game, although the Gophers were encouraged to see progress from Helge Pukema and end Bill Baumgartner. The latter was finally nearing his return to the field after suffering that broken leg in the season opener against Washington six weeks earlier.

Even in a non-conference game, Minnesota had a point to make against Nebraska this weekend. Though Bierman didn't acknowledge it, the writers had disrespected the Gophers by dropping them a spot in the AP poll. Jack Guenther of the United Press, however, dealt an even nastier blow to Bierman's ego that week when he published his own rankings. He agreed that Texas was, without a doubt, the best team in the country, followed not by Minnesota but by Fordham, an Independent team coming off a Cotton Bowl appearance the year before. The Rams were certainly a respected power and, like Minnesota, had not lost or tied a game so far in 1941. The mere fact that Guenther ranked the Gophers a spot below the Rams was not necessarily offensive, but the United Press writer may have taken it a little too far when he published the following comment: "From what I've seen of previous Minnesota teams the present Fordham eleven would score twice on the current Golden Gophers before their headguards were adjusted."[8] Those were fighting words. They would not play well in Minnesota over the coming days, as fans across the state sent Guenther angry letters in protest of his attitude toward their beloved Gophers.

✿ ✿ ✿

A day before the Minnesota–Nebraska game, an open letter to the Huskers appeared in the student newspaper, signed by the University Alumni Association, the Lincoln Chamber of Commerce, the Nebraska Press Association, the Nebraska State Teachers Association, and about a dozen other local organizations. "Those guys from Minnesota are only human. They can be whipped," the letter stated, "and you're just the team to do it."[9]

The Huskers arrived in St. Paul early Friday morning around 7:30, before heading to the St. Paul Hotel for breakfast. Unlike other opponents, who typically stayed overnight in the Twin Cities before games, Nebraska opted to spend Friday evening east of Minneapolis in Stillwater, on the banks of the St. Croix River. The team booked rooms at the Lowell Inn, a small Colonial venue built at the beginning of the Great Depression. Whether he knew it or not, coach Biff Jones had placed his team exactly three miles away from the Gophers' team hotel, the White Pine Inn in Bayport, where Bernie Bierman liked to escape the night before games.

In his weekly column, Bierman issued a stern warning to his team and to the Gopher fan base. Overconfidence, he said, would be a sore mistake. "Every one of Biff Jones' boys know what it would mean," Bierman wrote, "to beat our unbeaten Minnesota team."[10] Jones, for his part, expressed optimism in the days leading up to the game, telling Minneapolis writers that his team seemed loose, focused, and prepared. Still, he knew the odds were not in his favor: no Husker team had won in Minneapolis since 1902.[11]

Luckily for them, the Cornhuskers would not face the same raucous atmosphere that Northwestern had seen just seven days earlier. The university, no longer needing any temporary seats at Cooke Hall, expected much lighter attendance for the Nebraska game, probably in the range of forty thousand. For Dad's Day, many of the players' fathers (including Lucius Smith) would enjoy a special section to watch the game near the Minnesota bench. They might not see another epic brawl like Minnesota–Northwestern, but this game between two military men—Bernie Bierman the Marine and Biff Jones the Army major—still held some intrigue in light of international developments.

* * *

"Today," University of Minnesota president Walter Coffey said over the public address system before kickoff on November 8, 1941, "we dedicate this game to those men of the University of Minnesota who are serving our country in the armed service."[12] Coffey's speech followed a performance by five hundred members of the Army and Navy, in which cadets marched on the field and formed the words "U-S-N" (for the Navy) and "U-S-A" before a crowd of 42,893. These were times of high alert. Earlier in the week, Japanese media published a seven-point plan from the government, calling for the U.S. to unfreeze assets, leave the country alone in the Far East, and pull support for China in its ongoing conflict against Japan. Envoy Saburo Kurusu was on his way to Washington, via plane, for final diplomatic talks that the Japanese press said would decide "whether or not the entire world shall have peace."[13] In Russia, the Germans had just advanced into Crimea; at the same time, the Allies were concerned about the emergence of German U-boats near their bases in Newfoundland. Just one night before the Nebraska–Minnesota game, the Senate voted to scrap part of the Neutrality Act and authorize the arming of American ships in the North Atlantic. With these headlines in mind, Coffey took the microphone before kickoff and reminded the public that thousands of university graduates, including some former football players, were already serving in the military as prospects for peace seemed less and less plausible with every passing day. "Today, this is a greater glory," he told the crowd, "than could ever be achieved on the football field."[14]

There was no snowstorm in Minneapolis this weekend, but it was still a cold November afternoon with temperatures hovering around thirty degrees. Both Minnesota and Nebraska's offenses certainly looked frigid in the first quarter, perhaps thrown off by the early start time at 1:30 p.m. With Bruce Smith missing from the starting lineup for the second straight game, the Gophers again turned to Bill Daley at left half, Bill Garnaas at right half, and Bob Sweiger at fullback to gain some yardage on the ground. But the entire offensive attack was sluggish from the start as Bierman's worst anxieties about a letdown began to materialize. A clipping penalty ruined the first drive and forced Minnesota to punt. The second drive featured a thirteen-yard run by Sweiger and a twenty-two-yard sweep by Daley but stalled just past midfield. Another punt. On the third drive, Bud Higgins entered the game and found some running room with Sweiger and Daley as they marched to the Nebraska twenty-six. Turning to the air, Higgins threw an incomplete pass on first down, nearly had a pass intercepted on second down, lost three yards on a tackle by Fred Preston on third down, and then missed the mark again on fourth down. Turnover on downs. On the next drive, Higgins, Daley, and Garnaas combined to lose four yards. Another punt. The first quarter ended in a scoreless tie after a combined nine offensive possessions.

Nebraska's offense had not been any better. In fact, it had been much worse. Even with the mighty T formation in place to spread the ball downfield, the Huskers ended the first quarter with zero first downs and eight total yards, hardly a ringing endorsement of the offensive system Clark Shaughnessy had championed at Stanford. Minnesota's line was too big, too strong, and too good, especially Dick Wildung, whose name the public address announcer seemed to call over and over and over again throughout the afternoon. If only the Gophers could find a way to score.

Bud Higgins again came to the rescue, though not in as dramatic fashion as his forty-one-yard surprise a week before. On the first drive of the second quarter, Higgins twice connected through the air with Garnaas, the second of which saw Garnaas wrestle the football from an opposing defender at the twelve-yard line. On first down, four Nebraska defenders swarmed Sweiger at the line of scrimmage for no gain, but Higgins exploded left behind Wildung and Butch Levy on the next play, taking the ball all the way to the Nebraska one-yard line. On third down, Minnesota turned to Sweiger, the king of short-yardage situations. Refusing to be denied, he pummeled through a mob of defenders in red shirts as he crossed the goal line. Nebraska's Marvin Thompson blocked Bill Garnaas' extra point attempt, but the Gophers led 6–0. They had gotten the early lead they needed.

The rest of the quarter was a struggle. "From that point on," the *Daily Nebraskan* wrote, "the little-in-comparison Nebraskans tightened and the Gophers got not one more first down during the last 12 minutes of the quarter." The Huskers dominated time of possession and finally made their move during the final drive of the half. After Nebraska's Dale Bradley intercepted a Bud Higgins pass attempt, he took matters into his own hands on first down. On a pass fake, he sprinted right for a ten-yard gain, creeping into Minnesota territory just past midfield as coach Biff Jones called timeout. After a sack by Judd Ringer set the Huskers back seven yards, a Bradley-to-Thompson-to-Matheny lateral connection led to eight more yards. With time for only one more play on second down, Bob Ludwick caught a pass from Bradley at the Minnesota twenty-two and turned downfield with his eyes on the end zone—before Minnesota knocked him out of bounds as the buzzer sounded. "This," the *Daily Nebraskan* wrote, "was as close as the losers came to the goal."[15]

It was not for lack of trying. With limited subs, the Huskers fought tooth-and-nail after halftime to keep the game competitive. The Gophers did not look sharp. Higgins fumbled near midfield on the first drive of the quarter, and later in the third, the backfield suffered a major mental blunder when nobody knew who was supposed to grab Gene Flick's snap. With the ball flying loose, Daley rushed to grab the ball and lost sixteen yards. Minnesota gained a grand total of twenty-four yards in the third quarter.

Bierman would not stand for this sloppiness. In the fourth quarter, after sending Bob Fitch back into the game with Levy, he implored his end to *"go in there and raise that whole team!"*[16] The first drive resulted in a punt and the second drive ended in a missed field goal by Bill Daley. Minnesota finally showed signs of life on the next drive, using a power running attack to advance the ball to the Nebraska thirteen. After the Huskers stopped Daley and Garnaas in their tracks on three straight running plays, Bierman called upon Garnaas to try another field goal. He converted this time, extending the lead to two possessions at 9–0 with fewer than four minutes to play.

Bill Daley handled kickoff duties and booted the football toward the Nebraska twenty-two. Hoping the ball would dribble out of bounds, the Huskers let it roll without touching it. Big mistake. Herb Hein rushed all the way down the field on the kickoff team and fell on the football to give Minnesota possession in perhaps the most exciting play of the entire afternoon. After Garnaas gained two yards on a reverse, backup halfback Gene Bierhaus threw an interception on second down, a disappointment for the young Brainerd native but ultimately irrelevant. The

Huskers did not have enough time to score twice. On their final drive, they failed to advance past midfield and gave Minnesota the ball back with fifteen seconds to go. After running out the clock, the two teams broke from their respective sidelines to embrace each other at midfield. Bierman found Biff Jones in the crowd and shook his hand, telling his counterpart: "I don't know how we won this one."[17]

It was not a stretch to say that this had been the worst performance of the year for the Gophers, even in victory. The loss of Bruce Smith really took a toll; his teammates seemed lost on offense without him. "Without the running and passing of Capt. Bruce Smith," Joe Morgan of the United Press wrote, "the Minnesota team lacked a scoring punch."[18] Appearing on WTCN radio after the game, Smith quickly credited Dick Wildung and the defense for saving the game—and said voters would be foolish not to select the junior tackle as an All-American at the end of the year. "It just has to be Wildung," Smith said on the airwaves to a local audience in the Twin Cities. "He's been my choice ever since the opening game."[19] Wildung and the Gophers' defense earned this victory, especially with their smart second-half adjustments against the Huskers' cross-blocking and T-formation plays. They sniffed out Nebraska's attempts at every turn and held its offense to less than fifty total yards in the second half.

As the Minnesota players showered and the coaches reviewed the final statistics, other scores from across the country began to trickle into the locker room. The mood, downcast because of the lethargic performance against the Huskers, lightened immediately with the announcement of two stunning results. Top-ranked Texas, the AP voters' latest obsession, had apparently fallen quite short of its thirty-eight-point-per-game scoring average in a game against Baylor. The Longhorns scored just once and then managed to cough up the 7–0 lead late in the game, when Baylor reserve Bill Coleman caught a touchdown pass with eighteen seconds remaining. The game ended in a tie, a catastrophic result for the number one team in college football. "To the astonishment of many people," Weldon Hart of the *Austin American-Statesman* wrote, "the sun came up Sunday morning."[20] The fans in football-crazed Texas could hardly grapple with the disappointment, as the Longhorns' Rose Bowl and national championship hopes vanished overnight.

And then there was Fordham, the team Jack Guenther of the United Press said would roll Minnesota in a head-to-head matchup. Bierman wanted to know how the Rams fared the moment he walked into the dressing room: *"What was the Pitt–Fordham final?"*[21] Funny he should ask. Playing on the road at 0-5 Pittsburgh, Fordham unraveled in front of a lively and hostile crowd of twenty thousand, resulting in one of the most unbelievable upsets of the 1941 college football season. The Rams fell behind early in the first quarter and never gained any traction, losing by the embarrassing score of 13–0. The Pittsburgh Panthers, the same program Bernie Bierman's team had dominated start to finish in a 39–0 shutout in October, had just managed to spoil Fordham's undefeated season. Bierman could hardly contain his glee. So much for the Rams being able to score two touchdowns on the Gophers "before their headguards were adjusted," as Guenther had so boldly proclaimed a few days earlier. "I wonder," Bierman sneered in the locker room as if to mock his East Coast rival, "if they were selling buttons in New York and Pittsburgh today to send the Fordham team to the Rose Bowl?"[22]

✴ ✴ ✴

Bierman may have taken some joy in the misery of Fordham and Texas, but he knew it would be a mistake to gloat too much. His own team, after all, had nearly fallen flat against Nebraska and could take nothing for granted. So he ordered a full-pads workout two days after the game with a message on the bulletin board: *"REGULAR PRACTICE MONDAY."*

It was still unclear if Bruce Smith would be joining the team on the practice field. For the first time all year, he had sat out the entire sixty minutes against Nebraska, missing every single play due to that nagging knee injury. Only two games and a handful of practices remained in his college career, casting doubt about whether Smith could attain All-American status as so many had expected before the season.

More importantly, his absence would make life much more difficult for the Gophers, who needed to defeat Iowa and Wisconsin to cap off a perfect season but had shown little offensive firepower without their captain. Outside pundits with no knowledge of the actual situation soon began to speculate about Smith's future, such as columnist Bill Mandelcorn of the *Sentinel-Star* in Orlando, Florida. "Bierman had no right to let the injured Bruce Smith perform against Northwestern," he wrote in the Sunday edition of the newspaper on November 9. "Not only will he be out for this season . . . the chances are his football days may be over for good."[23] Those who knew Bruce Smith, however, knew this would not be the end.

11

FLOYD OF ROSEDALE

Faribault was ready. About one thousand folks crammed together outside the red-bricked Rock Island train depot on Friday, November 14, eager to erupt at any moment. With a loudspeaker and sound system hanging from the rail platform, the Faribault High School band broke into the Gopher fight song on multiple occasions, complete with a giant tuba booming musical notes from the back end of the crowd. They all waited breathlessly for a special train carrying Bruce Smith and the Minnesota Golden Gophers, as the team made its way south to the state of Iowa for the seventh game of the 1941 season. When the railcar finally approached the Faribault station late that afternoon, it slowed and came to a stop—but only for a moment. The whole town had prepared to give Smith the hero's welcome, to tell him how proud they were of him, and to encourage him as he attempted to return from his knee injury. Unfortunately, they never got much of an opportunity.

The train remained in Faribault for approximately sixty seconds—just enough time for Lucius Smith to hop off the platform and join his son's final road trip as a college player, but hardly enough time for the enthusiastic townsfolk to conduct their grand celebration. Some caught a glimpse of Bruce Smith in the brief moments during the stop, but he was literally there one minute and gone the next, off to Iowa with his dad and the rest of the Golden Gophers. J. H. Clarkson, the general manager of the Rock Island railroad, later apologized and said a telegram requesting the five-minute pit stop did not reach the company's Minneapolis office in time to adjust the itinerary. "The Rock Island intended no insult to the people of Faribault," Clarkson said, "and we regret that the Faribault people were disappointed in their plans to welcome Captain Bruce Smith and other members of his Gopher team."[1]

It was a shame, yes, but the people of Faribault saw the bigger picture. After a slow start to the week, Bruce Smith's right knee had been rapidly improving, to the point where he found himself donning full pads on Wednesday as the first-team left halfback. By Thursday, he ran "more freely than at any time since his injury," George Edmond of the *Pioneer Press* wrote.[2] And by Friday, he boarded his team's special train to Iowa—with that very brief stopover in Faribault—preparing to play significant minutes against the Hawkeyes, although he likely would start the game on the bench. Even so, Smith was thrilled with the progress of his knee and no longer feared the premature end of his college career. His All-American hopes hadn't vanished yet.

The triumphant return of their captain gave the undefeated Gophers a surge in confidence as they traveled from Minneapolis to Des Moines for the first leg of their journey on Friday evening. They would stay in Iowa's capital city overnight before heading to Iowa City early Saturday morning on November 15. Encouragingly, Herman Frickey and Helge Pukema also made the trip to Iowa after missing the Nebraska game with injuries. That was a good sign. And thanks to the stumbles by Texas and Fordham a week before, Minnesota had also returned to its rightful place in the Associated Press rankings: Number One. A win this week would clinch at least a share of the Big Ten title heading into the finale with Wisconsin on November 22.

The Hawkeyes, like Nebraska, hoped to play the part of spoiler. With three Big Ten losses, Iowa was out of the running for a league championship, but Dr. Eddie Anderson's group at least had some momentum on its side. The team had mounted a resurgence over the previous two weeks, knocking off Indiana at home before blanking Illinois 21–0 in Champaign. The modest success had apparently gone to at least one of the player's heads; an unnamed member of the Iowa roster had referred to America's top-ranked college football team as "Dem Gopher Bums" earlier in the week.[3] Iowa's two-game winning streak, if you wanted to call it that, hardly stacked up with Minnesota's fifteen straight victories stretching over three separate seasons. The last loss the Gophers suffered? It came during the second-to-last game of the

1939 season, against these same Iowa Hawkeyes in the same Iowa Stadium.

During a candid long-distance phone conversation with Gordon Gilmore of the *Pioneer Press*, coach Eddie Anderson acknowledged that Minnesota would be the heavy favorite this time around but warned outsiders not to count out his pesky Hawkeyes. Nonetheless, the former Notre Dame All-American and Knute Rockne protégé, celebrating his forty-first birthday that week, openly admitted that he would need to make some serious coaching adjustments to hang with the Gophers. Iowa, he said, must use the passing game to overcome Minnesota's weight advantage on the line. "Of course," Anderson said, "that's no secret."[4] Tom Farmer, a dual-sport athlete who played baseball in the spring for the Hawkeyes, stood out as the team's best passer. And Bill Green, who caught the decisive touchdown pass in 1939 to beat Minnesota for the first time in a decade, now had one more chance to duplicate the victory as a senior.

As the Gophers filed into Hotel Fort Des Moines on Friday evening, they spotted a curious and slightly infuriating sign in the front lobby: "*REMEMBER '39. IOWA IS READY.*" Similar signs hung on the doors of the players' rooms. "*Well fer crying out loud,*" the players were heard saying in the hallways. "*What's the idea? Who's responsible for that?*"[5] Apparently, it had been the handiwork of an Iowa alum, hoping to mess with the Gophers' heads the night before the game.

Minnesota was too psychologically strong to wilt in the face of a cheap fan trick like that, but truthfully, many of the Gopher seniors *did* remember that 1939 game against Iowa. The 13–9 loss to the Hawkeyes and Heisman Trophy winner Nile Kinnick two years earlier had been a bad memory during a frustrating losing season. It was, in fact, the only time Bierman ever lost a game to Iowa. During his tenure, Minnesota held an 8–1 advantage in the series, boosting the program to a 25–9 overall record against the Hawkeyes dating back to the first game in 1891. Since the very beginning, these two border schools had always fought hard against each other in a bitter geographical rivalry—but it rose to a whole new level in 1934 and 1935, when the rough treatment of Iowa's star African American halfback Ozzie Simmons caused an enormous rift and ultimately led to the creation of the "Floyd of Rosedale," a trophy similar in nature to the "Little Brown Jug" but born under much more serious and ugly circumstances. The tensions, though cooled, would linger into the late 1930s and early 1940s and very much remained top of mind when the two teams met for the thirty-fifth time in 1941.

* * *

Ozzie Simmons starred in track and football at I. M. Terrell High School in segregated Fort Worth, Texas, where he was unquestionably talented enough to play college football at white institutions in his home state, if not for Jim Crow. The state of Texas' loss was the Big Ten's gain. After correspondence with an Iowa alumnus, Ozzie and his brother, Don, moved north in 1933 to play for the Hawkeyes, where their hero Duke Slater—the school's first Black All-American—had played from 1918 to 1921. Head coach Ossie Solem, another Doc Williams pupil and teammate of Bernie Bierman's brother Al on the 1912 Minnesota team, agreed to let them join the Iowa roster. During his first varsity season in 1934, Ozzie Simmons quickly made a name for himself.[6] *The Pittsburgh Courier*, a powerful and influential Black newspaper with nationwide circulation, called him the "brilliant Iowa sophomore" after he scored two touchdowns against Northwestern in early October. "The Fort Worth, Tex., tornado, was easily the outstanding star of the day," the newspaper reported, "and almost beat Northwestern single-handedly."[7]

Two weeks later, the Hawkeyes hosted an undefeated Minnesota team on October 27, 1934, in front of a fiery crowd of more than fifty thousand at Iowa Stadium. Simmons lasted only about half the game. "Oze Simmons, Iowa's widely heralded Negro halfback, fizzled out completely," the *Minneapolis Tribune* wrote, "the Gophers smothering his every attempt to carry the ball."[8] He exited the field multiple times, reportedly suffering a neck injury during a lopsided 48–12 loss to the Gophers.[9]

Although nobody could prove it definitively, Simmons' skin color almost assuredly had something to do with the repeated hard hits. The Associated Press reported the very next day that Iowa fans "expressed the belief that Oze Simmons, Iowa's Negro halfback, was roughed unnecessarily by the Minnesota team early in the game,"[10] and a student newspaper on campus, the *Daily Iowan*, described Simmons' treatment as "a terrific battering verging on outright assault."[11] Following along from the East Coast, the *Pittsburgh Courier* credited Simmons for his courageous performance in the face of adversity. "They tried to bottle up Ozzie Simmons Saturday," the newspaper wrote, "but the 'Black Comet' is still flashing across the Big Ten skies and being heralded as one of the greatest backs since [Red] Grange." [12] A week later, when Minnesota faced Michigan's star Black player Willis Ward, the *Minneapolis Spokesman*—an African American newspaper founded by Cecil Newman—wondered whether "Bernie Bierman's bone-crushing Minnesota eleven will 'Simmons' Ward." [13]

It would take an entire calendar year for the tensions to truly boil between Iowa and Minnesota. When the Gophers, once again undefeated, returned to play the Hawkeyes in Iowa City on November 9, 1935, Iowa governor Clyde Herring said publicly the night before the game that if "the officials stand for any rough tactics like Minnesota used last year, I'm sure the crowd won't." [14] The statement infuriated Bernie Bierman, who strongly denied that the Gophers intentionally tried to hurt Simmons the previous year. [15] In response to Gov. Herring's suggestion, Minnesota's head coach requested extra police officers to guard his team at Iowa Stadium and said if any Iowa fans mistreated his players, he would cancel the Minnesota–Iowa football series. The controversy made front-page news in Minneapolis as enraged fans and public officials contemplated the future of the rivalry. Minnesota attorney general Harry H. Peterson told Herring in a telegram that his comments had been "unsportsmanlike, cowardly and contemptible." [16]

Minnesota's governor, Floyd B. Olson, sensed trouble and decided to intervene to ease the tensions. The morning of the game, he sent a telegram to his counterpart Gov. Herring with a somewhat silly proposal, one that allowed everyone to take a step back and calm down— although he used an especially repulsive term in the process. "Minnesota folks are excited over your statement about the Iowa crowd lynching Minnesota football players," Olson wrote to Herring. "I have given them my assurance that you are a law abiding gentleman and are only trying to get our goat. The Minnesota team will tackle clean but Oh, so hard, Clyde. If you seriously think the Iowa team has any chance to win I will personally bet you a Minnesota prize hog against an Iowa prize hog that Minnesota wins today. The loser must deliver the hog in person to the winner. You are getting odds because Minnesota raises better hogs than Iowa." In a separate telegram to Bernie Bierman, Olson said:

"Minnesota people expect the boys to tackle clean but hard. We are all with you and the team and know you will win."[17]

Gov. Olson's prized hog bet may have saved a whole lot of distress when the two teams took the field that Saturday afternoon in 1935 at Iowa Stadium. Ozzie Simmons carried the ball nineteen times for modest gains and played outstanding defense in a losing effort, but the Gophers did not initiate any confrontations or treat him especially rough this time around. "The real star of the day was Ozzie Simmons," Bierman wrote in his newspaper column a few days later. "He showed me more football than I ever thought he was capable of. I don't hesitate to say on what he showed offensively and defensively against Minnesota he must be rated as one of the best backs in the game."[18]

Bierman's players also avoided interaction with the raucous Hawkeye fans. "Minnesota earned this victory," the *Des Moines Register* reported. "And the Gophers earned it in a battle that was clean all the way."[19] Minnesota simply walked away from Iowa City with a 13–6 victory—and an actual live pig. Making good on his bet, Gov. Herring showed up at the state capitol in St. Paul four days later, carrying a 220-pound hog from Rosedale Farms to present to Floyd Olson. Nicknamed the "Floyd of Rosedale," the pig sadly died of cholera just months later, but a tradition had been established. Ever since, the two teams have traded a bronze replica of the hog for eight decades and counting. Although its unpleasant origins are all but glossed over now, the whole "Floyd of Rosedale" fiasco very clearly traces back to the Gophers' brashness toward college football's top African American sophomore in 1934.[20]

The treatment of Ozzie Simmons offered a glimpse into the enormous challenges Black players faced in college football before World War II. "Those were bad years," Simmons said in an interview with the *Iowa City Press-Citizen* in 1989. "We recognize those were not good years for us. We didn't have more than six or seven blacks playing major college football."[21] Although historically Black colleges and universities had vibrant football programs during that era, as they do today, integration across the country proved slow during the first half-century of college football. A number of Black football players had excelled at northern institutions dating back to the late nineteenth and early twentieth centuries—including Bobby Marshall of Minnesota, a childhood friend of 1941 Gopher assistant Sig Harris and one of the key figures in the 1903 "Little Brown Jug" game against Michigan—but opportunities remained limited and non-white players were often extremely isolated on rosters with all-white coaches, all-white administrators, and all-white teammates.

The University of Minnesota, for instance, did not appear to have any Black players on the varsity roster in 1941. However, Bernie Bierman had coached multiple Black players over the course of his career, both at Minnesota and in previous coaching stops. That included James Dorsey, an end at the University of Montana under Bierman in the early 1920s and the first Black graduate of the school. After a long and successful career as an attorney and civil rights activist,[22] Dorsey credited Bierman as the man who "personally shaped my life for me and through him I really learned what democracy means."[23] Ellsworth "Jack" Harpole, a native of Kansas City, Missouri, played for Bierman at Minnesota in the early thirties, and in the middle part of the decade, Dwight Reed of St. Paul and Horace Bell of Akron, Ohio, joined the program. In 1936, Reed and Bell earned regular playing time and helped the Gophers claim a national championship, despite facing racist taunts and other nauseating treatment in the same realm that Ozzie Simmons had experienced. In 1935, the *Spokesman* reported that a radio announcer—who remained unnamed—referred to Reed by using a racial slur. "Such fellows deserve either education or pity," the newspaper wrote. "If he had been near some of us, he would have obtained neither, but he would have received a nice sock on the jaw."[24]

The discrimination was not limited to the radio booth or the playing field. University policies also forced Black students like Harpole, Reed, and Bell to live in segregated housing. According to "A Campus Divided," a 2017 research exhibit that investigated racism and anti-Semitism at the University of Minnesota before and during World War II, the school practiced housing segregation under Lotus D. Coffman in the 1930s until the next president, Guy Stanton Ford, opened the dorms to students of all races in 1937. (After Ford's retirement in 1941, the ensuing administration under President Walter Coffey again supported a segregated "International House" on campus, which led to a major backlash from student activists during the first year of the war and ultimately a reversal of the policy in 1942. As the research team for "A Campus Divided" found: "By 1942, the University of Minnesota was one of the last Big Ten schools to still have segregated housing.")[25]

During the 1930s, Minnesota's administration and coaches also caved to segregationist demands and withheld Black athletes from competition against southern institutions with Jim Crow policies, drawing significant criticism from civil rights groups and Black journalists. Reed sat out a game against Bierman's old team, Tulane, in 1935, and both Reed and Bell missed a contest against Texas in 1936 because their opponents refused to play in a football game that featured Black players. Minnesota officials never offered an explanation for the benching, but the NAACP and the *Pittsburgh Courier* immediately took notice and sent messages to Bierman expressing their displeasure. "You used Reed and Bell in every game this season except last Saturday," the *Courier* wrote to Bierman in a telegram. "Why weren't they used against Texas?"[26]

Although she certainly did not agree with the benching of Black players, pioneering African American journalist Nellie Dodson of the *Minneapolis Spokesman* offered a slightly different perspective in a 1935 column, where she defended Bierman's character. "Those who have accused Bierman of being a prejudiced coach are not aware of the many things he has done to help colored players at Minnesota," Dodson wrote. "It was Bierman who wanted [Iowa star] Homer Harris to come to Minnesota; it was Bierman who persuaded Dwight [Reed] to follow up his career at Minnesota. He has done any number of things for Jack Harpole, and he and Jack are good friends now, even after Harp's football service is over. The question may be asked: 'Why does Bierman encourage Negro players and then stand for the discrimination that southern schools advocate?'"[27] Dodson explained that "gentleman's agreements" between northern and southern schools had, unfortunately, become standard practice in college football during the years leading up to World War II, not only in the Big Ten but also across the sport as a whole.

Public opinion shifted somewhat at the end of the 1930s, however, with the emergence of UCLA in the Pacific Coast Conference. Led by four Black players—Jackie Robinson, Kenny Washington, Ray Bartlett, and Woody Strode—the 1939 Bruins team finished undefeated and altered the landscape of college football moving forward.[28] Two years later, in 1941, Robinson and a few of his former teammates from UCLA were floated as possible additions to the "Negro All-Star" roster that would compete against the New York Yankees of the American Association on November 30, after the college football season ended. Eleanor Roosevelt would serve as the honorary committee chairwoman.[29] The idea for the game, organized by Yankees' owner Douglas Hertz at the Polo Grounds, had been praised by the *Pittsburgh Courier* as "making it possible for nationally-known Negro stars to engage in a football game for charity against a professional league team."[30] Proceeds would help Black, Jewish, and Catholic charity groups. The final roster included Ozzie Simmons, as well as several other names from the Big Ten, both past and present: Charley Anderson of Ohio State, Bernie Jefferson of Northwestern, and Jim Walker of Iowa.

Walker had started at tackle for three straight years under Dr. Eddie Anderson in 1939, 1940, and 1941, proving himself as one of the best in his position in the Big Ten. Illinois players would say after the season that Walker was the toughest opposing tackle they saw all year.[31] Originally born in Georgia, Walker spent his high school years in South Bend, Indiana, and now looked to finish his college career on a high note at the University of Iowa. A Big Ten title may have been out of the question in 1941, but Walker and his fellow seniors felt a wave of momentum heading into the final two games of the season. They looked more cohesive, more confident, and more dangerous in their back-to-back wins over Indiana and Illinois to start the month of November. Now, they had a chance to extend their winning streak to three games, as the seventh-annual battle for the Floyd of Rosedale loomed on November 15, 1941.

※ ※ ※

"Underdogs love to knock off the favorite," Bernie Bierman wrote anxiously in his regular column the day before the game. "I believe that we'll find Iowans in that mood Saturday when we take the field for our annual meeting."[32] After spending the night at Hotel Fort Des Moines, located downtown at Walnut and Tenth, the Golden Gophers caught yet another train on a picturesque fall Saturday morning and headed one hundred miles straight east to Iowa City. They arrived at Iowa Stadium around 12:00 p.m., giving the Hawkeye fans enough time to recover from a rowdy Friday evening pep rally that had spilled an estimated ten thousand people into the streets and blocked traffic.

On game day, the highway patrol brought in reinforcements to avoid the same problems, stationing twenty-one officers for traffic duty as the police doubled their force for the day. Roughly 43,200 people finally made their way into Iowa Stadium, some overflowing onto a grassy hill above the end zone, before the 1:30 p.m. kickoff. Seven thousand of those fans wore rival Maroon and Gold colors, arriving from Minneapolis on a dozen special trains. They must have cheered wildly as the visiting Gophers sprinted out of their locker room, emerging from a small, concrete overhang near Iowa Stadium's northwest corner. Built in 1929 just steps from the Iowa River, the facility sat below a steep hill on the southern end, where a wobbly set of stairs led up to a chain-link fence and a grass-covered parking lot. Unlike the illustrious Michigan Stadium, the Hawkeyes played on a more modest home field, with the majority of the fans packing tightly into diagonal bleachers facing east-to-west.[33]

As the nation's top-ranked team, Minnesota remained on high alert for an upset. It could not afford a slow start against Iowa if it wanted to avoid the kind of humiliation Texas and Fordham had experienced a week prior, but the opening kickoff began in ominous fashion as the Gophers lost a starter before the first snap of the game. After Bill Daley booted the football to Iowa's Bill Green downfield, Helge Pukema collided with a blocker and roughed up his knee, giving Bernie Bierman no choice but to replace Pukema at guard with John Billman, the former Central High standout. The crowd at Iowa Stadium apparently cheered loudly after the kickoff, which Bierman construed as an inappropriate celebration of Pukema's injury. Iowa journalists would later dispute this claim, but the point remained: these two teams were not on friendly terms.

After forcing a punt on the first drive, Minnesota opened possession at its own twenty-two with yet another new backfield look. Bill Garnaas returned to his natural quarterback position as the primary play-caller, Bill Daley lined up at fullback, and Bob Sweiger moved to right half. This time, Bierman tapped Bud Higgins as the starting left halfback, with the expectation that Bruce Smith would replace him eventually. Higgins received the first carry of the game but managed only two yards behind Butch Levy. A reverse by Sweiger on second down resulted in a loss of one yard as Iowa's captain Bill Diehl came crashing through the line. Higgins got the call again on third down—this time trying his luck to the right side, behind tackle Ed Lechner—but he again made little progress and gained maybe a yard, if that. Higgins punted on fourth down.

The baseball star Tom Farmer fielded the football for Iowa in his own territory, before racing to the Minnesota thirty-four to give his team outstanding field position and an early spark for the upset bid. Instead of an aggressive aerial attack, Dr. Eddie Anderson's offense committed early to the running game. Green slammed right for nine yards. Bus Mertes converted the first down with a four-yard run and then gained six more on the next play to move the ball to the Minnesota fifteen. Here came trouble. Minnesota called a timeout and sent Urban Odson into the game at right tackle for Lechner. The reigning All-American's presence did not scare the Hawkeyes, as they continued to pound the football on the ground. On the sixth straight rushing play of the drive, Bill Green—the nemesis of the 1939 game—took a reverse toward the left sideline and overpowered a much smaller Bud Higgins on his way to the end zone. Touchdown. Six minutes into the game, Iowa led 7–0. Trailing for only the second time all season, the Minnesota seniors remained calm. "All the teams we play are pepped up," Bob Sweiger later said, "but to us it is always just another game and it sometimes takes us time to get going."[34]

Sweiger earned some rest midway through the first quarter as Bierman replaced him with a fellow senior, Warren Plunkett. After the two teams traded three-and-out possessions, Bud Higgins fielded a punt and returned the ball to the Minnesota forty-two. After two short runs by Daley, the Gophers faced a third down and six yards to go as the 43,200 fans suddenly turned their attention to the visitor's sideline. There had been a development in front of Minnesota's bench: Bruce Smith was starting to warm up.

According to an oft-told legend, Smith begged Bernie Bierman to place him at left halfback during this first quarter, arguing that his sluggish teammates might be doomed if he remained on the sidelines any longer. No version of this tale appeared in any of the press reports or game recaps in 1941, but it would not be far-fetched to imagine Smith approaching his head coach with the composed, cool demeanor that had typified his four years at the University of Minnesota. Bierman, who had fully planned for Smith to play at some point anyway, must have obliged without hesitation. So the Faribault Flash continued his warm-ups in front of the bench, ready to enter the game, as the coaching staff huddled a few feet away, hoping privately that the return of the Minnesota captain would offer a much-needed lift. [35]

The crowd was astonished. Nobody expected to see Smith in action so early. The home fans in Black and Gold cringed, while out-of-town folks in Maroon and Gold yelled at the top of their lungs from the nosebleed section of Iowa Stadium. With his injured right knee wrapped in a bandage, Smith ended his stretches and jogged from the far sideline toward his teammates, staring straight ahead toward the playing field with a stoic expression on his face. Crouched and loitering near the line of scrimmage, the Hawkeye defenders downplayed the moment and pretended as though nothing extraordinary was occurring. Then Iowa's Ross Anderson, with his head cocked toward the sideline, raised his left arm and pointed to number "54"—just to make sure his teammates knew who was coming into this football game.

Smith took his familiar place at left halfback, lining up next to Daley at fullback and Bob Sweiger at right halfback. Guarding against the run, Iowa stacked the line of scrimmage with eight men and got burned when Bruce Smith took the snap and fired a pass downfield intended for Bill Garnaas. Iowa's Bill Green got his hands on the ball—or at least his right hand, which had been bothering him due to a sprain—and batted it up in the air. The football flew several yards above his head before dropping directly into the hands of Garnaas again for an improbable completion. Garnaas took off running as Green, in a daze, chased and tackled him with two other defenders at the sixteen-yard line. The *Daily Iowan* begrudgingly described the play as a "lucky pass," [36] but Minnesota would gladly accept it. Unorthodox or not, Bruce Smith's first pass attempt of the game had netted forty yards. Three plays later, on a fourth-down attempt, the Minnesota captain tossed another rocket to Garnaas at the three-yard line. Bill Daley capped off the drive on the next play as he fought through a crowd and strutted past the goal line for the tying score.

After the kickoff, it took only two plays for the Hawkeyes to drive into Minnesota territory. On third down from inside the forty, Farmer lofted a pass downfield but saw his end Bill Parker tumble to the grass as the ball fell incomplete. A physical encounter of some sort had occurred between Parker and a few Gophers, possibly interference, the *Waterloo Courier* argued. "The officials, however, either didn't see the tripping of the Iowa end or they didn't call it," the newspaper wrote. "The protests from the crowd and from the Iowa bench were numerous and loud."[37] The Hawkeyes punted on fourth down, pinning Minnesota at the eight-yard line. Lining up in punt formation, the Gophers ran a fake on first down for three yards as the quarter ended in a 7–7 deadlock.

Bruce Smith and his bandaged right knee led the charge from there. On the second play of the quarter, he converted a third down on a marvelous thirty-one-yard scamper, reversing from the right side of the field to the left as he shook multiple Iowa defenders. Riding Ed Lechner on the next snap, Smith then powered his way through the line for a five-yard gain to the Minnesota forty-seven. Same old Bruce. After a few more rushing attempts and a couple of penalties on both ends, Smith again used his right arm to make some magic happen through the air. This time, he connected with a reserve end named Cliff Anderson, who caught the ball at the Iowa twenty-two and then added seven yards after the catch. First down. Feeling a wave of momentum in front of a jeering Iowa Stadium crowd, Dick Wildung paved a gigantic hole through the left side on the next play, giving Bill Daley more than enough space to zoom into the secondary without a single Iowa defender getting a hand on him. Daley waltzed into the end zone for a twenty-two-yard touchdown. After missing a point-after attempt, the Gophers led 13–7—and then had a chance to run away with the game when Iowa's Tom Farmer immediately fumbled on first down inside his own territory on the ensuing drive. Unfortunately, after the Minnesota offense marched all the way to the Iowa eight, Bill Garnaas gave the football right back to the Hawkeyes with a fumble of his own.

Iowa landed the next punch moments later on one of the odder plays of the season, outside of "The Talking Play" against Northwestern. On third down, Bus Mertes hauled in a Farmer pass with his fingertips near midfield and continued running for a few steps before the football escaped from his hands and scooted ahead about ten yards. Assuming the officials would rule the pass incomplete, the Minnesota defenders failed to pursue before realizing they had made a huge mistake. The referees never blew a whistle. Sprinting ahead, Iowa's Al Coupee scooped the ball near the thirty-seven and hurried toward the end zone stripe. After conferring for a few moments, the officials signaled for a touchdown, even though game film would later show without question that Coupee never had control of the football. An incomplete pass had turned into a seventy-seven-yard score, tying the game at 13–13 after Farmer missed the extra point.

Minnesota might not have been able to keep up in such a fast-paced game in previous weeks, but with Bruce Smith back on the field, there were no longer any limits to the Gophers' offensive firepower. "Smith's return," Bierman said later, "put zip in our play."[38] His mere presence made a difference. On the second-to-last drive of the half, Smith, Daley, Garnaas, and Sweiger pounded, pounded, and pounded some more on a clinical ten-play drive. They showed no mercy, churning out gains of two yards, four yards, and six yards before Daley finally broke free into the open field, tumbling into a referee by accident before the Hawkeyes brought him down at the Iowa twenty-five. Daley, Sweiger, and Smith combined for five more rushes in a row, driving the ball to the Iowa three-yard line after Jim Walker made a touchdown-saving tackle. Then Bill Daley went back to work. With one minute and fifty seconds left to play in the second quarter, Daley followed a block from Smith into the end zone for his third touchdown of the afternoon. The Iowa Stadium crowd instantly transformed into a mix of deflation and agony; some frustrated supporters of the home team even taunted the Gophers with boos and drowned out the visiting fans' cheers as Garnaas converted the extra point. On the ensuing kickoff, the Hawkeyes continued to deteriorate. Four Gophers swarmed Mertes and blasted him on the return, forcing a fumble. Bob Fitch came up with it at the Iowa thirty-one, but Gordon Paschka misfired on a field goal attempt before halftime. Minnesota led 20–13 at the break but must have been irked at the wasted opportunity. It wouldn't have made much of a difference in the second half, as it turned out.

Over the final two quarters, the Gophers played focused, determined, and powerful football, controlling the game on the ground behind Garnaas' astute play-calling as they ravaged the Iowa line on both sides of the ball. It was vintage Bernie Bierman football, the style he learned as a player under Doc Williams and later implemented as a part of his "Minnesota system" when he returned as head coach in 1932. With bruising play by the usual suspects on the frontline, as well as some added punch from reserve Bob Smith, the Gophers held Iowa to just one first down in the third quarter and dominated time-of-possession with the running game. They waited until the second drive of the fourth quarter to deliver the final blow, leaning on the original starting halfback—Bud Higgins—to once again run wild. "When standing by his mates," the *Courier* wrote, "[Higgins] looked like a kindergarten youngster who had strolled away."[39] And yet Iowa still didn't have an answer for the Minnesota sophomore. Utilizing both sides of the field, Higgins carved up the Hawkeye defense and capped a forty-seven-yard drive with a two-yard touchdown rush.

With a two-possession advantage, this game was all but over. After forcing another punt, Minnesota stayed aggressive on offense and left the majority of its starters in the game. On a reverse play from the Iowa seventeen, Garnaas added an insurance touchdown to increase the lead to 34–13. Now this game was *really* over. The lopsided score gave some reserves a chance to play, including backfield mates Mike Welch and Gene Bierhaus. The latter nabbed his first career interception on Iowa's final drive—surely causing his hometown of Brainerd to explode in cheers back in central Minnesota. It was quite an exclamation point.

After a tumultuous first half, the Gophers had somehow managed to notch a three-touchdown victory, fueled by a gigantic 378-to-103 advantage in rushing yards. Daley himself ran for more yards than Iowa's entire backfield before exiting the game with an injury. "It was Bill Daley," the *Courier* wrote, "who was the most brutal of the visiting ball carriers."[40] The Iowa coaches also raved over Daley's performance, but they still could not forget about Bruce Smith. "You can't stop [Minnesota]," Iowa's line coach Jim Harris said, "not with Smith in shape to play somewhere near his best." After several tense weeks, praying and worrying about the status of his knee, Smith could finally exhale.

"It's the happiest day of my life," he said after the game.[41] Although he did not record a touchdown, Smith played a direct role in setting up at least two of the Gopher scores and established an overall tone from the moment he stepped off the sideline. The forty-yard completion to Garnaas on his first pass attempt transformed the whole game, according to Bierman. Despite the early adversity, Bierman praised his team's performance against Iowa as the most balanced and well-rounded of the entire season. The victory clinched a share of the Big Ten title for the seventh time under Bierman; one more win against rival Wisconsin would ensure an outright Big Ten title and, in all likelihood, earn the Gophers another mythical national championship in the eyes of the Associated Press and other selectors. "They don't stop a tank corps with small detachments these days," Bert McGrane of the *Des Moines Register* wrote in his game recap, "so the Gophers rolled on in their national championship march here Saturday."[42] They were one game away.

* * *

As Minnesota celebrated its flawless 7–0 record, and as seven thousand fans in Maroon and Gold streamed back on trains to Minneapolis with smiles on their faces, career diplomats prepared for a showdown a thousand miles away in the nation's capital. After a weeklong journey over the Pacific, through Honolulu to San Francisco and across the mainland United States, a plane carrying Japanese envoy Saburo Kurusu had finally arrived in Washington, D.C., around 1:30 on the afternoon of Saturday, November 15.[43] Kurusu was no stranger to the United States, having previously lived here while serving as a Japanese consul in Chicago, as well as in New York City, where he met his wife, Alice Jay Little, and married her in 1914 during a ceremony at Grace Methodist Church on West 104th Street.[44]

Sporting a pair of glasses and a striped tie, Kurusu tipped his hat in the direction of an Associated Press photographer when he first set foot on the runway during a layover in San Francisco, reportedly carrying a personal message to Washington from Prime Minister Hideki Tojo. Kurusu would not reveal the content of that message to the American press, but he claimed to seek compromise with the U.S. as he prepared to meet with Secretary of State Cordell Hull and President Roosevelt himself in roughly forty-eight hours. The American public could not ignore the widely publicized visit. For many months, the actions of Germany—including recent North Atlantic disputes involving American ships like the *Greer, Kearny,* and *Reuben James*—had dominated the headlines and eclipsed some of the tensions with Japan. By mid-November 1941, that had not changed, but it was noteworthy that Kurusu's hat-tipping picture appeared on the front page of many U.S. newspapers on November 15, including major publications like the *Atlanta Constitution* and the *Boston Globe*. In the Twin Cities, readers of the *Minneapolis Star Journal* might have noticed the wire photograph of Kurusu on the far right margin of Page One under the headline, "Envoy Arrives," adjacent to a Halsey Hall story titled "Sunny Skies Answer Hawkeye Dreams as They Face Gophers." Coincidentally, prior to takeoff from San Francisco to Washington, Kurusu used a familiar football analogy as he expressed his desire to avert war with the United States. "I hope to break through the line," Kurusu said, "and make a touchdown."[45]

The complex discussions would hinge on Japan's military occupation of territories in Asia, the status of economic sanctions, and whether Prime Minister Tojo's government could distance itself from the other Axis powers. The latter would be an especially difficult point of conversation, for it had been Kurusu himself who signed the Tripartite Pact with Italy and Germany one year earlier as his country's ambassador in Berlin. "Mr. President, in regard to Mr. Kurusu's visit," a reporter had asked Roosevelt a day earlier, "do you think the American people realize the emergency in the Far East?" The president said he thought so.

Moments later, another reporter launched a similar inquiry:

Q: "Mr. President, do you think anybody over-rates the seriousness of the Far Eastern situation?"

THE PRESIDENT: "That is awfully difficult to know. It's a difficult question to answer. What do you mean by 'seriously'? What do you mean by 'over-rate'?"

Q: "There is going to be war?"

THE PRESIDENT: "What?"

Q: "That there might be war?"

THE PRESIDENT: "I sincerely trust not."[46]

In a November 15 memorandum, Division of Far Eastern Affairs chief Maxwell M. Hamilton suggested Secretary of State Hull take a firm tone with Kurusu in a meeting scheduled for Monday. "We cannot afford to make light of the tremendous seriousness of the present world situation confronting us," Hamilton offered as one talking point with the Japanese. "The entire world has been placed in a precarious position as a result of the havoc which has been wrought by the forces of aggression. Our common sense tells us of the extreme need that the world come back to ways of peace."[47]

Kurusu and his colleague, Ambassador Kichisaburo Nomura, met with Hull alone for about a half hour on the morning of November 17. Around 11:10 a.m., President Roosevelt joined the meeting at the White House Red Room. Discussions lasted for another hour before the parties separated.[48] "Peace or war between the United States and Japan," the *Philadelphia Inquirer*'s Washington correspondent wrote, "hung in precarious balance tonight at the end of the first day of negotiations between American officials and Saburo Kurusu."[49] With both sides remaining tight-lipped, the public knew little about what had been discussed. Pressing Kurusu for answers, an American reporter asked the envoy if he felt the two sides were any closer to that "touchdown" for peace that Kurusu had talked about prior to leaving San Francisco a few days earlier.

Kurusu replied: *"I don't know."*[50]

12

ON WISCONSIN

Thanksgiving Day came early in 1941, but not by any fluke on the calendar. Two years prior, President Roosevelt had moved the holiday to the second-to-last Thursday of November, rather than the last, to encourage Americans mired in the Great Depression to spend an extra week Christmas shopping. Despite his intentions of economic stimulus, the president's break with almost century-old Thanksgiving tradition led to confusion, some outrage, and even defiance from state executives, like Governor Arthur H. James of Pennsylvania, an ardent opponent of the New Deal who refused to recognize Roosevelt's Thanksgiving and instead issued a proclamation declaring his own holiday a week later. The president, to his credit, apparently understood the gravity of his error and committed to restoring regular Thanksgiving on the fourth Thursday of the month the next year.[1] The change, however, would not take place in time to adjust the current calendar. So on November 20, 1941, Americans carved turkeys, prepared stuffing, baked pies, and settled in for a relaxing four-day weekend, enjoying the last Thanksgiving in American history to be held on the third Thursday of November, and also the last Thanksgiving in American history to take place before the country entered the deadliest war of all time.

"Hovering war clouds were forgotten in Minneapolis," the *Tribune* reported on Thanksgiving Day, "as the city began its annual festival of Thanksgiving, in gratitude for passage of another year of peace and plenty."[2] Businesses closed across the Twin Cities in observance of the holiday, including gas stations and drug stores.

The University of Minnesota campus also remained mostly empty, with one notable exception: Northrop Field. It was full of activity as the Gophers ran through a light workout, marking their second-to-last practice of the season, and for fifteen seniors, the second-to-last practice of their collegiate careers. In forty-eight hours, they would face their archrival, the University of Wisconsin, for a chance to capture an outright Big Ten championship and a mythical national title for the second season in a row.

Entering the final week of the regular season, Minnesota had now proven itself as the overwhelming favorite among Associated Press pollsters. A grand total of 112 out of 123 voters placed the Gophers at the top spot, followed by undefeated Texas A&M and Duke at number two and three respectively (Texas fell out of contention completely after a home loss to TCU). National writers now seemed to agree that one last victory over Wisconsin would assure the Gophers of their rightful place in history. If only the Big Ten would allow its members to play in postseason games, Minnesota "would be sought after by the bowl promoters much more avidly than any other team in the country," Bob Considine of the International News Service wrote. "Those hard-bitten babies know a national champion—even if the title must be mythical—when they see one."[3]

The national press had taken notice of Bruce Smith's impressive return to action in Iowa City. Better yet, his knee no longer appeared to be an issue whatsoever, according to practice reports out of Minneapolis. Emboldened by his progress against Iowa, Smith appeared "markedly repaired physically, completely repaired mentally," Bernard Swanson of the *Tribune* wrote, "and primed for one last surge against Wisconsin to clinch an all-America berth that appears just around the corner."[4] With Smith as well as Herman Frickey in much better shape, the Gophers would enter the final game of their 1941 season stronger and healthier than at any time since perhaps the season opener against Washington. Their mission was clear: defeat the Badgers, and they would walk away as champions. A loss would knock them down from the top spot in the national polls, and even worse, would relegate them to a share of the Big Ten title with the winner of the Ohio State–Michigan game in Ann Arbor. Both of those teams carried just one conference loss, and in the event the Buckeyes won, Minnesota wouldn't even have bragging rights in a head-to-head tiebreaker because the two teams hadn't faced each other in 1941.

Fans could not bear the thought of sharing a Big Ten championship with another team. On Thanksgiving Day, local business owners and community members began to flood the Gophers with encouraging telegrams, hoping to boost their spirits before the last game of the season. Butch Levy received at least a half-dozen messages, including one from Stanley Andersch of the Minneapolis Elks Lodge. "Keep up the good work Saturday," he wrote, "and bring home the Big Ten and national championship."[5]

* * *

With the eyes of the nation on the Gophers, the Wisconsin Badgers sensed an upset opportunity. "The boys," coach Harry Stuhldreher said, "are ready."[6] To keep his team healthy, Stuhldreher ordered light contact in practice that week, opting instead to prepare mentally for the Minnesota attack. Though the Badgers entered the game with an overall losing record, they owned a 3–2 conference mark and had just shut out Purdue 13–0 a week earlier in their most impressive defensive performance of the season. If Stuhldreher's team could play that way again on the defensive side of the ball, they might have a shot on Saturday.

There was no question at all that Wisconsin could score: it boasted one of the most explosive offenses in the Big Ten, leading the league in points per game and trailing only Minnesota in rushing yards per game. Pat Harder, a sophomore fullback, had already surpassed the 1940 Heisman winner, Michigan's Tom Harmon, with fifty-two points scored through the first seven games of the season. He also led the Big Ten in total rushing yards, followed closely by the Gophers' own fullback Bill Daley. Then there was Bud Seelinger, a Great Falls, Montana, native who had played a state high school title game against Herb Hein and Herman Frickey a few years earlier. All season, Seelinger lit up secondary after secondary with his powerful arm. His completion rate was even better than Northwestern's Otto Graham.

One of his favorite targets, Dave Schreiner, could make a strong argument as one of the top ends in college football. Gopher fans knew this quite well, after watching Schreiner torch their team for a seventy-

eight-yard touchdown catch in the first quarter of the 1940 game at
Camp Randall in Madison. The Badgers' captain Tom Farris, who ran
back an interception for a touchdown against Minnesota in that very
same quarter, would also return to play the final game of his career
along with five other Badger seniors. "I can't think of a better way to
finish," Farris said, "than by beating Minnesota."[7]

Wisconsin had not fared well in recent years against the Bernie
Bierman dynasty. Like Michigan, the Badgers also remained winless
against the Gophers during the Roosevelt era, with eight straight losses
dating back to 1932—most of them uncompetitive. Wisconsin came
close to breaking the streak in 1940 by taking a two-score lead in the
first half, but after an inevitable collapse, Minnesota emerged from
Madison with a 22–13 victory to claim the national championship. It
was Harry Stuhldreher's fifth straight loss to his border rival since taking over the program in 1936.

If anyone could reverse the fortunes of the Minnesota–Wisconsin
rivalry—which dated back to 1890, among the oldest in the Midwest—
it was probably Coach Stuhldreher. Standing at just five-foot-seven, he
was not very physically imposing and probably wouldn't stand out in a
crowd, but college football fans needed no introduction to the legend.
Stuhldreher, just two decades earlier, had played quarterback for Knute
Rockne at Notre Dame as a member of the "Four Horsemen." The
pinnacle of his Irish glory came in 1924, when his team finished undefeated and beat Stanford in the Rose Bowl. Almost immediately after
his playing career ended, Stuhldreher gravitated to the coaching profession, first at Villanova for a decade before moving to Wisconsin. In
Madison for the previous six years, Stuhldreher had struggled to break
into the top half of the Big Ten, but an upset over Minnesota could at
least even the Badgers' overall record at .500 and stir a little momentum
heading into the next season. With that goal in mind, Wisconsin
planned to bring at least six thousand fans to the Twin Cities for the
weekend, and most of them had already arrived by late Friday evening.
Hours before kickoff on Saturday, famed Wisconsin columnist Roundy
Coughlin reported from Minneapolis that "a guy will see so many here
from Madison this morning that he will think some moved Madison
north for a few days visit."[8]

Since 1930, the two border rivals had competed each year to stake
claim to the "slab of bacon," a short-lived trophy made of walnut that

eventually gave way to Paul Bunyan's Axe in the late 1940s.[9] Coincidentally, in 1941, the governors of both states considered replacing the slab
of bacon with the "Dairy Bowl," an arrangement that would provide the
Badgers with famous Minnesota butter if they won, and the Gophers
with famous Wisconsin cheese if they won. "I would suggest you start
wrapping up the butter," Wisconsin governor Julius Heil wrote in a
telegram to Minnesota governor Harold Stassen before the game.[10] The
"Dairy Bowl," unfortunately, never really caught any traction—kind of
like Roosevelt's failed third-Thursday-of-November Thanksgiving idea.

✿ ✿ ✿

With the British continuing their advance in North Africa, the Germans
surging through the fields of Russia, and the Japanese still engaging in
futile peace talks with the United States, college students began to
ponder their fate. They did not know what to expect after Thanksgiving
and Christmas, but according to a joint poll by the University of Texas
and the University of Minnesota, 54 percent of college students said
men should have their draft status deferred until they could complete
their education. A total of 64 percent of respondents said they would
wait for the draft instead of voluntarily enlisting in the armed forces.[11]

Ahead of the Wisconsin game, the press continued to speculate
about the draft status of football players. Although the whispers were
highly unreliable, local newspapers reported to readers in the Twin
Cities that Bob Sweiger could be headed for preliminary examination as
early as Monday, November 24, just two days after the season finale.[12]
It was all unverified chatter, but the reporting illustrated the extent to
which the draft status of high-profile athletes became a wide topic of
discussion during the fall of 1941. Pundits and writers could not help
but begin to look ahead. "Possibility of war and defense demands,"
Charles Johnson wrote in the *Minneapolis Star Journal*, "may cut into
football heavily in the future."[13]

Despite the uncertainty, Minnesota's fifteen seniors took the field on
Saturday, November 22, 1941, in front of an official crowd of 52,894 at
Memorial Stadium. Grounds crews, caving to the demands of the fans,
put temporary seats back in place and brought load after load of hay to
the sidelines to provide warmth for the players as temperatures dipped
well below the freezing mark. Most of the players wore long socks and

long sleeves under their uniforms; when they exhaled, they could see their breath. Both coaching staffs sported puffy winter jackets. Luckily, the snow held off, and some bright sunlight even shined over the stadium to add a few afternoon shadows.

Ahead of the 1:30 p.m. kickoff, Mutual Broadcasting System planned to broadcast at least part of the Minnesota-Wisconsin game to listeners in every state. "Barring fire, flood or the worst upset of the year," Harry Ferguson of the United Press wrote confidently to a national audience, "this is the day when Minnesota clinches its claim to the title of national champion."[14] With the crowd buzzing outside, the Badgers huddled in their warm locker room as long as they could. Beyond the door, they could hear their own band playing *On Wisconsin.* It was exactly the kind of motivation the team needed as it sought the most monumental upset in the history of the rivalry. When the players finally left the cozy locker room and marched into the frigid open-air Memorial Stadium, senior captain Tom Farris lined up at midfield with Minnesota's captain, Bruce Smith, for the final coin toss of their respective careers. Minnesota won the flip and chose to defend the west end zone with a favorable wind pattern. Smith did not end up starting at his regular left half position, but the coaching staff planned to insert him early in the first quarter.

The game did not start with much action. Wisconsin went three-and-out on its first possession, and Minnesota did the same. Then the two teams traded fumbles; Harder for Wisconsin and Sweiger for Minnesota. After five combined lifeless possessions, the Gophers again had the ball in their own territory in a scoreless game. Bernie Bierman called for a substitution. Number "54" would take over at left halfback.

It is impossible to know what Bruce Smith felt or thought as he jogged onto the field at Memorial Stadium for his final game in a Minnesota uniform. His mind may have drifted to early boyhood memories, back to the 1920s when he and his brother George plucked the grass from this same playing surface because they thought they found Bronko Nagurski's cleat mark. Maybe he thought about his first varsity game as a sophomore in 1939, when he caught the opening kickoff against Arizona and fulfilled a lifelong dream of playing for his father's alma mater. Maybe he felt a wave of emotions; maybe he saw a whole highlight reel of memories, of touchdowns and tackles and runs-in-the-mud against Michigan, all playing over and over again in his head as he trotted out in front of fifty-three thousand fans. Or maybe Bruce Smith ignored all of that and simply focused on Wisconsin and the task ahead. The Minnesota captain, after all, was not one for theatrics—but no doubt, this was an emotional moment for him personally, for his parents, for his siblings, and for everybody back home in Faribault who had watched him grow from a toddler at 415 Division Street to an All-American candidate at halfback. Smith now had one last chance to show the nation that, with a fully healthy knee, he was among the best college football players in the country. Bruce Smith proved all of this, beyond any doubt, in just two plays on the very first offensive possession of the game.

He started with the arm. On his first pass attempt, Smith launched a rocket to a leaping Bill Garnaas downfield for a forty-five-yard gain to the Wisconsin twenty-one. Two plays later, Smith bolted left, reversed field to follow his blockers, and streaked through the hole for an eighteen-yard touchdown; 7–0. And that was just the beginning. Smith's heroics continued a drive later, when he faked a pass downfield, cranked right, and sprinted thirty-nine yards before running into trouble; at the eight-yard line, Smith smartly spotted Bob Fitch and tossed him a lateral, which Fitch caught and ran into the end zone. Touchdown. It was 14–0 and the crowd sensed a rout in the making. Even Antonia Bell, a British teacher from Hartsfordshire, England, attending the game as a guest of her host family, said that Smith's sprint and lateral was the most exciting thing she ever saw in the two American football games she had attended. "Most thrilling!" Bell said, although she didn't know Smith's name. Whoever he was, he "made that long run and pushed people aside with his hand!"[15]

After trading possessions, Harry Stuhldreher's team tried to crawl out of the deficit by turning to its vaunted air attack early in the second quarter. It didn't work. Bud Seelinger, on first down, attempted a pass over midfield, but Bruce Smith leapt in front of the receiver and intercepted the football before running it back deep into Wisconsin's territory at the eleven-yard line. Smith then deferred to Bill Daley on three straight rushes, allowing his teammate to score the third touchdown of the day; 21–0.

Wisconsin, not one to roll over, managed to add six points on the next drive on a nine-yard run by star sophomore Pat Harder, who padded his league-lead in points to fifty-eight. With an ensuing chance to cut the lead to one score, however, the Badgers' momentum came to a halt when Minnesota's Vic Kulbitski, a reserve from the small town of Red Wing, intercepted a Tom Farris pass and returned it for a touchdown; 28–6. And it was only halftime.

After the band and cheerleaders took over the field during the break, in which they arranged themselves to spell out an "M" as a part of their performance, the Badgers attempted to mount a comeback but could not muster much luck. Wisconsin's first drive of the half began in shambles when Dick Wildung plunged through the frontline to sack Bud Seelinger for an eight-yard loss. Seelinger would make up for it with a couple of nifty passes later in the drive, helping the Badgers finally venture deep into Minnesota territory—but they again stalled near the goal line. With a chance to score from inside the ten-yard line on third down, Farris threw an errant pass wide left of his intended target in the end zone. On the next play, Farris ran a downfield route as a receiver toward the middle of the end zone. Mark Hoskins, dropping back to pass after a wild offensive shift, threw a low pass to Farris, who appeared to possibly catch the football cleanly for a touchdown. Butch Levy and Bob Sweiger, trailing Farris, both signaled "incomplete" with their arms as they pleaded with the officials. They agreed and ruled the touchdown no good, much to the displeasure of Farris as he emerged from the grass. "*How come*," he asked the referees as he threw his hands up in the air to protest.[16] His teammate, Dave Schreiner, came running toward the line of scrimmage with a similar gesture of discontent. Their pleas did nothing to change the referees' decision. Minnesota took over on downs with a three-touchdown lead and proceeded ruthlessly on the next drive.

Sweiger broke into the secondary on first down for seven yards. Smith, galloping with his long legs, pushed forward on the next play to secure the first down. Daley plunged up the middle twice in a row for a total of six yards, then took the snap on third down and handed it to Garnaas for a reverse. First down again. This was the kind of football that drove opposing coaches like Harry Stuhldreher crazy. Seemingly at a loss for answers, he smoked a cigarette and pranced around the sidelines the entire game without taking a seat. Members of the Twin Cities press said they had never seen a coach spend an entire sixty-minute football game on his feet. Stuhldreher soon realized he was in for more pain, when he saw Bernie Bierman send big Urban "Fireman" Odson back into the game for some power football. Odson's mind must have raced, too, as he played across the street from his Fire Station 19 living quarters for the final time.

Bruce Smith used the opportunity to catch the Badgers by surprise. Instead of taking off on another reverse, he tilted back that cannon of a right arm and connected with Bob Fitch downfield for a twenty-five-yard gain near midfield. The Gophers were in business again. A combination of a few more running plays, along with another pass completion from Smith to Judd Ringer, advanced the ball near the twenty-yard line. Shortly before the third quarter ended, Bruce Smith took another snap and immediately ran into chaos, as it appeared he was trapped with nowhere to go. Then he heard Bill Daley screaming at him downfield, shouting at the top of his lungs. He wanted that football, so Smith threw it to him and Daley grabbed it with a wide-open path to the end zone. Easy touchdown. Smith, overcome with excitement, dropped to his knees before getting up with a smile on his face. He had just thrown the final touchdown pass of his collegiate career, to give his Gophers a resounding 34–6 lead. Bierman felt Smith needed a short rest, so he substituted Herman Frickey at left halfback as number "54" jogged over to the bench. The crowd gave polite applause as a photographer snapped Smith's photo on his way to the sidelines. He would return a few possessions later.

Bierman let all of his seniors play in the final quarter, with the exception of the injured Helge Pukema. They were Bruce Smith, Bob Sweiger, Warren Plunkett, Bob Fitch, Judd Ringer, Joe Hirscher, Gene Flick, Butch Levy, Gordon Paschka, Bob Smith, Neil Litman, Howard Straiton, Urban Odson, and Ed Lechner. At one point near the end, some of the seniors huddled on the field in full view of the fans, as though to savor their final minutes together. This crowd would miss them.

✲ ✲ ✲

The final moment for Bruce Smith came on the second offensive drive of the fourth quarter. On first down from his own twenty-five, Smith lined up at his regular left halfback position and took a direct snap. Bob Sweiger, the lead blocker, dove under a defender in a cut block and bought Smith some open running room on the right side of the line. Smith drifted toward the sideline but then ran into a brick wall of

Wisconsin tacklers. Len Calligaro, a physical fullback who played on the frontline occasionally, dove toward Smith's right side but failed to bring him down or jar the ball loose. An end named Gene Lyons then got his hands on him, before another end named Ray Kreick suddenly appeared after sprinting over from the original line of scrimmage. Kreick, on a clean tackle, bear-hugged Bruce Smith as he fell to the ground. Smith was knocked out. Every single player on each team, all twenty-one of them, quickly huddled over the fallen senior with looks of concern on their faces. Bob Sweiger collapsed to his knees and consoled Smith, appearing to whisper a message as he placed his head right next to his captain's ear.

After a few tense minutes, a trainer rushed to Smith's side. With assistance from Bob Fitch, they helped Smith walk off the field from Memorial Stadium for the last time as the crowd rose to its feet, preparing for a thunderous send-off. Almost fifty-three thousand people, including even the Wisconsin fans, roared together in appreciation of their beloved senior as he limped away. Bruce Smith received the "noisiest ovation any Minnesota individual ever got in the long and colorful football history of this school," according to Charles Johnson of the *Minneapolis Star Journal*.[17] The crowd seemed to believe Smith had reinjured his knee, but this was not the case. "I got knocked out with a bump on the head," Smith later revealed.[18] He said he didn't remember anything—not the play, not the ovation, and not the slow walk to the bench with his helmet off and arms draped around Fitch and a trainer. Smith didn't regain a real sense of consciousness until he finally reached the sidelines. It was at that point he realized that his career at the University of Minnesota was actually over. Gene Bierhaus replaced him at left halfback.

Bierman emptied his entire bench late in the fourth quarter, with reserves like Bierhaus, Mike Welch, Earl Eli, Bob Sandberg, and Dave Thomas carrying the ball in the backfield. The Gophers didn't miss a beat. According to an account from the *Pioneer Press*, Bruce Smith, Bill Daley, and Bob Sweiger, probably looking to warm up a little bit, headed to the locker room with a few minutes left on the clock. Once inside, they began to hear the intensity of the crowd increasing again. The reserves were driving into Wisconsin territory. Sweiger ran to the door to see what he was missing. *"They're marching again!"* he told Smith.[19] There were forty-two seconds left on the clock when Thomas rushed for a modest one-yard gain. The final touchdown of the 1941 season came next. Bud Higgins, naturally, connected at the seven-yard line with young Bob Sandberg—a future Gopher captain—who marched into the end zone for the first score of his career. Nine seconds remained. By mere formality, Minnesota kicked the ball away to Wisconsin for the last time. Not a single person inside Memorial Stadium took a seat. They all stood, delighted, as Minnesota put the finishing touches on a second consecutive undefeated season; 41–6 was the final score.

The feeling of overwhelming joy was contagious in the Minnesota locker room after the game. The players hugged, slapped each other on the back, shook hands, and cried tears of joy. Yet there was also a feeling of melancholy and a sense of closure. As they put their equipment away for the final time, Gordon Paschka and Judd Ringer sobbed, both celebrating and mourning the end of their football careers. Urban Odson, who had battled through a pesky knee injury all season, sat solemnly in the corner. "Just wish I had one more season," the big man said.[20]

Bruce Smith, conscious again after that fourth-quarter blow, smiled cheek to cheek. "I feel the happiest, right now," Smith said, before realizing he had said the exact same thing a week earlier after the game against Iowa. "Well, it's just that way, that's all. I want to say this, too: We beat a darn good team by a good margin," Smith said, "and that is why it is so satisfactory to wind things up that way. This has been the swellest gang of fellows . . . " Smith stopped suddenly in the middle of his sentence, hanging his head. He could speak no more, so Bernie Bierman spoke for him: "The play of Bruce Smith and the seniors . . . the fact that we could wind up unbeaten . . . is glory enough for anyone without singling out individual stars."[21]

Over in the Wisconsin locker room, coach Harry Stuhldreher boldly pronounced that Bruce Smith was an All-American by his standards. "As long as we had to take a licking, I was glad to see Bruce have such a great day to wind up his college career," Stuhldreher said. "He was entirely deserving of such a fine finish."[22] Earl Hilligan of the Associated Press summed it up this way in his opening paragraph: "Minnesota's mighty tide of football empire—with Captain Bruce Smith brilliantly riding the crest of the wave—swept over Wisconsin Saturday to carry the Gophers to the Big Ten and national football championships," he wrote. "The season which ended today capped a remarkable record for the 10-year Bernie Bierman regime."[23]

Bierman had done it again. He staked claim to his seventh shared or outright Big Ten title. He completed a fourth undefeated and untied season. And he would likely earn a fifth national championship, as long as the pollsters voted as expected in a few days. Bierman's concerns about backfield depth, about injuries, about his team taking success for granted, about every little thing that could possibly go wrong during a hunt for a second straight undefeated season—it all turned out to be unfounded. None of it mattered because Bernie Bierman was a champion again. Amid the wild celebration in the Memorial Stadium locker room after the eighth and final victory, athletic director Frank McCormick rushed through the crowd to find Bierman and commend him on another job well done. "Thank you, thank you," Bierman must have said in some fashion. Then McCormick, an Army veteran, asked the Marine Corps reservist a final question as the 1941 season came to a close.

"What are you going to worry about now?"[24]

13

CHAMPIONS AGAIN

Two days after his collegiate football career officially ended, Bruce Smith hobbled back to Memorial Stadium, on his one good knee, for a trip down memory lane. Although the Faribault Flash would never again don the gold uniform, he forced himself back to the field on this hazy Monday afternoon to take a peek at the next generation of Golden Gophers, as the freshman football team lined up for its annual end-of-the-year scrimmage. Smith couldn't help but vividly recall his own freshman game, back in the fall of 1938, when he experienced the thrill of breaking into the open field on his first rushing attempt. Joe Mernik threw a nasty block for him that day, Smith remembered. Nostalgia rushed through his veins. "Gosh," Smith said, "the years go by fast, don't they!"[1]

Joined by a few hundred spectators in the bleachers, Smith and his varsity teammates stood together on the sidelines to watch Dallas Ward's "Green" squad face Babe LeVoir's "Gold" team. Warren Plunkett rooted for his younger brother Dick at left guard on the Golds, while varsity assistant Bert Baston beamed with pride at the sight of his son, Fred, playing end. Jack Spewak, the promising lineman out of North High School in Minneapolis, started for the Greens at center. His former North teammate, Don Johnson, saw action at right halfback opposite Red Williams at left half. In a spirited, competitive scrimmage, the Gold squad claimed a narrow 7–0 victory on the strength of a sixty-yard touchdown run by fullback Bob Kula of Jackson, Minnesota.

Sizing up his prospects for 1942, Bernie Bierman kept a close eye on the scrimmage from the press box. "I had my first look at the freshman squad Monday," Bierman told a crowd of 1,200 people at the Minneapolis Athletic Club later that night in his first public appearance of the off-season. "Physically, they were impressive, but we cannot tell anything about their football ability until spring practice rolls around." No longer bogged down by the stress of the season and finally able to reflect, Bierman lauded the accomplishments of his 1941 team, praising the players for overcoming injuries and for brilliantly meeting the expectations that came with trying to win a second straight national title. He would sorely miss his fifteen seniors—and he knew more players could be lost in the coming months. "Regarding our prospects for 1942," Bierman told the crowd, "it is difficult to say because of uncertainty of things due to the war situation."[2] News broke the next day that advancing Nazi forces sat within twenty miles of Moscow, as the British struggled with Axis troops in Libya.

✻ ✻ ✻

On Tuesday, November 25, the University of Minnesota invited students and faculty members to Northrop Auditorium to celebrate the accomplishments of the 1941 football season. Addressing the overflow crowd, Bierman said his 1941 team "did as fine a job as any has ever done" considering the adversity it faced. University of Minnesota president Walter Coffey, taking center stage next, credited the team with having a "wholesome influence" on the school at large. "It will have a lasting place in the history of the university," Coffey said. "Its spirit will be remembered as even greater than its playing performance."[3]

After the speeches ended, the students witnessed an annual tradition: the much-anticipated Passing of the Torch ceremony between captains. This time around, Bruce Smith handed off his captaincy to the stellar Dick Wildung, providing his successor with an actual flaming torch that carried the names of past captains on the barrel. *Bruce Smith, Bill Johnson, Bob Bjorklund, Win Pedersen.* The torch also featured an "M" inscribed on the base. With his proud mother Dale in attendance, Wildung held the torch high in his right hand, gladly accepting the position of captain as a result of his teammates' secret ballot vote. Dale beamed in the audience. "How well, I know, how worthy you are—and of how diligently you worked to make your boyhood dreams come true," Dale wrote to her son in a dedication. "You have always rated 'All-American' on my team and I'm proud of 'all my boys.' You have given me much happiness and—in times of trouble—strength and courage. My hopes and prayers have always been for your health, success and happiness—and shall be—through the uncertain future that lies ahead."[4] Having already watched her late husband suffer upon his return from France after World War I, Dale must have agonized over the thought of Dick potentially seeing combat if the U.S. entered another war overseas. For now, though, Dick still had one year of football left to play at Minnesota. He just hoped that he would not let down the program in 1942. "I believe that if the draft and ineligibility doesn't hit the squad," Wildung said, "we should have a pretty strong starting team."[5]

At the same time, the media continued to speculate about the future of the outgoing seniors like Bob Sweiger, whose teammates named him Most Valuable Player in 1941 as a credit to his versatility in moving from fullback to halfback. "Well, as long as I am called," Sweiger told Joe Hendrickson of the *Minneapolis Star Journal* in response to press reports about his possible role in military life, "I plan to make the Army my career. There is no sense to going in just to serve your time. I may try to get into the marines, and then I'll go to work at it. There are opportunities for a fellow with Uncle Sam."[6] Bruce Smith, meanwhile, prepared to place his NFL aspirations on hold, even though the Cleveland Rams reportedly expressed interest in selecting him number one overall in 1942. Another draft might take precedence. "Yes, if I'm not drafted into the Army," Smith said, "I want to see what the pro league is like next year."[7]

The players remained optimistic, but they could not ignore the alarming newspaper headlines, not only about ongoing battles in Russia and North Africa but also about the deteriorating peace talks with Japanese envoy Saburo Kurusu and Ambassador Nomura. The diplomatic discussions between the U.S. and Japan had become front-page news throughout November, reminding the American public that Germany was not the only path to potential conflict. In the "Hull Note" on November 26, the United States responded to Japan's so-called "Proposal B" with a list of stipulations, including but not limited to a demand that the Japanese "will withdraw all military, naval, air and police forces from China and from Indochina."[8] Japan found those terms impossible. Days later, at the 8th Imperial Conference, the country authorized war against the United States, the United Kingdom, and the Netherlands, solidifying plans for a surprise attack.[9] In fact, the First Air Fleet, directed by Vice Admiral Chuichi Nagumo, had already left the Japanese harbor, traveling across the Pacific toward the American naval base Pearl Harbor.[10]

Times were uncertain, but "the fifteen seniors who played football," Bernie Bierman stated at the Passing of the Torch ceremony, "are now better prepared for whatever lies ahead."[11]

☆ ☆ ☆

As the country veered closer to war in late November and early December of 1941, the Minnesota Golden Gophers earned just about every accolade imaginable for their undefeated season. "For the first time in years," Eddie Dooley of the International News Service wrote, "the football world is in agreement, generally speaking, as to the team that merits premier national honors."[12] In the final Associated Press poll of the season, experts awarded Minnesota the top spot by an emphatic margin, as the Gophers took home 84.5 first-place votes. The second-place team, Duke, earned just 9.5 first-place votes despite also finishing undefeated. Writers respected coach Wallace Wade's Blue Devils, but they had faced a much softer schedule than Minnesota. With zero losses, Notre Dame could have also made a strong claim for a mythical national title—if not for one blemish in a scoreless tie with Army. The Irish finished third in the AP poll. Texas, which tied Baylor and lost at home to TCU in November, surged back to fourth after knocking Texas A&M from the ranks of the undefeated. And familiar Big Ten foe Michigan, having tied Ohio State on the final weekend of the season, took a formidable fifth-place spot in the AP poll. Fordham, Missouri, Duquesne, Texas A&M, and Navy rounded out the rest of the Top Ten.[13] It should be noted that the AP released the poll prior to some teams playing their final regular season contests, and it did not take into account the slate of post-season bowl games.

Although college football fans still engage in lively debates over mythical national titles of the past, the NCAA to this day officially recognizes Minnesota as the national champions of 1941 based on the

Associated Press as the designated selector. In total, a dozen contemporary and modern ranking systems (all listed in the NCAA's official record book) now view the Golden Gophers as worthy of the 1941 title. Alabama, which lost two games and finished twentieth in the Associated Press poll but won a bowl game over Texas A&M, still claims a share of the 1941 national title based on one first-place selection from the "Houlgate" system. The University of Texas does not claim a title but received top designation from the "Berryman" and "Williamson" systems. Reasonable observers can form their own conclusions.[14]

Minnesota certainly didn't lack individual accolades either in 1941. Dick Wildung, Bruce Smith, Butch Levy, Bill Daley, Helge Pukema, Bill Garnaas, and Bob Fitch earned All-Big Ten honors in some form. As the prestigious All-American teams began to trickle out from media outlets and football publications, Wildung and Smith were also quickly recognized as "consensus" All-Americans for placing on so many lists among experts. Many other Gophers saw their names in honorable mention categories at the national level; the United Press, for example, extended that award to Fitch, Pukema, Levy, Garnaas, Daley, Gene Flick, and Urban Odson.

The most prestigious individual award, however, was not All-American: it was the Heisman Trophy. As the *Sheboygan Press* in Wisconsin explained: "The Heisman memorial football award is college football's equivalent to baseball's most valuable player award—no small distinction."[15] In 1941, the trophy was still in its relative infancy, having been awarded annually to the top player in college football for only the previous six seasons. As hundreds of sportswriters and experts nationwide began receiving their ballots in the mail during mid-November 1941, the race appeared as wide-open as ever. Since leading candidate Bruce Smith missed time due to injury, some voters looked elsewhere for their Heisman Trophy choices. The *Casper Tribune-Herald* in Wyoming selected Frankie Albert, the splendid left-handed passer from Stanford. The *Medford Mail Tribune* picked Steve Juzwik of Notre Dame, whereas the *Ogden Standard-Examiner* in Utah chose the Irish's sophomore stud Angelo Bertelli. With the voting split into five regions, Frank Sinkwich of Georgia, Jack Crain of Texas, Bill Dudley of Virginia, and Steve Lach of Duke carried a large portion of the southern vote. Harvard's Endicott Peabody, the future governor of Massachusetts, was a popular choice among eastern writers.[16] In small towns across the country, there were even some wild card selections thrown around: the *Dispatch* in Moline, Illinois, for example, chose Dick Wildung! "It's about time a lineman reached the throne," sports editor Lynn Callaway wrote.[17]

Most writers and broadcasters eventually gravitated back to Bruce Smith. It was true that Smith missed some significant moments, including the second half of the Michigan game and most of the Northwestern game, and it was true that Bill Daley—not Smith—led the team in rushing. Yet those who followed Minnesota all year knew that the Gophers' captain had been their sparkplug. "It seems to me that Smith is the ideal man for the Heisman award," wrote Edwin Moore Jr. of the *Courier* in Waterloo, Iowa, "simply because he inspires his mates to achievement on the football field."[18] Smith's intangibles proved the difference. With 554 votes, the experts selected Bruce Smith on Friday, November 28, as their 1941 Heisman Trophy winner. Notre Dame's Bertelli finished in second place, followed by Stanford's Albert, Georgia's Sinkwich, Virginia's Dudley, and Harvard's Peabody. The United Press reported that Smith won the Heisman by the narrowest vote in the award's young history.[19]

It took a few hours for the news to reach Smith himself. That Friday, he had been traveling back to Faribault, where he volunteered to operate the scoreboard inside his old gym on Saturday evening for the big Faribault–Waseca basketball game. Before he even arrived in Rice County, Smith received a telegram asking him to call a representative in New York City prior to 4:30 p.m.—only then did he learn voters had selected him as the most outstanding player in American college football. "I have to pinch myself every five minutes; I can't believe it's true," Smith said. "There are hundreds of other guys who deserve it—not me."[20]

The newspapers in his home state weren't so modest. "Bruce Smith," the *Tribune* in Minneapolis wrote, "was accorded the highest honor a Minnesota football player ever has won."[21] In his hometown of Faribault, the *Journal Weekly* proudly republished a letter its office had received from one of Smith's youngest admirers. "Dear Santa," the boy had written to *Journal Weekly* editors, "Please send me a moving picture reel that shows all of the runs that Bruce Smith made while he was playing at Minnesota."[22] Organizers in Faribault had originally planned a testimonial banquet for Smith the next week, but they decided to postpone it so he could receive the Heisman in New York City on the evening of Tuesday, December 9, at Manhattan's Downtown Athletic Club. They didn't want to rush him home from his first trip to the Big Apple. Smith's sister, Olive, and father, Lucius, along with Governor Harold Stassen and Bernie Bierman, planned to accompany him to New York City for the Heisman Trophy presentation on December 9, which the Mutual Broadcasting System planned to air live on its radio affiliates across the United States at 9:45 p.m. EST.

The pressure Smith faced as a young, fresh-faced twenty-one-year-old must have felt overwhelming. The *Faribault Journal Weekly* reported that mail carriers in town were "working overtime" to deliver all of Smith's fan mail to the family home on Division Street. Congratulatory letters and autograph requests, often from complete strangers as far away as Massachusetts, just kept stacking higher and higher on the Smiths' front doorstep. According to the *Journal Weekly*, two companies also offered Smith movie contracts, hoping to produce a motion picture about his life—similar to "Harmon of Michigan," a movie released that same year about 1940 Heisman winner Tom Harmon. Smith's decisions about the future rested largely on his draft number, which the *Journal Weekly* reported as 2,700 in early December.[23]

Before he could think about the future, Smith would need to focus on his busy few weeks ahead. Finals were looming back on campus in Minneapolis, and his fame continued to grow with extracurricular commitments. Now, in addition to receiving the Heisman on December 9, Smith would also receive the Eversharp "Man of the Year" award from sportswriter Grantland Rice in Chicago a few days prior. Smith and his family adjusted their itinerary to include time for a stop in the Windy City, so they left in their car from Faribault in the early morning of Sunday, December 7, 1941, en route for Minneapolis, so they could catch the Hiawatha passenger train east to Chicago and New York.[24]

14

PEARL HARBOR

On the sixth day of December 1941, a boisterous group of twenty-five thousand football fans in Honolulu powered the University of Hawaii to a 20–6 victory over Willamette, a small college from Oregon. It was the largest crowd to ever watch a college football game at Honolulu Stadium. On that balmy, 75-degree Saturday afternoon, the island's annual Shrine game for charity had been the center of social activity, drawing three thousand more fans than the previous year. Many of them arrived an hour ahead of kickoff, hoping to catch a glimpse of a 1:15 p.m. band performance showcasing several local high schools and the U.S. Marine Corps. After falling behind 6–0 early, Hawaii stormed back to score three unanswered touchdowns, the last of which came with four and a half minutes remaining in the fourth quarter. The record-breaking crowd, delighted by the home team's performance, left the stadium with happiness in their hearts.[1]

They would forget all about it on the next morning of December 7, shortly before 8:00 a.m. local time, when 353 Japanese aircraft torpedoed and bombed Pearl Harbor and various other military sites on the island of Oahu. With sounds of explosions and endless smoke plumes filling the Hawaiian landscape, panicked citizens sheltered in place as the territorial government declared martial law.[2] Despite mass confusion, the *Honolulu Star-Bulletin* was initially able to report that as many as 1,500 people had been killed in the attacks, although that number would grow exponentially in the coming weeks and months as the government discovered the true extent of the carnage. Within twenty-four hours, the newspaper had even tallied some of the names of the dead, including forty-nine Oahu civilians. Patrick J. Chong, twenty-eight years old. Peter Lopes, twenty-four. Toshio Tokusaki, five years old. William Benedict, fire chief, lost in the bombs at Hickam Field.[3]

Still grieving and agonizing over the now-uncertain future, the island shut down phone lines and banned vehicular traffic except for emergencies, leaving Oahu in a frightening state of paralysis. And all of those football players in town for the Shrine charity event—both from Willamette and another visiting team, San Jose State University—suddenly found themselves stranded with no way to reach the continental United States. So they joined forces with the local police department and began protecting the island. "We're happy to help," Willamette coach Roy Keene said. "If they equip us with rifles or guns I hope our boys will shoot straighter than we did with our passes against Hawaii Saturday."[4]

It was early afternoon when news of the attack on Pearl Harbor reached the mainland. News bulletins interrupted three NFL games as they were in progress, including the New York Giants' matchup against the Brooklyn Dodgers at the Polo Grounds in New York City. George "Sonny" Franck, the Gophers' All-American of 1940, started at left halfback that day for the Giants. With fifty-five thousand people watching from the stands, the Dodgers raced to a 7–0 lead in the second quarter and promptly kicked the ball away to Ward Cuff, a Redwood Falls, Minnesota, native who had played college football at Marquette. Cuff fielded the kick at his own three-yard line and cut left for about twenty-five yards before he was brought down. *Bruiser Kinard made the tack*—WOR Radio in New York City broke into coverage before the announcer could finish his sentence. "We interrupt this broadcast to bring you this important bulletin from the United Press. Flash, Washington. The White House announces Japanese attack on Pearl Harbor. Stay tuned to WOR for further developments which will be broadcast immediately as received."[5]

Although radio listeners across New York City had now been informed of the developments, the players, coaches, and fans at the Polo Grounds were kept largely in the dark as the football game continued. In the second half, the Brooklyn Dodgers added two more touchdowns to polish off a 21–7 victory over the Giants as the sun began to set on this cold, wintry evening. As they searched for the Polo Grounds exits, the fifty-five thousand fans in attendance heard a thundering announce-

This photograph of the USS *Arizona* symbolizes the devastation of December 7, 1941, a "date which will live in infamy." *National Park Service Photo*

ment from the public address system: "All Navy men in the audience are ordered to report to their posts immediately. All Army men are to report to their posts tomorrow morning. This is important." The announcement left the spectators puzzled as they prepared to leave the gates. "What had happened?" Tommy Holmes wrote for the *Brooklyn Daily Eagle* the next day. "No one knew, not until he got close to the nearest radio or within hearing range of newsboys yelling in the streets."[6]

My grandfather, many years later, told my family that he learned of the attack on Pearl Harbor while he was studying and doing homework in the upstairs room of his Thomas Avenue home in North Minneapolis. Although it is impossible to say with any certainty, one could imagine that my grandfather's Gopher teammates probably had similar experiences. Finals were approaching, and most if not all of them were likely hunkering down that Sunday afternoon to prepare for exams. Come

Monday, around 11:20 a.m., the university canceled fourth-hour classes as students converged on Northrop Auditorium to listen to President Roosevelt's "date which will live in infamy" speech to Congress as he asked Congress to declare war on Japan. "The students listened quietly and attentively to the President's words," the *Minnesota Alumni Weekly* reported that week. "There were no demonstrations."[7] An account in the *Minnesota Daily* described absolute silence, with the exception of Roosevelt's booming voice over the loudspeakers and some intermittent applause when the president struck a tone.

When Roosevelt's address to Congress ended, the students broke into another hearty round of applause and then hushed so they could listen to the national anthem. "The tension broke like rain breaks on a sultry night," Gareth Hiebert of the *Daily* wrote, "as the students poured out of the auditorium—all of them leaving their first war convocation."[8] Thomas Okuma, an education major and junior from Hawaii, could hardly grasp the news. "The attack by Japan is unbelievable—incredible," Okuma said. "The islands were on a war time basis when I left three months ago, but the attack was entirely unsuspected."[9]

The four thousand U of M students under Selective Service registration monitored the developments with apprehension. Within days, they heard the news that a 1940 graduate, Ensign Ira Jeffery, had indeed perished in the bombings. He was reportedly the first known casualty of Pearl Harbor from the University of Minnesota. Jeffery's friend, Harry A. Wilmer, memorialized the fallen ensign in *Alumni Weekly* as "a brilliant student, a loveable person, and a gallant and courageous Naval Officer. . . . Let the University bow the head and bend the knee in memory and eternal pride."[10] Max Shulman, a University of Minnesota senior who later enjoyed an illustrious writing career, penned a chilling *Minnesota Daily* column a few days after the attack that perfectly encapsulated the Greatest Generation. He wrote: "Starting with 1929 we have lived under constant tension—the crash, the breadlines, the bank holiday, the NRA, the occupation of the Rhineland, the Spanish war, the rape of Austria, Ethiopia, Munich, the fall of France, conscription, Dunkirk, lend-lease, national defense, the invasion of Russia. . . . Now we are in a war. We did not ask for it; we could not avoid it. . . . This is it."[11]

✦ ✦ ✦

Bruce Smith, his sister Olive, and father Lucius learned of the attack on Pearl Harbor while en route to Chicago on December 7, as they looked forward to the Eversharp "Football Man of the Year" dinner and presentation at the Stevens Hotel that evening. Smith earned the award based on votes from a half-dozen prominent college football coaches, including Minnesota alum and Stanford head coach Clark Shaughnessy. The event, which included a 9:00 p.m. national CBS radio appearance featuring Smith himself, proceeded as scheduled despite the developments from Hawaii. Grantland Rice, the famed sportswriter, presented Bruce Smith with a gold trophy to commemorate his leading role on the undefeated 1941 national championship team. "America," Rice said over the national airwaves, "is truly proud of you, Bruce."[12] Shortly after the event, around 11:00 p.m., the Smith family boarded a train for New York City, absent Governor Harold Stassen, who accompanied the family to Chicago but now decided to return to St. Paul due to the national emergency.

Following a grueling nineteen-hour train ride, the Smiths arrived in New York City late Monday afternoon—their first trip ever to the nation's largest city. Representatives of the Downtown Athletic Club took Bruce, Lucius, and Olive to dinner that night before parting ways to catch some much-needed rest. After all, the Smith trio had big plans on Tuesday: a meeting with Mayor Fiorello LaGuardia, visits to Yankee Stadium and the Statue of Liberty, and the big Heisman Trophy presentation in Lower Manhattan.

During their sightseeing tour on the Tuesday afternoon of December 9, two air raid alarms blared across New York City, the first at 1:25 p.m. and the second at 2:05 p.m., as the petrified Eastern Seaboard braced for potential attacks over the Atlantic Ocean. Within the hour, it became apparent these were false alarms, but not before New York City schools sent more than a million children home out of an abundance of caution. "The symbol of war came to us Tuesday," wrote *Minneapolis Tribune* sports editor Bernard Swanson, who was covering the Heisman presentation on assignment in New York City. He described the "distraught, fearful looks on people's faces something akin to hysteria."[13]

Although rattled by the false alarms, Smith and his contingent of friends and family finished their tourist activities in the late afternoon before flocking to the Downtown Athletic Club for the Heisman Trophy festivities. The reception would begin at 6:00 p.m. EST, with a dinner to follow at 7:30, a presentation at 8:45, and a nationally broadcast acceptance speech at 9:45. Fresh off his CBS appearance with host Bob Hawk and Grantland Rice in Chicago a few nights earlier, the modest college senior was getting the hang of this whole publicity thing. "Radio observers remarked on the adaptability of his voice to radio," the *Tribune* noted of Smith's Sunday night appearance, "although he had not had the experience that Tom Harmon enjoyed."[14] The stakes, however, would be much higher Tuesday evening for Bruce Smith. The Heisman Trophy was no small deal. Millions might be listening through the Mutual Broadcasting System.

At some point on Tuesday, the White House announced that President Roosevelt would address the nation in a fireside chat that evening at 10:00 p.m. EST. On Mutual Broadcasting System affiliates, this meant the president's speech would immediately follow the Heisman presentation. In afternoon programming guides published across the country on Tuesday, December 9, many MBS stations indicated they would air Bruce Smith's acceptance speech before pivoting to President Roosevelt. (For example, WOR in New York placed the "Heisman Trophy Award" and "President Roosevelt" next to one another on back-to-back listings.) In Minnesota, WLOL served as the local Mutual Broadcasting System affiliate and announced it would broadcast Smith's Heisman acceptance at 8:45 p.m. CST.

To this day, it is unclear exactly how many Americans heard the live broadcast of Smith's speech on their local radio affiliates. Years later, June Smith, Bruce's youngest sibling, recalled huddling around the radio at home in Faribault in a room their family called the "library," only to be disappointed when the speech was replaced by static and war news.[15] Indeed, the next day, the *Faribault Daily News* reported that the entire town had heard the same thing—static and war news—instead of their hometown hero Bruce Smith's voice.[16]

Even if listeners missed the initial broadcast, they could at least catch a *recording* of the Heisman presentation thanks to the revolutionary concept of "transcription." Through this duplication process, radio stations across the country received copies of Smith's address and played it following Roosevelt's fireside chat, in which the president confidently predicted that America would "win the war" and "win the peace that follows," as the largest radio audience in U.S. history listened from their living rooms.[17] If sixty to ninety million Americans reportedly tuned into Roosevelt on the radio that evening, then we can say with confidence that at least a portion of them, perhaps several million, heard Bruce Smith's voice as well—either right before or right after the president's speech. Yet only a privileged group of fewer than one thousand people heard Smith's address in-person that evening, inside the Downtown Athletic Club in Lower Manhattan.

❋ ❋ ❋

Throughout the long history of the Downtown Athletic Club, the evening of December 9, 1941, still remains one of the most consequential. Just hours removed from the terrifying false air raids across New York City, more than five hundred people filed into the Heisman Room on this chilly but not unbearable winter evening. The Minnesota contingent, about 150 strong, was quite vocal. Lucius and Olive Smith received hearty ovations from the crowd when they were introduced. Bernie Bierman also gave a speech and called Smith the most versatile football player he had ever coached in twenty-five years, telling the crowd that his star halfback "typified the courage and spirit of our football team the last two years."[18]

All of the speakers and visitors praised Bruce Smith effusively that night, including Bill Edwards, the head coach of the Detroit Lions, who had first met Smith in October after cornering him in the Michigan Stadium locker room. Edwards gave Smith a copy of John Heisman's *Principles of Football*, autographed by Heisman himself. Edwards had added his own touch with yet another autograph on the interior of the book: "From John Heisman to Big Bill Edwards to Bruce Smith," he wrote.[19] After a glitzy reception, a formal dinner, and heartfelt speeches, lasting all but a few hours, it was finally time for the main event. Joseph R. Taylor, the head of the Downtown Athletic Club, officially presented Smith with his personalized, forty-five-pound bronzed Heisman Trophy, carrying the famous mold of a football player stretching his right arm outward and tucking the ball under his left.

With his trophy in hand, Smith prepared to deliver the evening's closing remarks. He was told he could not speak long, because under no circumstances could he overrun the president. In Washington, D.C., Roosevelt was about to make his way from the White House doctor's office to the Diplomatic Reception Room on the South Grounds, where he would deliver his first fireside chat since the declaration of war on Japan. Needless to say, Bruce Smith had no time to waste. Dressed sharply in his tuxedo, feeling the weight of five hundred pairs of eyes staring at his every move, Smith looked out at the Downtown Athletic Club audience with his sheet of notes shortly before 9:45 p.m. Whitney Martin, a prominent Associated Press journalist who had covered the Heisman Trophy presentation for three straight years, described the halfback as "smiling" and "reticent," someone "whose appearance in civilian clothes belied the fact he packed 195 pounds of bone and muscle and was a terror in the backfield for Minnesota."[20] The moment had arrived.

Speaking with a serious and reflective tone, the twenty-one-year-old college football star gave the following address at the Downtown Athletic Club on that evening of Tuesday, December 9, 1941:

Mr. Chairman, Mr. President and members of the Downtown Athletic Club, ladies and gentleman: So much of emotional significance has happened in such a brief space of time that the task of responding on such an occasion leaves me at a loss to assign relative value. No college football player could ask for a greater honor or thrill than to have his name added to the list of Jay Berwanger, Larry Kelley, Clint Frank, Davey O'Brien, Nile Kinnick and Tom Harmon, who preceded me in winning this coveted Heisman Trophy. My gratitude is sincere and my appreciation deeply felt. I can really only accept this trophy on behalf of my great Minnesota teammates and one of the greatest coaches of all time Bernie Bierman.

Our team was good this year and literally carried me along to this honor. It was a year which was so productive with successful, outstanding and colorful players. The sportswriters and radio ambassadors had to make an exceptionally difficult decision, as was indicated by the small margin of votes between Angelo Bertelli of Notre Dame and myself. I hope I can justify your decision of the majority. My dad, who is here this evening, is a lawyer back in Faribault, Minnesota. He tells me that the proper way to explain it is that I would be holding the trophy in trust of my teammates. Since I seem to be getting elaborate, however, I want to openly and firmly thank those teammates and my coach for without them this honor would have been absolutely impossible. To them I owe everything. Football certainly has become an important part of American life. It even seems to have a place in diplomacy. I remember reading in the newspapers that Mr. Kurusu, the Japanese envoy, told the newspapermen on arriving here that he expected to carry the ball for a touchdown. As you all know by now, it didn't work out that way. It looked as though he tried a quarterback sneak before the field was ruled. Those Far Eastern fellas may think American boys are soft, but I have had, and even have now, plenty of evidence in black and blue to show that they are making a big mistake. I think America will owe a great debt to the game of football when we finish this thing off. If six million American youngsters like myself are able to take it and come back for more, both from a physical standpoint and that of morale. . . . It teaches team play and cooperation and exercise to go out and fight hard for the honor of our schools, and likewise the same skills can be depended on when we have to fight like blazes to defend our country. This is my first visit to New York and I find it very exciting. To the members of the Downtown Athletic Club, I offer my sincere thanks. [21]

Bruce Smith became coast-to-coast famous for a brief period after the speech, as radio stations rushed to broadcast his transcribed address and newspapers across the country frantically published snippets of the speech for the Wednesday morning editions. The next day, a local reporter from New York's *World-Telegram* approached Smith at the corner of Fiftieth and Madison, hoping to meet America's new football darling as he made one final stop to St. Patrick's Cathedral. As he watched Smith gaze at the back end of the church, the reporter peppered the deeply religious Heisman Trophy winner with a few questions. "You asked me what impressed me most about New York," Smith told the reporter. "This cathedral is the answer."[22] New York City made a wonderful impression on Bruce Smith—but it worked the other way, too. Bruce Smith had made a wonderful impression on New York City. "It's most refreshing," the wife of a city official said after the Heisman banquet, "for us supposedly austere New Yorkers to see a boy so refreshing."[23] At the same time, however, Smith felt overwhelmed by the spotlight and struggled to keep up with the never-ending commitments that accompanied the Heisman Trophy. "Been having time of life, but it's wearing me out," Smith wrote home to Faribault in a postcard, three days after the ceremony. "It was 3:30 one morning to 4:00 the next."[24]

When he finally departed from New York City, Smith shifted his focus to an uncertain future. With speculation rampant that he could be

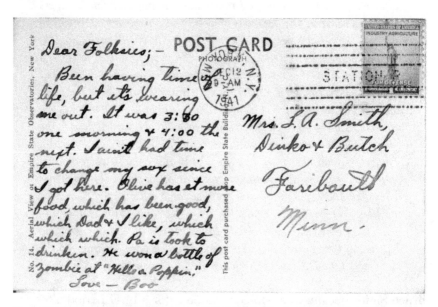

Bruce Smith writes about the stress of New York City in a postcard to his family in
Faribault, signing his name as "Boo." The letter was stamped on December 12,
1941, three days after the Heisman Trophy ceremony and five days after Pearl
Harbor. *Rice County Historical Society Collection, Faribault, Minnesota*

headed for the National Football League, the Associated Press reached
out for a brief comment. "The war is on top of us and no one seems to
know where he's headed," Smith told the AP. "I think I'll be in a bigger
game than pro ball by next fall."[25] NFL coaches feared the same. Assuming the Gopher halfback would forego pro football for military service, they allowed Smith to slip to the Green Bay Packers in the thirteenth round of the annual player draft in Chicago on December 22,
1941, even though the previous three Heisman Trophy winners had all
gone in the first two rounds. In fact, Michigan's Tom Harmon had been
the Chicago Bears' first overall selection the year before. But these
were not normal circumstances. As predicted, Smith would not play a
down of football for the Packers in 1942.

Seven other senior members of the Minnesota national championship team also heard their names called during the NFL Draft: Urban
Odson and Gene Flick (Green Bay Packers), Judd Ringer (Chicago
Cardinals), Bob Sweiger (New York Giants), Gordon Paschka (Philadelphia Eagles), Butch Levy (Cleveland Rams), and Bob Fitch (Washington). Although quarterback Warren Plunkett managed to play for the

Cleveland Rams prior to enlisting in the Navy, most of the Gopher seniors like Bruce Smith wound up missing the 1942 pro football season. There was a war to fight.[26]

* * *

As the days wore on in December 1941, bowl committees began to feel some pressure about their upcoming post-season games. Lt. Gen. John DeWitt, the commander of the Fourth Army on the West Coast, soon requested cancellation of the Rose Bowl on New Year's Day due to Southern California's perceived vulnerability to air attacks over the Pacific Ocean. DeWitt, later one of the driving forces behind President Roosevelt's atrocious Executive Order 9066 and the internment of Japanese Americans,[27] made his initial request through California governor Culbert Olson, "for reasons perfectly clear to any straight-thinking American."[28] The Rose Bowl committee complied and moved the game from Pasadena to Durham, North Carolina, where Duke University would host the Pacific Coast Conference representative Oregon State on its home campus in front of a much smaller crowd.

Meanwhile, organizers of the East–West Shrine charity game—an All-Star contest featuring Judd Ringer, Urban Odson, and Bernie Bierman as co-coach—resisted calls to cancel the event outright. "It is too fine a contest to abandon," they said. However, they too moved their game from California—in this case San Francisco—to New Orleans, on the campus of Bierman's former school Tulane. With a storm moving through New Orleans, only thirty-five thousand people showed up to the contest on January 3, 1942, which ended in a 6–6 tie.

Bierman had likely coached all sixty minutes in a complete daze. "Shortly before game time," the *Shreveport Times* reported, "Coach Bernie Bierman had been summoned for service with the United States Marines."[29] A telegram, sent to Bierman prior to kickoff, had been vague and included no specifics about what his duties would entail, but the message was unambiguous in its request: the Marines ordered Bierman to report to Quantico, Virginia, in just two weeks.

Quantico was at least familiar territory for Bierman. As a member of the reserves for so many years, he had made frequent trips to the base in Virginia, even embarking on a two-week training session as recently as the summer of 1940. Frankly, Bierman knew the barracks at Quantico as well as anyone in America, having also trained there during its inception in the spring of 1917 before deploying to Cuba during the First World War.

Suddenly, Bierman found history repeating itself. No longer a young twenty-something, the grizzled head football coach planned to leave for Quantico late in the evening on Friday, January 16, 1942, immediately following his farewell banquet at the Nicollet Hotel. Exactly one decade earlier, in this very same hotel, alumni and boosters had thrown a raucous welcoming ceremony for Bierman upon his arrival from Tulane. In a coincidental twist, many of those same people would now bid him farewell. "Football will go on despite the war," Bierman told the audience of about seven hundred people, "because it is a game that is vitally important in training young men mentally and physically for the war."[30]

15

A NEW REALITY

The U.S. Navy, with great fanfare, announced in the spring of 1942 that it had assigned Bernie Bierman to lead the athletic program at a new military school widely known as "Iowa Pre-Flight," where young cadets would build up necessary physical conditioning before heading to basic flight training. Bierman's wartime duties would include serving as the head football coach of a varsity team that would play a full schedule against collegiate teams in the fall of 1942. "That news that Bernie Bierman will coach the navy's pre-flight training school at the U. of Iowa," popular sportswriter Hugh Fullerton wrote, "may be the hottest thing that has hit the sports headlines in a long time."[1] Iowa Pre-Flight in Iowa City and three other similar institutions in Georgia, California, and North Carolina, essentially renting shared space at nearby universities, paved the way for thousands of young men to participate in athletics as a part of their rigorous exercise regimen. Football, after all, was the "closest thing to war," said Lt. Commander Tom Hamilton, a top Navy official and former head football coach of the Naval Academy. The Navy believed the sport incorporated some of the inherent skills needed to fly planes. "Air fighting nowadays requires a high degree of teamwork and a spirit of aggression," Hamilton said. "Football in my opinion is the nearly perfect means of giving a cadet those qualities."[2]

Bierman, though on record as supporting football as a wartime endeavor, emphasized that "no one will come here for the purpose of competing in athletics." Instead, he said, his duty was to "turn out physically-fit men with a competitive and aggressive spirit."[3] To help him accomplish this goal, Bierman would lean heavily on a group of assistants, consisting of more than two hundred athletic coaches from across the country. These assistants for football included Dallas Ward and Babe LeVoir, both of whom had coached the Gopher freshmen under Bierman.[4]

Although only a select group of players would compete in varsity football, hundreds of other cadets would participate in intramural sports and might even be eligible to crack the traveling squad if they were good enough. Their stays, however, would be temporary. The Navy called for a brief, months-long training schedule in the pre-flight schools before they would report to aviation bases, where they would learn how to actually fly. As Bierman put it, "our cadet personnel is in constant flux and we will have no single cadet from the first practice until the final game."[5]

At the start of September 1942, the roster totaled about seventy players-in-training, including Gene Flick and Judd Ringer from the '41 Minnesota squad. It was a strange mix of pro football stars and college players, many of whom also had competed in the Big Ten at one point. Familiar names like Michigan's Forest Evashevski and Iowa's Al Coupee reported to Iowa Pre-Flight. So did Dick Fisher of Ohio State and George Benson of Northwestern. Together, this assortment of players would compete as one unit, under Bierman's direction, during a regular ten-game college football schedule. They would be nicknamed the "Seahawks." Their regional opponents would include the likes of Kansas, Nebraska, Missouri, Notre Dame, Indiana, Ohio State, Northwestern, and, yes, Minnesota. Regardless of the talent level, merging a bunch of unfamiliar cadets into one cohesive squad would be an enormous undertaking. "This," Bierman said before embarking on his unusual 1942 schedule, "is the greenest team I've ever had."[6]

The arrangement was not unique to Iowa Pre-Flight. Many other service teams, located on military training bases throughout the country, would compete alongside Iowa Pre-Flight on the national football stage with the same mission of morale-building and physical fitness as the nation mobilized. In some ways, though, it was almost unfair from a competitive standpoint. The service teams would have older, more experienced players—including some professional players—and they would almost exclusively face college teams with depleted rosters due to the draft and voluntary enlistment. Even so, leagues like the Big Ten were more than happy to collaborate with the military squads and even rearranged their 1942 schedules to accommodate them. The service teams, though ineligible for the Associated Press poll, technically competed independently in an unaffiliated "military" division. They would barnstorm across their regions, facing some of the top competition in college football, for as long as the wartime conditions demanded. "These teams," Eddie Dooley wrote in the pre-season publication *Football Illustrated*, "are the big excitement of the year."[7]

Iowa Pre-Flight would face only one other military team in the fall: Fort Knox, based in Kentucky. So there would be little chance for the Seahawks to prove their worth in head-to-head matchups against other service squads. Still, with a coach of the highest caliber at the helm and a fierce roster filled with remarkable athletes, most intelligent observers pegged Iowa Pre-Flight as one of the top service teams in the country. Bierman's men were a step ahead of fellow pre-flight squads in Georgia, North Carolina, and California, not to mention the Naval Air Station team in Corpus Christi, Texas, and the Army trainees at Camp Grant in Illinois and Camp Davis in North Carolina, among others. But there was one squad even the mighty Seahawks might not be able to touch: a powerful team north of Chicago known as the Great Lakes Navy Bluejackets, featuring Bruce Smith, Bob Sweiger, Urban Odson, and Butch Levy.

※ ※ ※

The old-timers remembered the Bluejackets. Just a few decades earlier, when the First World War broke out, the Great Lakes Naval Training Station fielded an intimidating football team during the 1917 and 1918 college football seasons. As regular college programs folded left and right, the Great Lakes naval team excelled above all others, qualifying for the Rose Bowl on New Year's Day in 1919 just six months before the Treaty of Versailles. Despite the Bluejackets' rousing success, Americans surely hoped they would never have to see them compete during a wartime football season ever again. As it turned out, the Great Lakes Navy team would resurrect itself under unfortunate circumstances in the early part of 1942.

The Great Lakes Naval Training Station, situated on a large swath of land overlooking Lake Michigan, billed itself as the largest such training facility in the world and later claimed to have trained a full one million sailors during World War II.[8] Bruce Smith stood out above most. Fresh off the Heisman Trophy and a national championship, Smith spent the summer out in California filming a Columbia Pictures movie about his life, named "Smith of Minnesota." It was set for release in the fall. "I got a tremendous kick out of my first motion picture experience," Smith told the *Star* in Minneapolis that summer. But even movie stars had to play their part in the war effort. Smith bid farewell to Faribault on Independence Day, July 4. "Off for Great Lakes," the *Star* wrote, "and the biggest battle of his career."[9]

Just like the Iowa Pre-Flight cadets, the football players reporting to the Great Lakes station did not come for a picnic. To prepare for eventual deployment, they would follow an extremely strict training and academic regimen, starting at the crack of dawn each day and extending until the sun went down. Football was probably the only fun part about it. The rest was grueling. "Just a short note to let you know that I am still alive," Butch Levy wrote in a letter to his parents after arriving at Great Lakes in the summer of 1942. "Time really goes slow around here."[10]

Levy had faced some adversity after the Gophers' national championship run, namely an ankle injury during the winter that hobbled him in his quest to repeat as the NCAA heavyweight wrestling champion. Luckily, Levy recovered in time to capture the Amateur Athletic Union title in New Orleans in April, helping him draw continued interest from pro wrestling promoters. Yet Levy, like everybody else, would instead have to focus his efforts on the military as he finished up spring classes and prepared for graduation at the U of M. A letter from Bernie Bierman reveals that Levy inquired that spring about a position at Iowa Pre-Flight, but Bierman informed his former guard that it appeared all the slots had been filled. "Much as I would like to am afraid there is not much I can do for you," Bierman told Levy. "Any time you want a letter of recommendation for this on anything . . . feel free to call on me."[11]

Levy eventually landed at the Great Lakes Naval Training Station, though he would later tell his family he had to memorize the eye chart to pass a physical examination because his eyesight was so bad. When he arrived in Illinois at the vast Great Lakes complex in July 1942, Levy learned quickly that military life had significant downsides. "The food here is terrible," he reported to his parents. Even worse, the coffee tasted awful, too, and the Navy didn't provide milk. "What I wouldn't do for about 4 qts," Levy wrote.[12]

Levy, Smith, Odson, and Sweiger, the four members of the 1941 Golden Gophers, headlined an outstanding group of naval trainees at Great Lakes under the direction of Lt. Paul "Tony" Hinkle, a respected

Butch Levy played football for the Great Lakes Navy Bluejackets during his military training. *Upper Midwest Jewish Archives, University of Minnesota*

basketball and football coach at Butler University in Indianapolis. "The Lakes squad," *Football Illustrated* observed, "will have no shortage of stars."[13] Besides the Minnesota greats, the Bluejackets also welcomed Pete Kmetovic of Stanford, Rudy Mucha of the University of Washington and Cleveland Rams, Carl Mulleneaux of Utah State and the Green Bay Packers, and a back named Steve Belichick from the Detroit Lions and Case Western Reserve University in Cleveland (he would later have a son named Bill). Before reporting to Great Lakes, Mucha had been quoted by the syndicated Wide World about the challenges of playing football while training for war: "There is nothing in football comparable to the shock of falling out of a Navy hammock and landing flat on one's pus while sound asleep," Mucha said.[14]

Truth be told, it was a strange idea, this concept of star athletes competing in football while the future of the world was at stake. It made some people uncomfortable. Navy physical fitness leader Gene Tunney, who rose to national fame as a boxer after serving overseas in the Marines during World War I, blasted the emphasis on team athletics during wartime: "You can't train a man to be a fighter by having him play football or baseball," Tunney said in a quote that appeared in dozens of newspapers in August 1942.[15] The quote drew a forceful response from Bob Zuppke, the former Illinois coach who had just retired after the 1941 season. "So Gene Tunney has decided again that football's no good and we can't have competitive athletes fight a war," he said, before taking a shot at the sport of boxing. "I'm just wondering what Tunney knows about football and other sports that require cooperation."[16]

Richard Beamish, the public utility commissioner in Pennsylvania, spurred further outrage that fall when he proposed banning football and other sports during the war. He argued that large events, like those at college stadiums on fall Saturdays, could disrupt vital transportation lines. "American adults who gather by thousands on football fields or on racetracks set a bad example for the youth of the nation," Beamish said, "in addition to wasting oil and gasoline."[17] Zuppke's old Big Ten counterpart, Northwestern coach Lynn Waldorf, did the heavy lifting this time and laid into Beamish. "That guy, whoever he is, doesn't carry enough weight to merit a reply," Waldorf was quoted as saying by the International News Service. "If there wasn't merit to football in war-

time, the army and navy would place less accent on it and other competitive sports."[18]

In defense of football, Rear Admiral John Downes underscored the
military's belief that the sport could play a role in the war effort, just as
the leaders at Iowa Pre-Flight had argued. "The United States Navy,"
Downes said at the start of football practice for Great Lakes, "always
has recognized the worth of athletics of the body contact type in developing men for rigorous sea duty."[19] Like Iowa Pre-Flight, the Great
Lakes Naval Training Station felt it could prepare for battle by putting
its football players through an intense college football schedule in 1942,
including games against Michigan, Iowa, Pittsburgh, Wisconsin, Michigan State, Missouri, Purdue, Marquette, Illinois, Northwestern, and
Notre Dame. As members of the Bluejackets, the Gopher boys would
return again to Ann Arbor; they would face the Badgers at Soldier
Field; and they would play in the familiar confines of Northwestern's
Dyche Stadium, Iowa Stadium, and Memorial Stadium in Champaign.
Six of the Gophers' eight 1941 opponents were on the Great Lakes
schedule, with only Washington and Nebraska missing. Odson, Smith,
Sweiger, and Levy must have been licking their chops, as they got one
more chance to relive their college glory days.

Still, the players knew that nothing would be the same. The war had
impacted every facet of daily life in 1942 and profoundly shifted the
landscape of college football. "On last December 7th, the U.S.A. jetti-
soned football-as-usual," *Football Illustrated* wrote before the season.
"As the season opens there is no such thing as comparative form. The
player roster of every team in the land is black with question marks.
Coaching changes are marked on every college program."[20]

✿ ✿ ✿

The Minnesota Golden Gophers, now under the careful tutelage of Dr.
George Hauser following the departure of Bernie Bierman, kept their
1942 roster somewhat intact because players could enroll in military
reserve programs on campus. "Despite the loss of football's foremost
tactician and the greatest back he ever coached, plus the departure of
other massive stars," *Football Illustrated* predicted, "the Gophers are
title-bound once more."[21] Winners of seventeen straight games, they
still returned twenty lettermen, including All-American candidates

Dick Wildung, Bill Garnaas, and Bill Daley. Their new coaching staff included a former Gopher star by the name of Bud Wilkinson, who would later achieve great fame as a coach at Oklahoma. "Use whatever measuring stick you please," Tommy Devine of the United Press wrote. "Minnesota rates as the pre-season favorite to win another Big Ten football championship."[22]

Minnesota began the 1942 season in familiar fashion, blasting Pittsburgh 50–7 to win its eighteenth straight game as a program. Fueled by the new offensive star Bill Daley, who scored or played a part in four touchdowns, George Hauser emptied his bench in the blowout. Jack Spewak, the backup sophomore center, earned his first varsity snap. Gene Bierhaus, the Brainerd sensation who had played mostly halfback in 1941, saw some action at end. In total, thirty-seven substitutes entered the game as the Gophers, once again, flexed their muscles against Charley Bowser's outclassed Panthers.

That's about all that really seemed familiar in Minneapolis that afternoon. Ten months earlier, Memorial Stadium barely had enough space to contain the overwhelming demand from fans in the Twin Cities; now, under wartime conditions, just twenty-two thousand fans attended the season opener for the two-time defending national champions of college football. With travel restrictions and rationing gasoline, it was difficult if not impossible for some fans to attend sporting events. College football attendance as a whole dropped 19 percent that season.[23] "During the 1942 football season," a team official wrote after the season, "the war held first claim on the minds of college players and their partisans."[24] Almost every single player on the team had enlisted as a reserve in the Army, Navy, or Marines.

After defeating Pittsburgh handily, the players and coaches immediately faced an awkward situation in the second week of the season. Bernie Bierman was coming to town with Iowa Pre-Flight on October 3, setting up a mind-boggling scenario in which the man who helped build an eighteen-game winning streak at Minnesota would now attempt to snap it himself. In total, at least four former Gopher coaches and six former players would join the Seahawks on their trip to Memorial Stadium, fresh off victories over Kansas and familiar foe Northwestern.

It couldn't have been easy for any of them to return to Minneapolis in this fashion. They would dress in the visiting locker room. They would wear different uniforms. Their beloved crowd in Maroon and Gold would cheer for their opponents, not them. It was going to be weird, if not downright upsetting. Yet they had a game to play. In front of a slightly larger crowd of more than thirty-seven thousand people on October 3, the undergraduates at Minnesota held strong against the experienced and older Seahawks in a close-scoring affair, although the Gophers missed the services of the injured Bill Garnaas.

Bill Daley electrified Memorial Stadium with a fifty-four-yard touchdown run in the first quarter, but Iowa Pre-Flight blocked Vic Kulbitski's extra point in a crucial turning point. That proved the difference in the game when the Seahawks added a score and extra point later in the quarter. Iowa Pre-Flight's Dick Fisher, formerly of the 1940 Ohio State team that had lost to Minnesota in Columbus two years earlier, notched the touchdown on a thirty-five-yard punt return. The 7–6 score held for three more quarters, although the Gophers nearly stole a victory in the final two minutes. From his own forty-nine-yard line, Daley once again broke free in the open field before a Seahawk tackler pushed him out of bounds near the goal line. In a demoralizing twist, Kulbitski fumbled on the next play, giving the ball right back to Iowa Pre-Flight. The Seahawks punted out of precaution, giving Minnesota the ball at the opposing thirty-four—but the Gophers, no longer in goal line position, threw three straight incomplete passes. On fourth down, Kulbitski missed a desperation field goal as time expired.

The winning streak was over. Iowa Pre-Flight 7, Minnesota 6. Bernie Bierman was responsible.

"Those kids," Bierman said of his old players, "certainly haven't lost any of their spark."[25] He barely knew how to react. Joe Hendrickson of the *Minneapolis Star Journal*, penning his up-close observations of the game, reported that Bierman seemed anxious and befuddled throughout the contest. "He left the bench for the first time, very excited, when Daley scored to put Minnesota ahead," Hendrickson wrote. Yet when his own Seahawk, Dick Fisher, scored a touchdown, Bierman apparently "didn't move from his seat."[26] In the Gophers' locker room, Kulbitski was "disconsolate" over his fumble and missed field goal. His teammates, who had never before experienced a defeat at the varsity college level, tried to handle the disappointment as best they could. Still, they could not escape the irony of losing for the first time since 1939 against a Bierman-led service team. "Thanks Bernie," John Billman said after the game. "Thanks a lot."[27]

It would get much worse for the Gophers. A week later, with Garnaas still sidelined, the unthinkable happened when Minnesota stumbled in a 20–13 loss to Illinois on homecoming in Champaign. Not only was Minnesota's winning streak over; now it had suffered a *losing streak*. The 1942 season marked the end of Minnesota's dominance over the Big Ten and national college football. Marred by injuries, like the one that kept Bud Higgins out the whole year and hobbled Garnaas and Daley for portions of the schedule, the Gophers finished fifth in the league, although at 5–4, the Associated Press still ranked them tied for nineteenth in the final poll. Dick Wildung also earned consensus All-American honors after a spectacular senior season.

One can only wonder how the Gophers' 1942 season would have turned out, had they set a different tone against Bernie Bierman's Iowa Pre-Flight in Week Two. The Seahawks, navigating their own difficult schedule, played pretty good football the rest of the way, although they were not immune from their own stumbles. Bierman, Gene Flick, and Judd Ringer lost three games themselves in 1942, all on the road—at Notre Dame, at Ohio State, and at Missouri, the last of which came during the final game of the season before just 7,600 fans in Kansas City, after a foot of snow buried Ruppert Stadium. Despite the losses, Bierman remained committed to the concept of service-team football without an end to the war in sight. "It is our intention to carry on football at the pre-flight schools," Bierman said after the season, "as long as it does not interfere with our program."[28] The pre-flight teams would continue in 1943, but Bierman himself would never again coach the Seahawks. The military had other plans for him.

☼ ☼ ☼

The former Gophers at the Great Lakes Naval Training Station also failed to carry on the perfection they'd become accustomed to during the 1940 and 1941 seasons. On September 26, 1942, the Great Lakes Bluejackets opened their wartime campaign in Ann Arbor, Michigan, against Fritz Crisler's Wolverines. Bruce Smith, Urban Odson, Bob Sweiger, and Butch Levy saw a much different Michigan Stadium that day. There were no record-breaking crowds this time, no intimidating screams from supporters in Maize and Blue, no eighty-five thousand people in the bleachers. Michigan and Great Lakes played before a meager crowd of seventeen thousand to start the 1942 season, probably a result of restrictions on fans traveling from the Detroit metro area. The star-studded Bluejackets apparently fed into the lethargy of the crowd, falling 9–0 in a lifeless shutout to a team most expected them to defeat handily. The Bluejackets threatened late, after Sweiger returned a kickoff thirty-two yards and teamed with Bruce Smith to march to the Michigan eight-yard line, but they would go no farther. Great Lakes' twelve-game winning streak, dating back to World War I, had been broken. Bruce Smith totaled only twelve yards on the ground and forty-four passing yards, losing to Michigan for the first time in his football career.

Meanwhile, that same weekend, Smith's hometown of Faribault prepared for the event-of-a-lifetime: the release of a Hollywood movie, "Smith of Minnesota." The film made its world premiere on Friday, September 25, 1942, at the downtown Paradise Theater. Advertisements in the local newspaper hyped the event: *"It's All about Faribault! It's about Faribault People! It Stars Faribault's Favorite Son!"*

The premiere had long been sold out, raising $15,000 for war bonds in conjunction with ticket sales. June Smith recalled rainy and dreary weather that night, though it certainly didn't place a damper on the excitement. "We had the big spotlights and all this stuff," Smith said years later. "It was quite a group of people, in our little theater." The whole town was eager to see how Columbia Pictures had depicted their beloved Bruce Smith. Although he would play himself in the movie, well-known Hollywood actors portrayed the rest of the "characters," which included Smith's family, friends, teammates, and coaches. Don Beddoe played Lucius Smith; Arline Judge played a local reporter at the fictional *Faribault Standard*; and Roberta Smith played June Smith, the sporty younger sister. "We used to communicate back and forth," June said. "It was fun."[29]

"Smith of Minnesota" broke the mold of traditional football movies, even for that era. Instead, the producers opted for a more creative "movie-within-a-movie" storyline, focusing on Bruce Smith's family life and upbringing, with only brief football clips intertwined. Although the sixty-six-minute film was not a masterpiece or Academy Award winner, it did capture a valuable snapshot of wartime America just nine months after Pearl Harbor. In one of the movie's final dialogue scenes, for example, a fictional Lucius Smith told the real Bruce that he had "a lot of big games ahead" on a team led by General Douglas MacArthur. "A lot of Minnesota men on that American team all over the world. Wherever you go in the Navy, they're not gonna ask you about football," Lucius told his son in the movie, "they're gonna ask what you can do to help win the war. It's a big job, Bruce, for you and a lot of other men."[30]

The movie also elevated Bruce Smith and the Golden Gophers to even higher national prominence, prompting one fan from Mount Vernon, New York, to nervously request an autographed photo. "Dear Mr. Smith," the fan wrote in November 1942, "after seeing you play in many football games and especially after seeing 'Smith of Minnesota,' I have finally gotten up the nerve to write you."[31] Smith appreciated the interest but remained forever uncomfortable with the big-screen attention. He even shied away from the film when replays appeared on television in the sixties, according to his youngest sister and children. For Smith's family, friends, and fans, however, the movie was a source of pride. The rest of the country seemed to like it, too. "The new Columbia film," a Pennsylvania newspaper wrote in a 1942 review, "is far more than a mere recital of stadium triumphs, backgrounded by cooing co-eds. It is a dramatic restatement of the American way of life, as that way of life directly affected one individual to mold him into a nationally-respected athletic idol, and a dynamic leader of men."[32]

Following the film's release, Smith continued his stellar football career against college competition, leading the Great Lakes Bluejackets in points, rushing yards, and passing yards. Although not quite the Heisman Trophy, Smith did manage to earn an award from the "Touchdown Club" as the most outstanding service player of the 1942 season. His Navy commanders, including Ninth Naval District captain F. J. Lowry, granted Smith a leave of absence to attend a celebratory dinner in Washington, D.C., on the evening of January 5, 1943. "It took real courage and initiative to work as hard as he did on the football field," Captain Lowry said, "while at the same time carrying on his normal and routine duties in recruit training."[33] With an estimated seven hundred people in attendance at the Touchdown Club testimonial dinner— roughly the same size as the Heisman crowd at the Downtown Athletic Club thirteen months earlier—Smith took home a modest, bronze trophy and was pictured in an AP wire photograph the next morning staring at his prize with a look of astonishment. "Great Lakes had a good football team this year," Smith was quoted as saying by the AP, "and that's why Mr. Smith finally got to Washington."[34]

Pretty soon, though, Mr. Smith's military duties would send him to the opposite side of the country, where he would continue to play football and fly planes on the West Coast. In fact, Smith, Bob Sweiger, Urban Odson, and Butch Levy would all disperse from Great Lakes and find themselves in different locations yet again in 1943, as the war began to really take hold.

o o o

About three million men were drafted into the United States military in 1942, followed by 3.3 million in 1943 after Congress approved lowering the draft age to eighteen.[35] With the United States now directly engaged in the war for more than a year, ongoing Selective Service requirements left colleges and universities reeling. At the University of Minnesota, fewer than ten thousand students showed up for classes at the start of the 1943 winter semester—representing a steep 15-percent drop compared to the previous semester. "The enrollment of the regular students of collegiate grade will continue to shrink," the *Minnesota Alumni Weekly* admitted, "as calls for men are made by the Selective Service organization." The university remained open, however, and did not close a single department during World War II. The loss of men to the service also provided new opportunities for women, who formed more than 40 percent of the student population in 1943 for the first time in recent memory.[36]

Those who remained on campus could only pray their fellow classmates would come home. Many did not. In early 1943, Minnesota students and alumni learned that Private Allen B. Samuelson, a St. Paul native who had served as a student manager for the Gopher football team, died in action in the Pacific. Gilbert O'Hallaran, a 1935 U of M graduate formerly of Butch Levy's West High School in Minneapolis, had been killed in a traffic accident while serving with the Army in North Africa. Lt. Ralph Rich, who had been on Minnesota's campus as recently as 1939, earned a Cross of Honor award after losing his life in the Battle of Midway in June 1942. "Rich led a section of fighters assigned to cover the approach of our attack group toward the main

Japanese invasion fleet," the Navy reported. "For one hour, planes under his capable and aggressive leadership maintained continuous flight over enemy naval units."[37] Countless other students were reported either missing or as prisoners of war.

Three months before the 1943 college football season, the nation was stunned to learn that former Iowa legend Nile Kinnick, the 1939 Heisman Trophy winner, died after his plane tumbled into the water during a training exercise near Venezuela. "Here was one of the finest contributions intercollegiate football ever gave to the world. He typified college sports—yes on the same order as Bruce Smith and many other gallant competitors who are carrying on for Uncle Sam with the same enthusiasm as they did on the football field," Charles Johnson wrote in the *Minneapolis Star Journal*, recalling Iowa's victory over the Gophers in 1939. "Like Iowans, Minnesota gridiron enthusiasts will never forget Nile Kinnick. He was the spark who carried an average Hawkeye football team to the heights in 1939."[38]

However insignificant sports seemed after the death of Nile Kinnick, it was undeniable that the war dramatically disrupted college football in 1943, much more so than even 1942. Major conferences, including the Big Ten, made freshmen eligible for varsity competition in order to fill in the gaps caused by wide-scale departures. A few hundred schools shut down their football programs in 1943—including big-name institutions like Michigan State—and even the remaining teams were shells of their former selves. With most college men shipped off to war by this point, the eligible players still on campus basically fit into a few select categories: (1) seventeen-year-old freshmen too young for draft age, (2) older players with some type of medical deferment that prevented them from serving in the military, or (3) players enrolled in training regimens on campuses across the country, such as the V-12 Navy College Training Program. Teams looked stranger than ever before. Ohio State's roster entering September 1943, for example, featured sixty freshmen, seven juniors, and no sophomores or seniors.[39]

In a further twist, star college football players began to suddenly switch teams as they were transferred to different V-12 programs. Thanks to extremely loose eligibility requirements during wartime, they would be allowed to play football at their new schools. Minnesota's Bill Daley, incredibly, found himself packing his bags for the V-12 program in Ann Arbor, meaning he would join archrival Michigan and Fritz

Crisler. Herb Hein and Herman Frickey also left the Twin Cities after earning assignments with Northwestern's Marine Corps officer training program. Vic Kulbitski and Ed Trumper, who could not crack Bernie Bierman's starting lineup in 1941, wound up at Notre Dame in 1943 and won a national championship.

At Minnesota, where civilian enrollment had further tumbled to seven thousand in the fall of 1943, the emergence of Navy V-12 and other military training programs helped add an additional four thousand trainees to campus. The pre-flight cadets in the Army Air Forces housed themselves in the bowels of Memorial Stadium, while the Navy V-12 enrollees stayed in fraternity houses. Despite the turmoil, the Gophers' 1943 squad would still carry at least two familiar faces: Bill Garnaas and tackle Ed Lechner, a Navy dental student who was eligible for a special fifth season in 1943 after competing for the New York Giants professionally.

The Gophers missed Bill Daley. That became evident immediately, as the Gopher-turned-Wolverine rushed for 531 yards in the first four games of the season. "Daley has been living up to those monikers and all the other nommes de plunge conjured since his arrival in Ann Arbor," the *Detroit Free Press* wrote.[40] In the fifth game of the season, on October 23, 1943, Daley scored two touchdowns at Michigan Stadium *against* Minnesota in a 49–6 debacle, handing the Gophers their first loss of the season. It was, and remains, the only time in the history of the Michigan–Minnesota rivalry that a player has captured the Little Brown Jug from both sides. "Gosh," Daley said after the game, "it's too bad it happened to those fellows."[41] Without missing a beat, Daley then joined the Gophers' team train—yes, he did that intentionally—so he could ride home to the St. Cloud area. He planned to spend furlough time with his mother.

A week later, at Dyche Stadium in Evanston, the Gophers lost a second straight game—this time to Herman Frickey, Herb Hein, and the Northwestern Wildcats. Otto Graham, now a senior, started at left halfback opposite Frickey at right half and Hein at left end. The Wildcats, or "Minnesota Transfers" as Bernard Swanson of the *Minneapolis Tribune* wrote in jest, led by two scores at halftime and ran away with a 42–6 victory. Hein and Frickey both tallied a touchdown. Hauser's second season did not get any easier from there, as the Gophers dropped two more games to Purdue and Iowa Pre-Flight to finish 5–4 overall and fifth in the Big Ten—an identical record to the previous season. The final loss of the 1943 season against the Seahawks, a 32–0 calamity at Memorial Stadium in late November, came against a Don Faurot–led service team, not Bernie Bierman. Faurot, who had gained fame at the University of Missouri, took over the coaching duties for Bierman in 1943 and led the Seahawks to a sensational 9–1 season, earning them the second spot in the Associated Press rankings after military teams became eligible for the polls. Bierman was missing from the Iowa Pre-Flight sidelines because the Navy reassigned him to a non-coaching role, although Minnesota fans surely must have laughed at the sight of a little halfback playing for the Seahawks that afternoon. Bud Higgins joined the squad in 1943 and rushed for forty-six yards on nine carries against his former team. No trick plays were reported.

Nobody seemed to stay in the same place from 1942 to 1943. Three of the Gophers from the 1942 Great Lakes Bluejackets team—Sweiger, Levy, and Odson—were transferred to naval bases in Idaho by 1943. "Going to Farragut Idaho possibility of coming home Love Len," Levy wrote in a telegram to his parents in April 1942.[42] Bruce Smith spent the 1943 season playing football for St. Mary's in California and, for the remainder of his service, flew Corsair fighter planes and became a flight instructor with a rank of Lieutenant Junior Grade. "Like thousands of others who had stood by awaiting an immersion in the crucible, he had flown his Navy fighter through unchallenged American skies," Tom and Sam Akers wrote in *The Game Breaker*, "and wondered when the die would show his number. By V-J Day he was still waiting."[43] During the entirety of the war, Smith never left the United States, although there is no indication that he received any special treatment because of his celebrity status. The military simply assigned him, and some of his teammates, to stateside roles. Bob Fitch, for example, spent 1943 in the U.S. Coast Guard near the Atlantic Ocean, playing football for a service team at Camp Lejeune in Jacksonville, North Carolina, before embarking on a long coaching career that included a three-decade stint as head golf coach at Indiana University. Ed Lechner, a dental school graduate who later established himself as a longtime Twin Cities dentist, spent time on active duty in Idaho and Bethesda Naval Hospital in Maryland.

Many other members of the 1941 Minnesota football team, however, served abroad—and in some cases saw direct combat. During the final years of World War II, these men would experience the horrors of real battle, not the trivial ones versus Michigan or Northwestern, but rather the ones on the beaches of Normandy and the shores of Iwo Jima.

16

NORMANDY

The Allied invasion of northern France has been discussed at considerable length over the past seven and a half decades, perhaps more so than any other episode in American military history. Hundreds upon hundreds of books, movies, documentaries, television shows, and video games have portrayed the events of June 6, 1944, from the paratroopers who soared through the midnight sky to the boatloads of men who stormed the five beaches of Normandy as they embarked on an assault that would liberate Western Europe and deliver a blow to the Nazi forces. At least 160,000 Allied troops, almost half of whom came from the United States, landed at Normandy to participate in D-Day.

Most of us know generally what D-Day was, what it did, and why it stands to this day as a defining chapter in this country's history. And yet there's still so much many of us never bothered to learn—like, say, about the role of the minesweepers, the smaller vessels that provided critical support in the operation by detecting enemy mines near the beaches before they could blow up their fellow Allied forces. "It can be said without fear of contradiction," Rear Admiral Alan Kirk said in late July 1944, "that minesweeping was the keystone of the arch in this operation."[1] This unprecedented invasion simply could not have occurred without the work of a few hundred minesweepers near the beaches of Normandy, including the diligent efforts of the USS *Tide*, which carried a former University of Minnesota football player, First Lieutenant George Michael "Mike" Welch.

Nineteen months earlier, in November 1942, the reserve fullback wore the number "73" for the final time at Memorial Stadium after spending three years backing up Bill Daley and Bob Sweiger. Now he suddenly found himself thrust into the most dangerous situation of his life, witnessing indescribable carnage that would remain seared in his consciousness for decades to come. After canvassing the waters during the late evening of June 5 and early morning of June 6, quietly and inconspicuously checking the English Channel for mines ahead of an oncoming wave of Allied troops, the USS *Tide* drifted away from the shore shortly before 6:30 a.m. Their preparatory work, for the moment, was complete. During the actual invasion, minesweepers were told to keep their distance and shift to a protective role, in order to prevent German E-boats and U-boats from disrupting the waterways. So the roughly one hundred men aboard the *Tide*, stationed defensively a few hundred yards offshore, could do nothing at that moment but watch the onslaught of D-Day.

"When dawn came, it was tremendous," Mike Welch said in an interview many years later for a book titled *The Fate of the USS Tide: The Forgotten Sailors of D-Day*. "There was this roar of hundreds of airplanes overhead. We could look around; we had a grandstand seat."[2] With his eyes glued to the beach and his ears fixated on the radio, Welch could see and hear battleships firing. Planes kept coming. He saw a church explode. It was abhorrent. Fellow *Tide* sailor William Daniel, a second-class naval radarman from Alabama, said the "sky turned black all at once . . . like a swarm of locusts, but thank the Lord it was our own planes."[3]

Positioned just far enough away to remain safe, the *Tide* crewmates survived the rest of D-Day without incident, but they knew their mission would continue long beyond June 6. Later that night, the Germans littered the shores of Utah Beach with more mines, forcing the *Tide* back to overnight sweeping duty. The crew needed to eliminate the threat before dawn. Running on pure adrenaline and very little sleep, they encountered a German E-boat at some point during early daylight hours of June 7 but continued sweeping. After the *Tide* completed that mission somewhere in the English Channel near Utah Beach, on the eastern edge of Cotentin Peninsula, shipmate William Daniel left his radar post around 8:00 a.m. to catch a much-needed nap on the deck. A few hours later, the young Alabaman's eyes burst open. "Something told

The **USS** *Tide* **sinks after striking a mine off the coast of Normandy, France, on June 7, 1944. Former University of Minnesota fullback Mike Welch, a two-time national champion, served as a first lieutenant on the minesweeper.** *Public Domain, work of the U.S. government in the National Archives (Catalog number: 80-G-651678)*

me to wake up," he said. "Just as I opened my eyes, the ship hit a mine and exploded."[4] Without any warning whatsoever, the 221-foot-long vessel burst forcefully five feet into the air above water level, breaking the back of the *Tide* as the ship burst into flames and flooded from the bottom. The devastation was unthinkable. "Everybody got injured and the first thing I did was I saw the captain was killed immediately," First Lieutenant Welch said. "Then I thought of survival."[5]

※ ※ ※

Although it is difficult to verify all these years later, Mike Welch liked to tell a story about the 1941 Minnesota Golden Gophers and Uncle Sam. Shortly after Pearl Harbor, Welch claimed that he and about a dozen of his teammates crammed into two separate cars and drove to the Marine

Recruiting Office at the corner of Washington and Second in downtown Minneapolis. Infuriated by the attack on U.S. soil and eager to join the war effort, they hoped to enlist along with thousands of other young men in the Twin Cities. There was just one problem, Welch said: all but one of the Golden Gophers failed the physical. "Out of a championship football team," Welch said, "we weren't fit for the Marine Corps."[6]

So, Welch found another way to participate in military life while remaining enrolled at the University of Minnesota. He applied for the Navy reserves on campus, although he worried he might fail that test due to poor eyesight. Welch blamed the problem on a hit he suffered during the second-to-last game of the 1941 season in Iowa City. Toward the end of that 34–13 win over the Iowa Hawkeyes, remembered best as the afternoon Bruce Smith triumphantly returned from injury, Bernie Bierman sent Welch into the game late in the fourth quarter for mop-up duty in the backfield. He played one snap on defense and then closed out the game for Minnesota on offense with two consecutive carries, both for no gain. Somewhere along the way, a Hawkeye defender slugged him in the eye.

Ever since, Welch had struggled with his vision, so he employed the same strategy that Butch Levy used to gain entry into the Great Lakes Naval Training Station. He memorized the letters on the eye chart. And it worked. Welch remained on campus in Minneapolis in the fall of 1942, officially joining the naval reserves as he completed his final year of school. Even better, it afforded Welch an opportunity to play his senior season of college football. After appearing sparingly in the backfield during the 1940 and 1941 seasons, Welch dressed for most home games in 1942 but still did not see much meaningful action under coach George Hauser. Although he certainly would have liked to play more, Welch had achieved his wildest dreams by participating in three full varsity seasons with the Gophers.

The son of a railroad foreman, Welch had split his high school years between St. James, Minnesota, and Eau Claire, Wisconsin, starring in football at each stop as his father moved jobs. "And as he tells the story, he had a decision," his daughter, Deb Welch, recounted. "*Do I go to the U of M or go to the University of Wisconsin?* Ultimately, he decided to go to the University of Minnesota."[7] Despite the lack of varsity playing time under Bierman and then Hauser, the decision paid some dividends. Shortly before he graduated, the Green Bay Packers selected

Welch in the sixteenth round of the 1943 NFL Draft, although surely the organization knew there was little chance he would don a football uniform that fall because of the war.

The Packers' interest flattered Welch, and the feeling was mutual, so he signed a contract to play for the legendary Curly Lambeau. As expected, it never came to fruition. Needing to fulfill his obligations to the United States Navy, Welch reported for commissioning at the Navy Pier in Chicago, got married the next day, and then received an order to attend mine warfare training, which would lead him to a position on the USS *Tide*. In 1944, the *Tide* drew convoy escort duty and sailed from the coast of South Carolina straight east to Bermuda through the Atlantic Ocean, then to the Azores approaching the coast of Portugal, before taking a sharp northeast turn toward Wales. The minesweeper would remain in the United Kingdom for another few months as the Allied forces targeted early June for a massive invasion of German-occupied northern France.

When the *Tide* hit that magnetic mine near Utah Beach on the morning of June 7, 1944, about twenty-eight hours after the start of D-Day, more than twenty crewmembers died, in some cases almost instantly. "Suddenly, it seemed like the end of the world came," recalled *Tide* engineer Samuel Betros, a twenty-year-old Houston native working in the engine room during the explosion. "There were terrible crashes. All the lights went out. I bounced up and down. Water was coming in and diesel oil was burning over the whole shop." A dazed Betros stumbled to the deck "like a drunk" and desperately sought the first shipmate he encountered. Should they abandon ship? *The captain's killed; do what you want*, the shipmate responded.[8] That captain, Lieutenant Allard Heyward of Charleston, South Carolina, perished within seconds of the mine's detonation. Radarman William Daniel found him debilitated on the *Tide's* deck. "I turned him over," Daniel said, "and he took his last breath while I was looking at him."[9] Sinking quickly and threatened on all sides by bright orange fireballs and rushing floodwaters, surviving crewmembers sustained vicious spinal injuries, shattered bones, and blows to the chest, according to various published accounts.

The sheer force of the explosion on the *Tide* tossed Mike Welch violently toward the bow of the vessel, breaking two of his vertebrae. Surrounded by flames, Welch instinctively grabbed the first raft he could find on the boat and threw it as hard as he could into the water. A signalman named Jerry Harris, who was helplessly drowning in the English Channel after the blast knocked him off the ship, used the raft to secure himself. It was just the first life Welch would save that morning.

Writhing in agony from the shattered vertebrae, Welch and other sailors tried to tame the fire by pumping ocean water toward the flames, but their makeshift device did not work very well. Even after a "great big wave" finally knocked down the fire, Welch knew he needed to evacuate as quickly as possible before the ship descended to the bottom of the English Channel.[10] Luckily, help was on the way. A Patrol Torpedo (PT) boat, directed by Commander John D. Bulkeley, came to the rescue and pulled up next to the *Tide* to aid the crewmembers who had not died in the explosion. Welch, joined by the half-dozen men under his command as the first lieutenant, began to make his way toward Bulkeley's boat. Time was imperative. But Welch noticed a desperate situation unfolding just as he prepared to depart the sinking *Tide*. He paused.

"As men then clambered onto ships that pulled alongside, Welch went back on board and into the steward's mates cabin, quarters for five African-American men," the University of Minnesota news service reported in a newsletter sixty years later. "The Navy was segregated at the time; a steward, the only role available for African-Americans, did chores like cooking and cleaning for officers. In the rush to evacuate, the men had been left behind."[11] Welch noticed that the men had "leg bones coming out of their pants legs,"[12] and seemed to understand they would die if they did not receive some assistance. Although severe injuries hampered his mobility, Welch inched toward two of the sailors and let them grab the gun belt on his pants. They held tight. "Welch, who had played on the undefeated 1941 Gopher football team, then dragged them to the doorway and pulled them up onto the deck. He returned for two more men, and then the final survivor. All were evacuated before he, too, climbed aboard a waiting boat," the school's newsletter noted later. "Within 20 minutes, the *Tide* had sunk."[13]

Welch saw "chaos" when he finally reached Commander John D. Bulkeley's rescue boat. "Doctors were amputating, saving lives, doing emergency medical work," he remembered. "All those early wounded were glider pilots, paratroopers, and us." Welch ultimately landed inside a naval hospital in England before sailing across the Atlantic back to the United States, joined by about sixty other wounded troops. They received an epic welcome party upon arrival in New York City, complete with musical bands and a large contingent of WAVES, the Navy Women's Reserve. The supportive WAVES crowded around Welch and other injured soldiers until they received word that one of President's Roosevelt's sons had entered the Naval Headquarters. "Then all of the sudden," Welch said, "they left us."[14]

❊ ❊ ❊

For some reason, the story of the *Tide* remained elusive. Outside of the initial celebration, the larger public knew virtually nothing about the minesweeper's experience until mid-July 1944, more than a month after D-Day, when military censors released a photograph of the ship submerged in the English Channel. The picture ran in multiple U.S. newspapers, including the *News-Journal* in Mansfield, Ohio, and the *Daily Citizen* in Tucson, Arizona. A handful of news outlets also published short blurbs about the *Tide* in the summer, fall, and winter of 1944, but the ship's role in minesweeping operations and its tragic sinking on the morning of June 7 went largely overlooked.

Welch earned a Purple Heart for his heroic actions, but he, too, said little about the *Tide* in the years after the explosion. Once his wartime service ended, he worked in advertising, bouncing from Minneapolis to Illinois to Cleveland and finally to Denver, but rarely did his family ever hear anything about minesweeping, D-Day, or the trauma he endured on Utah Beach. That changed after a French diver named Corrine Erizo, excavating wreckage off the coast of Normandy in 1994, discovered the USS *Tide*'s log buried deep in the English Channel. "It was then that it was like the ship came alive!" she later described.[15] The rusted, dilapidated ship log, bottled up inside a container at the bottom of the sea, included dozens of unfamiliar names of *Tide* shipmates— including Mike Welch, listed near the end in alphabetical order. Using her sleuthing skills and an American phone book, Erizo found Welch's listed address and sent him a letter. They struck up a friendship, and within a matter of months, he would become the first member of the USS *Tide* to meet Erizo when he traveled to Normandy for the fiftieth anniversary of D-Day in June 1994.

Returning for the first time, Welch saw the English Channel once again. He stood at Utah Beach. It spurred difficult memories of gunfire and explosions and loud planes. Then he came across two things that truly astounded him: the French divers had recovered a gun in the water, which Welch identified as his own, and a toothbrush, imprinted with the name of a dentist, *Lewis Thom.* That was Welch's father-in-law. The toothbrush had apparently survived D-Day and the half-century that ensued. "I think that this whole incident with going to France, it was very emotional," his daughter said. "I think all of that really helped, him being able to talk about the memories. Because here were the French people, who were saying 'thank you,' directly to him."[16]

Welch gradually began to feel more comfortable talking about the war, particularly as the crew started to earn some long overdue recognition for their acts. On June 6, 2004, Welch and five surviving members of the *Tide* reported to the diamond of Wrigley Field in Chicago—two of them in wheelchairs—prior to a Sunday afternoon game between the Cubs and Pittsburgh Pirates. Wearing a red, white, and blue collared shirt, a grey-haired Welch, at that time in his eighties and living in California, listened as the public address announcer acknowledged the *Tide*'s role in aiding the invasion of Normandy and liberating France sixty years prior. "Forty thousand people rose as one and clapped and cheered," Welch said, "and every one of us had tears in our eyes."[17] Twelve years later, at the age of ninety-five, Welch earned the prestigious French Legion of Honor from Consul General of France Christophe Lemoine during a ceremony in San Diego. The former Gopher fullback and two-time college football national champion spent the final year of his life bestowed with France's highest military honor.

❊ ❊ ❊

Among his teammates on the 1941 national championship team, Welch was somewhat unique in that he served on the Western Front in Europe. Most of the other players from that squad, if they hadn't remained in stateside roles, shipped in the opposite direction to fight Axis forces in the Pacific Theater. Gopher end Judd Ringer, a nature lover with little inherent mechanical ability, learned how to fly a four-hundred-mile-per-hour Corsair as a fighter pilot. "He didn't really know a screwdriver from a pair of pliers," his son, Charles, would later say, "but he was a Marine and flew those Corsairs and was really good at it. It staggered me that he could do that—and not know how to fix his lawnmower."[18] Before setting sail toward Japan with the USS *Amsterdam*, Urban Odson would often recall his Navy chemical warfare training as "the worst experience he had in his whole life,"[19] far harder than any practice run by Bernie Bierman. Dick Wildung, just months after the Green Bay Packers selected him fourth overall in the NFL Draft, married Margaret on New Year's Day 1944—wearing his Navy uniform during the ceremony. In the coming months, he would become a boat commander in the South Pacific near the Philippines. Bill Daley, after finishing the V-12 program at Michigan and earning All-American honors in 1943, requested overseas duty in the Navy and also landed in the Philippines. Bill Garnaas followed suit as he traded Gopher football cleats for a rifle and a spot on a Navy tugboat, where he helped ships funnel in and out of the harbors. Although he did not directly confront the battlefield, Garnaas suffered a back injury after slamming against an underwater chain from a neighboring ship, leaving a lifelong scar. His top quarterback competition in 1941, Warren Plunkett, spent a few years on the USS *Sitka* in the Pacific as a Lieutenant Junior Grade Boat Group Commander. He later said he enlisted "to beat the countries that had attacked the United States, without any cause . . . I was glad to be able to join the Navy."[20]

With Gophers scattered on boats across the Pacific, American forces launched successful campaigns in the Mariana Islands in the summer of 1944, helping to wrest control of important strategic territories like Saipan and Guam. The United States then set its sights farther north in the Pacific Ocean, toward an eight-square-mile island about six hundred miles from the Japanese mainland. And so began perhaps the second-most prominent military invasion of the war: Iwo Jima. More than one hundred thousand American troops participated in the battle, including 5th Marine Division Lieutenant Gene Bierhaus and U.S. Navy Ensign Joe Lauterbach, formerly teammates in the same backfield at the University of Minnesota. "It is so incredibly unfortunate," Lauterbach's daughter, Ann Waits, said years later. "They journeyed from the gridiron into hell."[21]

17

I-W-O J-I-M-A

Although undiagnosed in those days, the horrors of Iwo Jima undoubtedly left Gene Bierhaus with some form of post-traumatic stress disor-
der, not to mention physical injuries that rendered him unable to walk
shortly after returning to the United States. In the decades following
the war, Bierhaus protected his family the best he could, revealing very
little about his month-long experience on Iwo Jima. "As a daughter,
that's something I never heard about," Kristy Bierhaus said, "literally
until it was close to the end of his life." In 2006, when Clint Eastwood
released *Flags of Our Fathers* and *Letters from Iwo Jima* in tandem,
Gene Bierhaus fielded an interview request from someone who wanted
a firsthand experience of the battle portrayed in the movies. He called
his daughter Kristy to glean more information about the Hollywood
films. In that phone conversation, Bierhaus revealed memories he had
repressed for decades. "It was the first time," Kristy said, "that he explained what it was like being on that island."

Shortly before he embarked on that trek to the Pacific Theater,
Gene Bierhaus had married the love of his life, Jeanne Broach, although not a single picture exists from the wedding because of an
inexplicable equipment hiccup by the photographer. The marriage, absent any visual evidence, occurred despite the warnings of Jeanne's
father. "You need to be fully aware," he told Jeanne, "that Gene could
come back crippled up, maimed, and a person you would have to take
care of for your entire life, if you get married before he goes off to war."
Jeanne did not listen.[1]

After initially meeting as youngsters in elementary school, Jeanne and Gene had dated on and off during their high school days in Brainerd, a small Mississippi River town in central Minnesota located about halfway between Minneapolis and the Canadian border. In their first official outing, Gene and Jeanne went down to the local dump in Brainerd—quite a romantic place—and shot rats together. Their love story evolved over the years, despite the fact they hailed from opposite sides of the socioeconomic spectrum. Unlike his future wife, Gene grew up on the poorer south side of Brainerd, in a strict traditional German household where his father struggled mightily to run his grocery store during the Great Depression.

The hardship fostered a rigid work ethic in Gene—and that helped him immensely when he started playing sports. During his high school years with the Brainerd Warriors, he shattered track and field records, captured golf trophies, and captained the 1938 football team, which made him somewhat of a local celebrity in central Minnesota. Hometown fans were extraordinarily proud when they learned he would attend the University of Minnesota to play football for Bernie Bierman's legendary Gophers. After a year of freshman football under Dallas Ward, Bierhaus caught Bierman's attention for the first time near the end of his sophomore year in 1940. During a 33–6 blowout victory against Purdue in November, Bierman and Dallas Ward marveled at the way Bierhaus performed off the bench at the quarterback position—particularly on the defensive end. "Say, he threw in one tackle out there that looked like [Bill] Daley," the coaches remarked.[2]

As a junior in 1941, Bierhaus mostly played halfback, serving as one of the many reserves in the Gophers' loaded backfield. He saw some action late in blowout victories over Illinois and Pittsburgh, while also landing a spot on the traveling team for road contests. His shining moment came at the end of the Iowa game, when he snagged his first career interception. A week later, of course, he also earned the distinction of replacing the injured Bruce Smith at halfback, after the Heisman Trophy winner left the Memorial Stadium grass for the final time against Wisconsin.

Still, as Bierhaus entered his senior season in the fall of 1942, folks back in Brainerd wondered why the Minnesota coaching staff hadn't given their hometown hero more opportunities. "We know Bierhaus can play football," they would say, according to the *Star Journal*, "and

Gene Bierhaus of Brainerd, Minnesota, played football at the University of Minnesota from 1939 to 1942 before heading to the United States Marines. *Family of Gene Bierhaus*

he will when he gets a chance."[3] George Hauser's staff moved the 180-pound Bierhaus from the backfield to the end position in 1942, but it still did not earn him regular playing time. Bierhaus had no regrets. "It's been a lot of fun for me," he said after his senior season. "I like football a lot and I think I've learned an awful lot to help me in my future physical education work."[4]

Coincidentally, his football career followed an eerily similar path to Mike Welch, another Minnesota reserve of the same age. In the 1943 NFL Draft, nine rounds after selecting Welch, the Green Bay Packers drafted Bierhaus, too, convinced the two Gophers could develop into professional football players with enough practice. Of course, just as Welch had joined the Navy instead of Curly Lambeau's Packers, Bierhaus headed for the United States Marine Corps and officer training school. He emerged as a first lieutenant and prepared to ship out from Quantico in 1944.

But first—his wedding. After leaving high school, Bierhaus and Jeanne Broach had dated long-distance between Brainerd and Minneapolis. Now that distance would be even longer. An entire ocean would separate them. So instead of waiting around, they got married—and then stayed in contact during the war with a secret communication system. Although the military censored mail in wartime to keep the troops' locations confidential from enemy forces, Gene and Jeanne bypassed the restrictions with a clever trick: in all of their written correspondence, Gene would spell out the 5th Marine Division's location in the first letter of every sentence. In February of 1945, the first letter of each sentence spelled out "I-W-O J-I-M-A."

※ ※ ※

Iwo Jima served a crucial purpose on both sides. For the Japanese, the tiny dot in the middle of the sea served as a line of defense against attacks on the mainland, helping them terrorize the Americans' B-29 Superfortress bombers as they traveled to and from Japan. For the U.S., however, a seizure of Iwo Jima promised strategic access to the mainland, providing landing strips and refueling opportunities for the vaunted B-29s. "Given these powerful incentives," James Bradley and Ron Powers wrote in the critically acclaimed book version of *Flags of Our Fathers*, "the island had to be taken at almost any cost."[5]

On February 19, 1945, the morning of "D-Day" for the Iwo Jima invasion, General Tadamichi Kuribayashi allowed the Americans to overtake his beaches, preferring to huddle his Japanese troops underground before opening an assault. "He placed his confidence in the elaborate defensive system," the U.S. Marine Corps History and Museums Division later wrote, "tunneled among the tortuous ravines of the northern plateau."[6] When Kuribayashi's troops finally emerged to open fire on the unsuspecting Americans, the combat was horrific, among the worst of the war. Gene Bierhaus did not document D-Day specifically, but he would later tell a newspaper reporter that his "arms, legs and shoulders were perforated with shrapnel" at some point during the invasion and that he saw fifteen Japanese soldiers burned with flamethrowers right before his eyes.[7]

In addition to Bierhaus, a number of other former college football players converged on the island with the United States Marines. Angelo Bertelli, the Notre Dame standout and runner-up to Bruce Smith for the Heisman Trophy in 1941, would later earn a Purple Heart for his campaigns at Iwo Jima and Guam.[8] Jack Lummus, an All-American at Baylor and member of the New York Giants, sailed to Iwo Jima with the USS *LST-756* on February 19 and reportedly told a medic a few weeks later, "Well, doc, it looks like the Giants have lost a good end," as he was bleeding out and dying after stepping on a mine.[9]

George "Sonny" Franck, Bierhaus' former teammate at Minnesota, also slogged through volcanic ash on Yellow Beach 1 as Iwo Jima's D-Day began. Franck, the All-American senior sensation for the Golden Gophers in 1940, had played just one season with the New York Giants in 1941 alongside Jack Lummus before the Marines came calling. He spent the majority of the war as a fighter pilot, but on this first day of the Iwo Jima invasion, Franck drew a ground assignment with seventy thousand fellow Marines. At one point, he lunged into a foxhole next to a fellow Marine named Jack Chevigny, a legendary football star himself at Notre Dame. As a player under Knute Rockne in 1927, Chevigny's famous tackle at the three-yard line of Cartier Field had preserved a 7–7 tie against Bronko Nagurski's Gophers; a decade later, in 1936, Chevigny coached the University of Texas football team that lost 47–19 to Minnesota at Memorial Stadium. Those days felt far away on February 19, 1945, when the thirty-eight-year-old 5th Marine Division fighter ducked into his own foxhole next to Sonny Franck. "After a while he called and asked me to come over to his foxhole. I happened to be kinda worn out at the time and told him I thought I'd stay where I was," Franck told a newspaper later that year in his home state of Iowa. "Ten minutes later Chevigny was dead."[10]

✿ ✿ ✿

Navy ensign Leo Joseph "Joe" Lauterbach, an intelligence officer at Iwo Jima and another former Gopher football player, never expected to find himself in the thick of this brutal fighting. His role changed when hundreds of American forces, such as Jack Chevigny, died at the start of the invasion, forcing the twenty-four-year-old into direct combat. It is unclear if Lauterbach knew that fellow Gophers Sonny Franck and Gene Bierhaus were on the island with the Marines, but as a Navy ensign, he faced similar danger. During the second day, while conducting ship-to-shore communication on a beach American forces mistakenly felt was secure, a surprise Japanese mortar shell landed about ten feet away from Lauterbach and unleashed a devastating explosion. The blast obliterated most of Lauterbach's left leg, detonating just inches above his knee in a moment that forever changed the course of his adult life and, without question, ended a football career that had started with such promise back in Redwood Falls, Minnesota.

Although he played his high school ball in a small community about one hundred miles outside the Twin Cities, the *Star Journal* in Minneapolis learned of Lauterbach's prowess and named him to the 1938 "All-Outstate" team,[11] which also included a fellow by the name of Dick Wildung and a kid from Brainerd named Gene Bierhaus. After arriving at the University of Minnesota, Lauterbach played some quarterback and fullback for Dallas Ward's freshman team before joining the varsity as a sophomore in 1940—where he had the unique opportunity to play alongside senior Bob Paffrath, another product of Redwood Falls.

As a junior on the 1941 team, Lauterbach competed with Bierhaus, Welch, and others for snaps behind the backfield stars, but he, too, found it difficult to earn regular playing time. During that same Iowa game, when Bierman reached deep into his bench to give Welch and Bierhaus opportunities, Lauterbach played one drive late in the first half before an injury forced him out of the game. Returning as a senior in 1942, Lauterbach finally carved out a niche for himself at fullback and earned praise from the press in the second half of the season. "Lauterbach, from Redwood Falls, showed up well in the Nebraska game at Lincoln," the *Minneapolis Tribune* reported, "and has been booming along ever since."[12] He broke through in a big way during the final two games of his career, carrying the ball fifteen times for eighty-three yards against tough Iowa and Wisconsin teams. Then it was off to the United States Navy. "Can you imagine how quickly they had to grow up?" his daughter Ann wondered in retrospect, long after her father's passing. "Incredible, just incredible. They would have had to grow up so fast."[13]

After the blast from the enemy mortar shattered most of Lauterbach's left leg at Iwo Jima, the military rushed him across the Pacific to Aiea Heights Naval Hospital, an extensive wartime complex overlooking Pearl Harbor in Hawaii. Most of the wounded service members from Iwo Jima landed there. Lauterbach lived on the first floor with three other patients in similarly dire straits, including Phil Roach, a former football player from Texas Christian University. In 1941, Roach's extra point provided insurance in a 14–7 victory over Dana Bible's Texas Longhorns, all but eliminating them from national title contention. Lauterbach might have thanked Roach for his championship ring as they recovered next to each other in traction beds at Aiea Heights.

Inside the hospital, they both encountered a storied *Chicago Times* war correspondent named Keith Wheeler, an embedded journalist receiving medical treatment after a Japanese soldier shot him in the throat at Iwo Jima. Wheeler portayed Lauterbach as one of the "sickest of the lot," describing his infection as "persistent" as he loaded up on penicillin longer than perhaps anyone else at Aiea Heights.[14] By April 1945, Lauterbach had spent a grand total of twenty-nine days in the traction bed and could hardly bear the thought of staying any longer. "I want to go home," Lauterbach apparently wrote in a poem, according to Wheeler.[15]

The two eventually parted ways after leaving Aiea Heights, but they remained in touch. Writing for the *Honolulu Star-Bulletin* in 1946 with a Shanghai dateline, Wheeler shared a letter he received from Joe Lauterbach, the "one time Minnesota university footballer." From his new facility on the mainland, the Great Lakes Naval Hospital, Lauterbach sent Wheeler an update about his left leg. It was not good news. "They did all they could to pass the clot but it wouldn't budge. We sat tight with the foot packed in ice but it became necessary to amputate the foot as gangrene was setting in. I reasoned that as long as the leg would never be much good even after two years of bone grafting, it might as well be removed above the fracture," Lauterbach wrote. "On January 16, the leg was removed about six inches above the knee. I am indeed happy that it has been done and that soon I'll be up and around. I'm sure that God intervened to give me an easy out in deciding, because it was a necessity."[16]

After earning a Purple Heart for his service at Iwo Jima, Lauterbach returned home with an artificial leg and enrolled again at the University of Minnesota. He received his degree in 1948 and then married Jean Ann Perrine a year later, while embarking on his post-war career as an insurance salesman with Old Northwest. Lauterbach's sales territory changed frequently, so the couple and their five children moved several times—from St. Louis Park, Minnesota, to North Dakota to Central Wisconsin and finally to Harlan, Iowa, in the summer of 1967.

Lauterbach spent the rest of his career in Harlan, enjoying life as a husband, father, rosebush caretaker, and avid singer who performed with a barber shop quartet in the community production of *The Music Man*. Through the years, he won company awards as an insurance salesman, brought his children to Catholic mass each Sunday where they sat in the front left row, and refused to sulk about the loss of his left leg at Iwo Jima, despite the pain and difficulty it brought to his life. One of Lauterbach's sons, also named Joe, recalled wonderful childhood memories of playing basketball with his father, and he remembered that other kids in school would often ask him why his dad walked with a limp. "He's got a wooden leg," the younger Joe would tell his friends. "Doesn't everyone's dad have a wooden leg?"[17] The Lauterbach kids had simply never known their dad without a prosthetic leg. It was a fact of life, something they knew had happened to him as a young man during the war. They did not learn much more. "Something he never wanted to talk about," daughter Ann said, "was Iwo Jima."[18]

* * *

The American public must have been shocked by the stories and images coming from Iwo Jima, especially through the newsreels that played in movie theaters across the country. Since Gene Bierhaus had informed his new wife that he was on I-W-O J-I-M-A via their special letter-writing arrangement, Jeanne watched those clips in horror back in Brainerd, knowing Gene was somewhere on that island. Perhaps it was better that she did not know the full extent of the situation, for surely she would not have wanted to know that her husband was sleeping at night directly above enemy soldiers hiding in bunkers, ready at any moment to open fire. Accompanied by native Navajo speakers to help them communicate in a language the Japanese could not intercept, Bierhaus at one point shouldered one of the injured code talkers on his back during battle and brought him down to safety as the battle raged for more than a month. Jeanne knew none of this, though according to family lore, she received one report in 1945 that her husband had died on Iwo Jima; this obviously turned out to be false. Still, Jeanne had to wait in agony for months—until the war was over later that year—to learn that Gene was safe on a British hospital carrier ship. Jeanne and Gene appeared together in a photo on Page Seventeen of the *Minneapolis Star Journal* on July 31, 1945.

"Invading an island is a lot like football. There are a number of plans, like plays, that have to be executed when you hit the beach," Lt. Gene Bierhaus told the *Star Journal*. "But plenty of times you have to call your own signals."[19] Although Bierhaus could draw some strategic comparisons between football plays and military operations, he knew that sports and war were not one and the same. On Iwo Jima, he had not simply been knocked cold by a tackle. He had fought for his life every minute of every day, and by the time he left the island he suffered injuries that would require intensive rehabilitation. Yet, at the same time, Gene Bierhaus had been so lucky.

By the time the U.S. seized Iwo Jima in March 1945, roughly twenty-five thousand American and Japanese troops had lost their lives. The catastrophic number of casualties earned Iwo Jima an infamous place in World War II history, but the fifth day of the battle also produced one of the most iconic military photographs ever taken. Joe Rosenthal of the Associated Press earned a Pulitzer Prize for the February 23, 1945, shot that "appeared on literally millions of posters and on a three cent postage stamp," capturing six U.S. Marines as they raised an American flag on the southern end of Iwo Jima, atop Mount Suribachi. Almost everybody in the United States saw that picture, but very few knew the truth: it was the *second* flag photographed on Mount Suribachi. The mounting of the first flag, captured in a picture earlier that morning by an obscure *Leatherneck Magazine* photographer named Sgt. Louis Lowery, happened around 10:20 a.m.

Lt. Col. Chandler W. Johnson had ordered a group of forty Marines to climb the mountain and place a fifty-four-by-twenty-eight-inch flag at the crest. After fending off Japanese soldiers, the men reached the top of the mountain and attached the flag, as ordered, on top of a water pipe. "Then all hell broke loose below," Corporal Charles W. Lindberg said. "Troops cheered, ships blew horns and whistles, and some men openly wept. It was a sight to behold . . . something a man doesn't forget."[20]

Gene Bierhaus was one of those U.S. Marines watching from the bottom of the mountain. Although he refused to talk about the actual

This snapshot of the second flag raising atop Mount Suribachi was among the most iconic World War II photographs ever taken. Lt. Gene Bierhaus witnessed the first flag raising earlier in the day, which still offered a tremendous boost to the troops at Iwo Jima. *Joe Rosenthal, Associated Press, Public Domain, National Archives Identifier 520748*

battles for most of his life, he never hesitated to discuss the moment he saw the first flag raised atop Mount Suribachi. "This part of the story we always knew," daughter Kristy said. "It gave these exhausted men a real boost in energy. He referenced that a lot." After returning home on the British hospital ship, Bierhaus began his rehab in Asheville, North Carolina, where doctors removed shrapnel from his body. He would later spend time in the dry heat of Camp Verde, Arizona, where he and Jeanne lived in the upstairs bedroom of a chicken coop. Eager to prove to his father-in-law that his injuries would not become a burden on Jeanne, Bierhaus overcame his arthritis and eventually recovered quite strongly.

Although Bierhaus had always dreamed of coaching football and held a degree in education from the University of Minnesota, he did not feel he could physically handle that lifestyle. He ultimately found his calling studying veterinary medicine at the University of California–Davis and Colorado A&M (now known as Colorado State). Jeanne and Gene Bierhaus then moved to Denver, where they built a small animal clinic. Over time, Dr. Bierhaus became a respected authority as the Colorado State Racing Commission veterinarian and left a distinguished mark on the profession with his development of medication protocol. Whether they knew it or not, the Bierhaus family settled in the same city as the family of teammate Mike Welch, who had pursued his career in advertising after coming home from Normandy. Two of the reserve backs under Bernie Bierman in 1941, each of them drafted by the Green Bay Packers but unable to play due to the call of duty, had miraculously survived the most intense fighting of World War II—and somehow ended up in an identical location. They, along with Joe Lauterbach and the rest of the 1941 Golden Gophers who returned home, could finally start rebuilding their lives in post-war America.

18

COMING HOME

After the worst experience of his life at chemical warfare training school in Edgewood, Maryland, the 247-pound tackle Urban Odson joined shore patrol on the USS *Amsterdam* as it sailed across the Pacific in June 1945. He likely left with the *Amsterdam* from Pearl Harbor and the Hawaii area on June 9, before reaching the Philippine Sea on July 1 along with Task Force 38 as they "headed for the combat areas off the Japanese homeland." According to U.S. Navy records, the *Amsterdam* engaged in a "series of devastating sweeps against Japanese airfields, factories and shipping," with the goal of "protecting the carriers from attack by the enemy, whether aerial or seaborne."[1] The crew, including Odson, had undergone extensive anti-aircraft training but did not encounter any attacks. A month later in mid-August, following an "all day alert" aboard the *Amsterdam*, the mission changed. "Word received that the Japanese have accepted defeat," the commanding officer noted in a confidential war diary. "All offensive United States operations are hereby discontinued."[2] Days earlier, in a move that has been debated vigorously by scholars ever since, the United States avoided using troops in a military invasion by dropping two atomic bombs on Hiroshima and Nagasaki, killing tens of thousands of Japanese people instantly with many more to die from the effects in the coming months and years. The final death toll, although still unclear, may have reached at least 200,000.[3]

The end of the war brought celebrations to the streets of Minneapolis, where police closed Hennepin Avenue to vehicular traffic due to the size of the crowds. With an executive order from President Harry S. Truman, along with announcements from Minnesota governor Edward J. Thye and Minneapolis mayor Hubert H. Humphrey, all government workers learned they would be given two holidays on August 15 and 16. But, truly, this was no joyous time. "It has been the sad duty of the *Alumnus* staff," the weekly alumni magazine reported in September 1945, "to report the deaths of nearly 550 Minnesota alumni in service."[4] In all, the state of Minnesota suffered more than 6,000 casualties during World War II.[5]

Across the country, several high-profile football players lost their lives, including Dave Schreiner of Wisconsin. After starting at end against Minnesota in 1940 and 1941, he earned All-American honors in 1942 before dying in action at the Battle of Okinawa during the final months of the war. Others had survived just barely: Hal Van Every, a star Minnesota halfback voted Most Valuable Player on Bernie Bierman's 1939 team, tasted freedom in spring 1945 after U.S. forces liberated him from captivity in a German POW camp. Enemy troops had been holding Van Every as a prisoner of war for an entire year after shooting down his B-17 bomber the previous spring.[6]

When Japan officially surrendered on September 2, 1945, at the USS *Missouri* in Tokyo Bay, Urban Odson and the USS *Amsterdam* were not far behind. The ship remained in the area for more than two weeks "to guard against any possible aggression,"[7] before Odson and his crew headed back to the United States on September 20. His Gopher teammates soon followed. Slowly, as they received their military discharges in the coming months, members of the 1941 national championship team began to regain their footing in society. War had brought their lives to a grinding halt for four years, but now they had an opportunity to press the restart button. Some, like Judd Ringer, Bob Fitch, and Herman Frickey, came back to school to finish their degrees on the GI Bill and wound up with eligibility remaining on the Minnesota football team—led once again by Bernie Bierman, who seamlessly transitioned from the Navy's physical education program to retake the Golden Gophers' head coaching position in 1945.

Helge Pukema, returning from the South Pacific with the U.S. Coast Guard, could no longer play football due to an injury he suffered falling off a ship mast—so he took a job teaching and coaching at the high school level in Michigan. According to family lore, Pukema may have saved his own life unknowingly during the war. While on shore leave in the South Pacific, which he was adamant about taking against the preference of his commander, Pukema's cargo ship, the USS *Serpens*, exploded near Guadalcanal in late January 1945. The blast killed two hundred and fifty people, considered the "largest single disaster in the history of the United States Coast Guard,"[8] but Pukema remained safe on dry land, far away from the destruction. Many years later, knowing how lucky he had been, the former Gopher lineman visited Arlington National Cemetery to pay homage to his fallen shipmates.[9]

Bill Daley, meanwhile, came home from naval duty overseas with plenty of stories to tell, including one from late 1945 when he played an Army–Navy football game in China before thousands of fans at a former greyhound racetrack. "So that was rather interesting, one of the high points of my career, and I was always very happy that I requested duty overseas so I could see that," Daley said. "I enjoyed the Navy very much."[10] Upon his return to the United States, Daley turned his attention to an emerging professional football league, the All-America Football Conference (AAFC), which immediately threatened the National Football League's reign when it launched in 1946. Daley spent time with the New York "Yankees," Chicago Rockets, Brooklyn Dodgers, and Miami Seahawks, while Minnesota teammate Bob Sweiger also landed on the Yankees (no relation to the baseball team). Don Nolander and Paul Mitchell, a pair of reserve linemen at Minnesota in 1941 whose roles increased under Hauser during the wartime years, headed west to play for the Los Angeles Dons of the AAFC in addition to having served in the Navy.

The All-America Football Conference, unfortunately, did not live to see the end of the decade. Despite the league's best efforts, it could not overtake the National Football League—where most of the top stars from the 1941 Minnesota national championship team landed after the war.

✿ ✿ ✿

Earl Lambeau could not contain his excitement—and that was somewhat rare for a man known to be abrasive and difficult at times. Known more commonly by the name "Curly," the co-founder and longtime head coach of the Green Bay Packers proudly announced in February

1945 that his franchise had agreed to terms with one of the most famous college football players of the decade: Bruce Smith, the one they made that Hollywood movie about. The University of Minnesota All-American and Heisman Trophy winner, originally drafted by Green Bay in the thirteenth round back in late 1941, would finally play for the Packers as soon as the Navy discharged him. "Smith is one of the greatest halfbacks in the country," Lambeau said after Smith signed a two-year contract, "and will be a valuable addition to Green Bay when he joins us. He can pass and run well and is one of the best team players to come out of college ranks in recent seasons."[11]

After launching the organization as a player-coach in his hometown of Green Bay in 1919, Lambeau had amassed six NFL championships with the Packers, including one most recently in 1944. The 1945 season was somewhat of a transition year—it started just weeks after the war ended—but the league quickly saw an influx of talent as players returned from military service. After his discharge from the Navy, Bruce Smith joined a 4–1 Packers squad for a game against the Chicago Bears at Wrigley Field on November 4. "The news that Bruce Smith has joined up with the Green Bay Packers," a New Jersey newspaper wrote, "will not spread any happiness around the National League. Smith is so good that [future Hall of Fame pass-catcher] Don Hutson can finally retire."[12]

During his professional football debut, Smith appeared briefly for a span of just two plays. In front of forty-five thousand fans, smaller than most crowds he encountered at Memorial Stadium, Smith fumbled his first touch on a punt return in the second half—although he avoided embarrassment when a teammate snatched the ball and retained possession. On the next play, the Packers fed Smith his first NFL carry. He gained five yards but did not see any more action the rest of the game, as the Packers fell 28–24.

Starting at left halfback a week later, Smith exited a contest against the Cleveland Rams with a neck injury and subsequently sat out the next game. He returned for the second-to-last game of the season, on November 25 at the Polo Grounds, where he dazzled a New York City audience of fifty-two thousand with his running game in a 23–14 victory over the New York Giants. It was his finest performance in the pros to date. "There was indication that another rookie, Bruce Smith, the ex-

Minnesota ace, will be heard from in 1946 and succeeding years," the *Green Bay Press-Gazette* predicted.[13]

Smith also prepared to take another big step in life by marrying Gloria Bardeau, a fashion model and designer. After the final game of the 1945 season in Detroit against the Lions, they planned to fly home to Faribault for a late December ceremony. According to an account in *The Game Breaker*, a snowstorm altered those plans, so instead they drove about seven hundred miles from Detroit to Faribault in Smith's 1943 Ford.[14]

The newlyweds would soon be reunited with more familiar faces. After a 6–4 season and the retirement of the great Don Hutson, Curly Lambeau bolstered his 1946 Green Bay roster in the off-season by signing two ferocious linemen: Urban Odson and Dick Wildung. Both had been All-Americans at Minnesota. Both had been first-round picks of the Packers before the war interfered. And both had played with Bruce Smith, meaning three members of the 1941 national championship team would now get a chance to wreak havoc on the National Football League. "The trio stood out," Dave Yuenger of the *Green Bay Press-Gazette* wrote, "when Minnesota elevens under Bernie Bierman were trampling opposition."[15]

The Gopher Trinity would remain intact for the next few seasons in Green Bay, strengthening the personal bond between the former college teammates. Urban Odson would even name a newborn son after Bruce Smith. But sadly, they could not duplicate the Minnesota magic in Green Bay, as the franchise tumbled into a downward trajectory. Unable to capitalize on the presence of three college national champions, the once-proud Packers toiled in mediocrity during the post-war years and would not win their next NFL championship until 1961.

✽ ✽ ✽

Wildung, Odson, and Smith lined up against several former college teammates during their pro years, including Bill Garnaas of the Pittsburgh Steelers and Butch Levy of the Cleveland and Los Angeles Rams. Although Levy did not experience direct conflict while stationed on the naval bases in Illinois and Idaho, his family and new wife Lucky were still reeling from the war. Lucky's brother, Peter Bellson, had died in combat just months earlier in the Battle of the Bulge. After his own discharge from the Navy, Levy inked a $4,000 contract with the Cleveland Rams and joined them in October 1945—just as the Rams were set to leave for a road game against the Green Bay Packers, not all that far from Minneapolis.

Although he had just arrived from the Navy and probably needed more time to acclimate himself with the franchise before he could play, Levy asked the team if he could travel to Wisconsin and take the train to Minneapolis from Milwaukee. He wanted to see his wife. *"You might as well suit up if you're gonna do that,"* the Rams told Levy. So they placed him on special teams.

The bruising lineman, more accustomed to playing in the trenches of Memorial Stadium, must have looked absurd making open-field tackles on the kickoff team for the Cleveland Rams. He later told his kids that he used a simple technique—he ran as fast as he could with his head straight down. One play in particular during his rookie season earned him some respect among the Rams' coaches. "I remember him saying it was like the parting of the Red Sea," son Peter Levy said. "Before he could react, he crushes the running back, somebody who was well-known. Knocked him out of the game. And that's how he made the team, and then the next year they moved to Los Angeles."[16]

After winning the NFL Championship in 1945, Rams' owner Dan Reeves said during the relocation process in January 1946 that Los Angeles had been his goal dating back as early as 1937. "I've wanted to go out there ever since," Reeves said, "and the current move is the product of long-range planning and the culmination of seven years of trying."[17] The move incensed local fans in Cleveland, including Chamber of Commerce president Herbert Ladds. "I'm terribly disappointed and sorry and I think owner Dan Reeves has made a mistake," he said. "I think Cleveland did a good job of supporting the Rams this past season and that the city took the Rams to its heart for their brilliant showing."[18] Once in Los Angeles, the Rams prepared to move into the massive Coliseum and signed Kenny Washington and Woody Strode, two of the first African American NFL players after World War II and former UCLA teammates of Jackie Robinson. Joined by Levy, who started often at guard, the Rams finished 6–4–1 and defeated the Packers' "Minnesota Trio" twice. Levy later joined the AAFC's Los Angeles Dons before the league folded, and then pursued a very successful career in professional wrestling.

After facing Levy in 1946, Bruce Smith spent another year in Green Bay but dealt with significant injuries, including one to his kidney that reportedly left him in dire condition at the hospital. In 1948, he wound up signing with the Los Angeles Rams himself. Coincidentally, he played under Clark Shaughnessy, the former Gopher and Dr. Henry L. Williams protégé. Smith played only one year in Los Angeles before he decided to retire from his injury-ravaged professional football career. After he left the Rams, sister June Smith said she drove cross-country with her father, Lucius, to pick him up and bring him back to Minnesota, where he would remain for the rest of his life with his wife and children in a variety of sales and business jobs.

By the end of the 1940s, almost every single member from the 1941 Gopher national championship team had finished playing professional football in either the NFL or AAFC. After spending a few years under demanding head coach Jock Sutherland, Bill Garnaas' time with the Pittsburgh Steelers came to an end in 1948. Urban Odson's career with the Green Bay Packers concluded in 1949. Dick Wildung, however, continued to play into the next decade and thrived as a tackle with the Packers. Appearing in more than eighty professional games and often playing both offense and defense, Wildung earned All-Pro honors twice, made the Pro Bowl in 1951, and was one of the last two-way players in the NFL.[19] He was also one of the lone bright spots during some of the darker days in the history of the Green Bay Packers. From 1948 to 1951, the franchise won only eleven games; Curly Lambeau resigned after a 2–10 season in 1949. Dick Wildung was "always disappointed that Green Bay wasn't a better football team than they were," said his son, Dave. Following his final season in 1953, Wildung returned to Minnesota and eventually took over his father-in-law's hardware store in Redwood Falls. "He was never sorry he went to Green Bay," Wildung's son said, "except that after the war, Curly Lambeau was not the same person he was before."[20]

That was the case for Bernie Bierman as well.

✿ ✿ ✿

While Bierman was away, the Gophers won fifteen games, lost eleven, and tied one under George Hauser from 1942 to 1944, but they anticipated a post-war boom when the Silver Fox returned in 1945. Loose eligibility rules also allowed players like Judd Ringer and Bob Fitch to play an extra year of football with the Gophers. ("I never have been able to figure out how I was eligible," Fitch later said.)[21] Bolstered by the reappearance of so many familiar faces, the 1945 team delivered an impressive 34–0 victory over Missouri in front of thirty-four thousand at Memorial Stadium. But after four straight victories to open the season, the Gophers buckled against tough Big Ten competition, suffering a disastrous five-game losing streak against Ohio State, Michigan, Indiana, Iowa, and Wisconsin. Minnesota, with a final record of 4–5, suffered its first losing season since 1939; Bierman had not lost this many games in one year as a head coach since his first year at Tulane. Fans expressed displeasure. "The howling mob forgot to weigh the material," Bierman said after the season. "They just figured it was Minnesota and that there was no reason to expect other than a Minnesota victory. But they were wrong, weren't they?"[22]

Despite another mediocre 5–4 season in 1946—a team that featured veterans Herman Frickey, Herb Hein, and Bill Baumgartner, among others—Bierman managed to orchestrate a program turnaround, a final stand of sorts. The 1947 team won six games, and then the 1948 and 1949 teams, led by a stellar Superior, Wisconsin, native named Bud Grant, won seven games apiece. Bierman, aging into his fifties and still running the single-wing offense, did not feel the game had passed him by yet. He continued to shun the more explosive T formation, which had become the talk of college football during the war years, ever since Clark Shaughnessy and Stanford restored it to glory in 1940. "How can anyone call Bierman-type football old-fashioned?" a *Star* reader named George Mohn wrote. "It's about as old-fashioned as the atom bomb. Pictures clipped from the Minneapolis Star show good examples of blockers moving in a fashion I consider very up to date, even in 1949."[23]

This quickly proved untrue in 1950. Making a familiar, opening-season trek to Seattle and Husky Stadium, where Bruce Smith had scored a pair of touchdowns nine years earlier to launch another national championship run, Bierman's 1950 team opened with a 28–13 defeat by the Huskies. The season spiraled from there. Home loss to Nebraska. Loss at Northwestern. A shutout at the hands of Ohio State. A tie with Michigan. Two losses to Iowa and Michigan State by the combined score of 40–0. With a winless record of 0–6–1, Bernie Bierman announced during an 8:15 a.m. press conference on November 13, 1950, that he would resign as head coach at the University of Minnesota at the end of the season. "It wasn't an easy decision to make, but this is final," Bierman said, expressing hope for his alma mater after his departure. "Football conditions have been tough here ever since the end of the war. I won't say that the future is hopeless."[24] Bierman's wife, Clara, said that her mother-in-law wept when she learned the news. Lydia Bierman, who had been so delighted back in December 1931 when she learned via telegram that her son was coming home to Minnesota, had attended every single one of Bernie's games until illness snapped her streak in 1950. Neither Lydia nor Clara Bierman could grasp the concept of a Minnesota football team without Bernie in charge. "I knew this day was inevitable," Clara said. "I just didn't think it would come so soon."[25]

With two games still left in the 1950 season, Bierman coached his final home game at Memorial Stadium against Purdue the following weekend. It did not start well for the hapless Gophers as they fell behind 14–0. Bruce Smith, who would not have dared miss the final home game coached by his mentor, remained optimistic. "The boys are showing signs of life," he said as he observed from the grandstands. If only the Faribault Flash could wear a gold helmet again.

Sophomore halfback Kerm Klefsaas notched a touchdown in the second quarter, although the extra point failed. Trailing 14–6 at halftime, forty-three thousand fans at Memorial Stadium fixed their eyes on midfield, where the "M Club" honored Bierman for his contributions to the university. Over the public address system, the crowd heard a tribute: *The last home game at Minnesota for Bierman. A heritage of glorious memories . . . builder of character and maker of men.* Then Bierman took the microphone. "We've had a lot of fun, a lot of heartaches," he told the fans. "And right now we have an awful tough second half on our hands."[26]

From the locker room, the Gophers emerged a new team. Kerm Klefsaas, who had been in elementary school the last time his coach won a national championship back in 1941, punched in a one-yard touchdown in the third quarter and then another one in the fourth quarter. Minnesota extended the lead to 27–14, and from there, the Gophers refused to relinquish the advantage. Once time expired and the thrilling comeback victory became official, the players carried Bierman on their shoulders and escorted him out of Memorial Stadium for the last time ever.

A week later, the Gophers lost a road game at Wisconsin in unceremonious fashion, by the score of 14–0. And so ended Bierman's run at his alma mater, the place he had loved so dearly ever since he arrived as a wide-eyed freshman from Litchfield four decades earlier in 1912. He had accomplished so much, from his captaincy under Dr. Henry L. Williams in 1915 to his illustrious coaching return in 1932 to his five national championships, the last of which came two weeks before Pearl Harbor.

Nothing was the same after the war.

19

LEGACY

Long after the glory days of 1941, Butch Levy took his family to the slopes of Vail, Colorado, for a winter ski outing. Although the exact date of the trip has been lost, it occurred sometime after 1977, because Levy attended an event with *ex*-president of the United States Gerald R. Ford. The former president often vacationed in Vail and appeared at a formal event that Levy attended. Ford stood in a reception line, shaking hands with guests, when suddenly it was the hulking Levy's turn. As Levy approached the one-time most powerful man in the country, someone turned to Ford and asked him if he remembered this guy coming down the aisle, the guy nicknamed Butch who played football at the University of Minnesota a long time ago. Ford replied: *"Do I remember Butch? Of course!"* As a young man, Gerald Ford played football at Michigan and started at center against the Gophers in 1934, before spending the next several years coaching at Yale while earning a law degree. It was there, as an assistant football coach, where Ford somehow came across game film of a Minnesota–Michigan game while scouting for the Bulldogs. Ford remembered what he thought to himself all those decades earlier, when big Butch Levy kept popping on his screen at guard with huge blocks and tackles: *"He's everywhere!"*[1]

The fact that a person of Ford's stature remembered a player from the 1941 Minnesota national championship team was not all that surprising. Millions of Americans during that era read about the Gophers through wire reports in their local newspapers. They listened to their games on national radio networks, and they saw highlights on newsreels in the theaters. For years and years after their playing days, members of that team remained rock stars—particularly in the Twin Cities, where their children remember having to constantly answer questions about their last names. *"Hey, aren't you related to. . . . "* The names Sweiger and Smith and Daley and Levy and Garnaas and Odson and Wildung, heard constantly over the radio on fall Saturdays in Minnesota, elicited an immediate reaction from football fans through the 1940s, '50s, '60s, and beyond.

Unfortunately, the vast majority of people who lived through the 1941 season are no longer here. Only young fans, ones who watched or listened to the team's games as children, would still be alive today. After Warren Plunkett passed away at the age of ninety-eight in December 2018, it appears that most if not all of the players from the 1941 team have now died. Although they cannot tell their stories today, evidence of their success remains everywhere—you just have to look for it. The Bierman Field Athletic Building, which houses memorabilia from the 1941 team and other championship squads, stands proudly at Fifth Street Southeast and Sixth Street Southeast on the edge of campus near Dinkytown. Bruce Smith's retired number, "54," hangs next to the number of his boyhood idol, Bronko Nagurski, over the northwest corner of TCF Bank Stadium.

And in November 2019, when coach P. J. Fleck's undefeated Golden Gophers hosted fourth-ranked Penn State in front of six million American television viewers on ABC, play-by-play announcer Sean McDonough stirred memories of the Golden Decade in the opening seconds of his broadcast. "The University of Minnesota has a proud football history," McDonough said, as the camera showed images of Bierman's national championship banners. "But most college football fans know little or nothing about those long-ago accomplishments. They're certainly learning more about this year's Golden Gophers— 8–0, ranked number seventeen." Minutes later, when Fleck and his players stormed out of the TCF Bank Stadium locker room in front of 51,883 boisterous fans waving gold rally towels, McDonough had to raise his voice several notches to compete with the overwhelming crowd noise. "Here come the Gophers!" McDonough bellowed. *"8–0 for the first time since 1941."*[2]

Those young Gophers who faced Penn State, despite coming along nearly eight decades later, had at least some familiarity with the accomplishments of the 1941 team—thanks to an ongoing history lesson that P. J. Fleck first began teaching in 2017. Months after accepting the job at Minnesota, Fleck gave his players a break from grueling summer workouts and loaded them on a bus headed for Fort Snelling National Cemetery, where many University of Minnesota alumni and veterans were buried. "One of the most important Americans, one of the most famous Americans in our past," Fleck told his 2017 team in front of one particular grave, "is Bruce Smith." He instructed senior captain Steven Richardson to place a captain's coin on Smith's headstone, which read, *Bruce P. Smith Minnesota Ensign USNR World War II.* A year later, when the Gophers again returned to Smith's grave in August 2018, the coin miraculously remained in the very same spot. It had not moved from the top of the headstone, even after a long Minnesota winter. This second time around, Fleck invited Smith's youngest sister, ninety-one-year-old June, to witness the ceremony and meet the players. Rodney Smith, who bears the same last name by pure coincidence, presented June with a bouquet of flowers as the team circled around her brother's final resting place. "Two days after Pearl Harbor, he won his Heisman Trophy and then went right into the Navy," Fleck told the players. "How many of *you* would give up what you have right now to go do that? That's what type of man this was."[3]

✿ ✿ ✿

Bruce Smith (1920–1967) worked in a variety of sales ventures after his playing career, ranging from a sporting goods store to clothing to Foley Manufacturing (owned by Judd Ringer's family) and finally to Hamm's Beer in Alexandria, Minnesota, where he moved with his wife and four children. Smith worked as a distributor for Hamm's in promotions and advertising and spent a fair amount of time traveling. During one such trip up north, he brought his son Bruce to International Falls—where Smith's hero of the 1920s, the larger-than-life Bronko Nagurski, still ran a gas station. When Smith introduced his son to Nagurski, he simply could not stop gushing about the former Gopher behemoth and Chicago Bears legend. Of course, it had been Smith, not Nagurski, who won a Heisman and two national championships. But that was classic Bruce Smith: although he was proud of his accomplishments with the Gophers, he didn't dwell on the past. He talked rarely about his football days. "He was just a regular dad," his son said, although this regular dad could still punt and pass with the best of them in the backyard, even in his older age.[4]

Symptoms of intestinal cancer developed in late 1966, and by spring of 1967 it became apparent that Smith would not survive. He spent the summer in Alexandria. "He wanted to be home, where he could hear the boys playing basketball and watch the kids water skiing from our porch off the bedroom," his wife, Gloria, wrote to a friend. "He wanted everyone to have as normal a summer as possible, and whenever I would mention a miracle, he would say, 'I am having my miracle, I will have the summer with my family.' And he did."[5] Smith lost a significant amount of weight, dropping by some estimates to fewer than one hundred pounds.

During the late summer, by then under care at St. Barnabas Hospital, the Reverend William Cantwell encountered Smith in the facility but supposedly knew nothing of his background. In a story that has been spread long after Smith's death, Rev. Cantwell nominated Smith for sainthood due to his resiliency, humbleness, positive attitude, and kindness to other patients in his final days. Bruce Smith died on August 28, 1967, at the age of forty-seven. "I'm just shocked," Bernie Bierman said. "I don't know how I can tell you about Bruce. He was such an outstanding football player, and a great fellow in every respect."[6] Smith's funeral was held three days later, at Immaculate Conception Church in Faribault. Pallbearers included Dick Wildung. After his death, Faribault High School moved to rename its football venue "Bruce Smith Field." Smith was inducted into the College Football Hall of Fame in 1972. "As a player he did more to bring football glory to Minnesota than any other player ever has," Bierman said that year. "I have often said that leaving pure football technique out of the picture entirely that Bruce was one of the finest young men I ever had contact with."[7] Five years later, the Gophers retired his number and eventually inducted him into the "M" Club Hall of Fame. Bruce Smith remains the only football player in University of Minnesota history to win the Heisman Trophy.

Leonard "Butch" Levy (1921–1999) became an outstanding wrestler on the professional circuit after leaving the Los Angeles Dons—at one point competing with high visibility as far away as New Zealand. After moving back to Minnesota and starting a family of three children with his wife Lucky, he continued to moonlight as a wrestler, appearing at venues like the county fair and serving as a color commentator for local professional wrestling at WTCN-TV's old South Minneapolis studios. Levy also worked in the plumbing and heating business, in the insurance industry, and as a stockbroker. He kept in close contact with many of his former Gopher teammates, visiting them often during home games at Memorial Stadium and the Metrodome over the years. "They were just pretty proud," said his son, Peter. "They knew they were the winners."[8] Levy was inducted into the "M" Club Hall of Fame in 1994.

Urban Odson (1918–1986) played one season for Montreal in the Canadian Football League in 1950 following his NFL career. He then worked in the petroleum business in marketing for multiple companies and became active in the Fellowship of Christian Athletes, both in South Dakota and nationally. Many years after his father's playing career, while attending a sophomore geography class at the University of Wyoming, Bruce Odson (the son named for Bruce Smith) encountered a professor originally from the state of Minnesota. "My last name is not real common," Bruce explained, "so he says, '*are you related to Urban Odson?*'" The professor had attended the Minnesota–Northwestern game in 1941 at Memorial Stadium, where he watched Odson throw the key block on "The Talking Play" that helped Bud Higgins dance into the end zone. "He saw that play as a Boy Scout usher," Bruce Odson said. "We spoke about it for fifteen minutes!"[9] Nobody could forget a man of Urban Odson's stature. The Clark native is a member of the South Dakota Sports Hall of Fame and joined the "M" Club Hall of Fame in 2011. Odson's former quarters at Fire Station 19, where he lived all throughout college across from Memorial Stadium, has been converted into a Buffalo Wild Wings restaurant.

Bill Garnaas (1921–2002) worked in the insurance industry for many years, a change of pace from his physically exhausting time with the Navy and the Pittsburgh Steelers. "He loved the game of football," son Bob said. "He loved kids. He was always a park board coach and YMCA coach." Garnaas had an outstanding football mind; he diagrammed plays and mimeographed football fields well into adulthood. He also became a Minnesota Vikings season ticket holder and attended University of Minnesota reunions with his old teammates. In his later years, when he contracted Parkinson's-related dementia, Garnaas still retained many of the happy memories of his college football days. "He spent a lot of time there, in 1941," Bob Garnaas said. "He'd get his scrapbooks out and point, and say, *Dick Wildung, that's the toughest son of a gun you'd ever met!*"[10]

Dick Wildung (1921–2006) made a good living as one of the top players on the Green Bay Packers through the early 1950s, albeit a far cry from the multi-million-dollar contracts of today's NFL. At the end of his playing career, Wildung ran his father-in-law's hardware store in Redwood Falls, Minnesota, coincidentally the same hometown as teammate Joe Lauterbach. After selling the store, Wildung transitioned into a strong career as a heavy equipment dealer and returned to Minneapolis with his family. "He loved football, but he never talked about it," his son Dave said. "He was very humble in that regard." Yet Dave Wildung still remembers one night in particular, when the family lived in South Minneapolis and his father invited about a half-dozen former teammates, including Helge Pukema, to their house. "I sat there in that kitchen that night listening to those guys drinking whatever they were drinking and reminiscing about the days," the younger Wildung said, "and I learned more that night than I probably had ever known before, about what it was like to play football at Minnesota and for Bernie Bierman."[11] Dick Wildung is a member of the "M" Club Hall of Fame (1993), the College Football Hall of Fame (1957), and the Green Bay Packers Hall of Fame (1973). He is also buried at Fort Snelling National Cemetery, along with teammates Bruce Smith, Bill Daley, and Bob Sweiger.

Bob Sweiger (1919–1975) returned to the Twin Cities and worked for many years in the paper industry, including as the vice president and sales manager at Falk Paper Company, following his time in the All-America Football Conference with the New York Yankees and Chicago Hornets. He kept his wife and three children constantly entertained with jokes, humor, and a legendary barbeque chicken recipe. Sweiger followed the Gopher football program closely throughout his later years and attended games in the alumni section as a member of the "M" Club, where his teammates and friends often swarmed him during games. "He was a pretty popular person," his son Michael said. "It was kind of like being with a celebrity."[12] Bob Sweiger died from a heart attack at the age of fifty-six on November 1, 1975, the day Minnesota faced Michigan at Memorial Stadium. Just hours after learning of his death, play-by-play announcer Ray Christensen and athletic director Paul Giel honored Sweiger on the halftime radio broadcast, introducing a new generation of Gopher football fans to the Most Valuable Player of the 1941 national championship team.

Bill Daley (1919–2015) stayed involved with the Minnesota program as a radio announcer for the Gophers after his playing career ended in the AAFC, and he later did some work for the Vikings' broadcasts. Then, he pursued other passions in the art field. Daley worked for almost eighteen years at Jostens Company as a ring and yearbook designer before opening Daley Illustration Gallery in downtown Minneapolis with his wife, Melba, in the late 1970s. During a 1992 interview with Roger Paschke of the Melrose Area Historical Society, Daley recalled some of his favorite memories from Minnesota. "Well, we were national champs. I guess making the team and being part of the team was always great. I enjoyed it. I enjoyed all the moments I had. I enjoyed the practices. I enjoyed the team. I still have a lot of friends from the team."[13] Daley was inducted into the "M" Club Hall of Fame in 2004. Eleven years later, at age ninety-six, he died on October 19, 2015—just twelve days before Minnesota hosted his other former team, Michigan, at TCF Bank Stadium.

Gene Bierhaus (1921–2006) moved back from Colorado in the early 1990s after the death of his beloved wife Jeanne, choosing to spend the final two decades of his life at home in Brainerd, Minnesota, where he had been such a popular and well-known athlete in the 1930s and early 1940s. After his death in 2006, Brainerd High inducted Bierhaus posthumously into the school's Hall of Fame. Some of his track and field records in the Brainerd schools stood until very recently, said his daughter, Kristy. The district also created an award in his honor, the "Dr. Gene Bierhaus Athletic Scholarship," given to a high school senior athlete each year. "I can't even tell you the impact he had on my life," Kristy said. "He's a cornerstone of how I live my life."[14]

Mike Welch (1921–2017) remained in Denver after surviving the USS *Tide* disaster, working in advertising for Shaw-Barton as he rose to regional sales manager and later vice president. He lived in California after retirement and, late in life, attended a 2016 ceremony at TCF Bank Stadium alongside quarterback Warren Plunkett. Returning on the seventy-fifth anniversary of the national championship, they were two of the oldest surviving players from the 1941 Minnesota football team. Welch followed football in his later years but also had a wide array of other interests. "I would call him a Renaissance Man in a way," daughter Deb Welch said, "in the sense that here was a football player and World War II hero, but he also had an artistic talent and would paint. And, up until the week before he died, he played bridge three to four times a week. All of my dad's friends would say he was absolutely the best bridge player they had ever played with."[15]

Warren Plunkett (1920–2018) enrolled at the University of Minnesota's law school after returning from the Navy, courtesy of the GI Bill, and joined the Third Judicial District as a judge in 1955 following an appointment by Governor Orville Freeman. The Minnesota District Court Judges Association named him president in 1976, just one of many prestigious titles Plunkett would hold in the Minnesota legal community over the course of his storied career. During an interview for the Veterans History Project, the former quarterback said his experience on the USS *Sitka* in the dangerous waters of the Pacific forever shaped his perspective. "It made me very concerned for my country. I was willing to fight and die for my country. I'm just glad I didn't have to do the latter."[16]

Joe Lauterbach (1921–1996) and his wife moved from Iowa back to Minneapolis upon his retirement from the insurance industry. Before her death in 1989, Jean had been an outstanding figure skater and golfer, rivaling her husband's talents on the gridiron. Although he talked little about Iwo Jima or about the injuries that caused his leg amputation, Lauterbach took pride in his football career at Minnesota and stayed in contact with teammates like Don Nolander. "He didn't talk about specific plays or specific accomplishments, [rather] it was the camaraderie and the people that he played with," daughter Ann said. "I know that he was tremendously proud of being one of Bernie Bierman's boys."[17]

Bernie Bierman (1894–1977) remained active in the Twin Cities community following his resignation in 1950, making occasional public appearances and offering some radio and newspaper commentary. He reportedly turned down several offers over the years to coach at the professional level, saying the timing was never quite right. The College Football Hall of Fame inducted him as a member in 1955. Bierman's ninety-three victories at the University of Minnesota, during two stints from 1932 to 1941 and 1945 to 1950, still rank second all-time in program history, trailing only his mentor, Dr. Henry L. Williams. Although each of his five national championship teams held a special place in his heart, Bierman later admitted that his first (1934) and last (1941) stood out above the rest. "I believe our 1941 team was potentially as great a team as the 1934 eleven," he said. "The line was probably even better and the backfield could be more potent when all the men were in good shape."[18]

Bierman often marveled at how much college football had changed in the two decades since he left coaching, particularly the near-universal practice of athletic scholarships and the acceleration of pass-heavy offensive systems. Reflecting later on his rocky ending at Minnesota, Bierman acknowledged that he struggled to adjust to the game once he returned from the service. "The big changes came after the war," he said. "It was then that the battle of scholarships began and although it's wonderful that so many have gotten college educations out of it, it has multiplied the pressures of coaching and everything about it."[19]

In 1969, Bierman and wife Clara moved to a retirement community in Laguna Hills, California, receiving a farewell party at the Radisson Hotel before they departed. Bierman survived a heart attack in 1973 but died four years later on March 7, 1977, just four days before his eighty-third birthday. A few weeks after Bierman's death, University of Minnesota political science professor Millard L. Gieske penned a warm tribute to the "Silver Fox," reflecting on those five national championships that carried his home state from the depths of the Great Depression all the way through the remarkable 1941 season and World War II. "During the golden age of radio, tens of thousands of Minnesota boys clung to fictional heroes like Jack Armstrong, Captain Midnight, Tom Mix. Bigger than all of them was Bierman," Gieske wrote. "He was a real person, and his accomplishments, though legendary, were part of Minnesota life."[20]

NOTES

ACKNOWLEDGMENTS

1. *"On the Gopher Squad"*: Bernard Swanson, "Roamin' Round," *Minneapolis Tribune*, May 12, 1943, 16.

INTRODUCTION

1. The next day, a White House spokesperson estimated ninety million listeners ("Expect Long War, Roosevelt Warns," United Press, December 10, 1941), while later estimates put the total closer to sixty-two million ("CBS Says 25,217,000 Heard Truman Friday," *New York Times*, May 26, 1946).

2. "Transcript," Franklin D. Roosevelt Day by Day, A Project of the Pare Lorentz Center at the FDR Presidential Library, http://www.fdrlibrary .marist.edu/daybyday/daylog/december-9th-1941/.

3. "Substitute Draft," December 9, 1941, General Services Administration, National Archives and Records Services, Samuel I. Rosenman Papers, Franklin D. Roosevelt Library and Museum, version date 2013, 101, http:// www.fdrlibrary.marist.edu/_resources/images/msf/msfb0005.

4. Heisman speech quoted with permission from the Rice County Historical Society Collection; RCHS possesses Smith's original typed version of the speech as well as an audio recording.

5. "DiMag Named Top Athlete," Associated Press, December 17, 1941, and "Minnesota Named to Second Place," Associated Press, December 19, 1941.

6. Braven Dyer, "Grantland Rice Here to Cover Local Events," *Los Angeles Times*, December 12, 1941, Part 1, 21.

7. Howie Larson, "Bernie Bierman, Landmark of a Decade," *Minnesota Daily* via *Minnesota Alumni Weekly*, University of Minnesota Alumni Association, vol. 42, nos. 1–7 (July 1942–October 24, 1942): 110, retrieved from the University of Minnesota Digital Conservancy.

8. George A. Barton, "Sportographs," *Minneapolis Sunday Tribune and Star Journal*, November 16, 1941, 36.

9. "Gridder-Grenadier," *Minneapolis Tribune*, May 26, 1943, 15.

10. "Super Legacy," *New York Daily News*, January 31, 1993, 70.

I. RIGHT MAN FOR THE JOB

1. Bob Beebe, "'U' Spring Football Preview Today," *Minneapolis Tribune*, May 10, 1941, 8.

2. *Minneapolis Star*, May 10, 1941, 1 and 4.

3. "Lindbergh Quits Air Corps; Sees His Loyalty Questioned," *New York Times*, April 28, 1941, 1.

4. "Lindbergh Text, 'U.S. Being Led into War Unprepared,'" *St. Louis Post-Dispatch*, May 4, 1941, 2.

5. Charles Johnson, "Bruce Smith's Maroons Win, 20 to 0," *Minneapolis Tribune and Star Journal*, May 11, 1941, 29 and 38.

6. Charles Lindbergh, *Address / by Charles A. Lindbergh, Minneapolis, Minn., May 10, 1941* (New York: America First Committee, 1941), accessed via the Gale Family Library at the Minnesota History Center. Supplemented by "Lindbergh Talk Highlights," *Minneapolis Star*, May 11, 1941, 1.

7. Johnson, "Bruce Smith's Maroons Win," 38.

8. "Minneapolis City Directory 1941," Hennepin County Library.

9. Grantland Rice, "Sportlight by Grantland Rice," *Midland Journal*, August 8, 1941, 6.

10. Francis Powers, *Football Illustrated*, republished in *Minneapolis Star Journal* under the title, "Joe's Task Tough; 'U' Boom Continues," August 26, 1941, 18.

11. "University of Minnesota Sports Release," University of Minnesota athletics archive, March 27, 1941, retrieved from the University of Minnesota Digital Conservancy.

12. *Minnesota Alumni Weekly* (July 1940–October 19, 1940). Note: The Bierman information can be found in the "Sports" section, 16, and "Gophers Face Six Conference Teams," 98. The alumni magazine refers to Bierman as a

"captain" on multiple occasions, but other press outlets sometimes classified him as a "major."

13. Gordon Gammack, "Says Coach Bierman—Gopher Freshman Squads Mediocre," *Des Moines Tribune*, August 19, 1941, 12.

14. The timeline of his early life is largely described in the "Bernie Bierman's Life Story" series that ran in the *Minneapolis Star* in September 1936. Some of the unquoted information contained in this chapter has been derived from Bierman's own words in that published series, as well as the January 27, 1932, edition of the *Minneapolis Tribune*, which extensively covered Bierman's background when he first arrived to coach at the University of Minnesota.

15. Although some published reports about Bierman merely mentioned a bone infection, journalist Edwin Pope wrote in detail about an osteomyelitis diagnosis in *Football's Greatest Coaches* (Atlanta: Tupper and Love, 1955). The excerpt on Bierman was republished in the *Sioux Falls Argus-Leader* on November 20, 1960, 41.

16. "Football World Mourns Death of Dr. Williams," *Minneapolis Star*, June 15, 1931, 13.

17. Allison Danzig, *The History of American Football* (Hoboken, NJ: Prentice-Hall, 1956), 33.

18. Bernie Bierman, "Bernie Bierman's Own Life Story," Chapter No. Two, *Minneapolis Star*, September 9, 1936, 19.

19. *Minneapolis Sunday Tribune*, October 3, 1915, 19.

20. Andrew P. Keefe, "'Bashful Boy' Bierman Grabs Many Laurels," *Minneapolis Morning Tribune*, October 25, 1915, 10.

21. Melgs O. Frost, Special to the *Tribune* from New Orleans, "Bernie Bierman, Sensation of South, Unique among Ranks of American College Football Coaches," *Minneapolis Sunday Tribune*, October 25, 1931, 21.

22. James P. Quirk, *Minnesota Football: The Golden Years 1932–1941* (Grantsburg, WI: Self-published, 1984), 20.

23. Bernie Bierman, "Bernie Bierman's Own Life Story," Chapter No. Three, *Minneapolis Star*, September 10, 1936, 22.

24. Letter from Bierman to University of Montana administration, May 17, 1919, HR file and President's Office records related to Bernie Bierman provided by the University of Montana Mansfield Library Archives, Collection Number RG 30, Bierman, B.W.

25. Letter from University of Montana President Charles Clapp to University of Minnesota President Lotus Coffman, January 24, 1930, provided by the University of Montana Mansfield Library Archives.

26. Bernie Bierman, "Bernie Bierman's Own Life Story," Chapter No. Six, *Minneapolis Star*, September 14, 1936, 17.

27. Letter from Bernie Bierman to Tulane administration, September 17, 1928, Bierman, Bernard W., Information files collection, ua-01158, University Archives, Elmer Andersen Library.

28. Clark D. Shaughnessy, "Bernie Bierman to Take His Version of 'Old' Minnesota Shift Back Home as Football Coach at Gopher School," Associated Press via *Shreveport Times*, December 9, 1931, 11.

29. Chandler Forman, "600 'U' Fans Welcome Bierman Home as Head Coach," *Minneapolis Tribune*, January 19, 1932, 14.

30. George A. Barton, "Sportographs," *Minneapolis Tribune*, February 10, 1941, 12.

31. Bernie Bierman and Frank Mayer, *Winning Football: Strategy, Psychology and Technique* (New York: Whittlesey House, 1937), dedication page on opening flap.

32. John D. McCallum, *Big Ten Football Since 1895* (Boston: Chilton Book Company, 1976), 54.

33. McCallum, *Big Ten Football Since 1895*, 57.

34. Hubert H. Humphrey, "Chicago: Football Writers Association, August 6, 1965," accessed via Minnesota Historical Society digital archives, http://www2.mnhs.org/library/findaids/00442/pdfa/00442-01654.pdf.

35. Some of this information is based on the author's own interviews with family members of the Gopher players (supplemented by published accounts of recruiting rules, including descriptions by Quirk in *The Golden Years*, 8–9).

36. "Atherton Outlines New Purity Policy," United Press via *Oakland Tribune*, January 7, 1941, 13.

37. Robert M. Hutchins' 1954 piece for *Sports Illustrated*, "College Football Is an Infernal Nuisance," was one helpful resource for this information. The article was originally published in the October 18, 1954, edition of *SI* and has been added to the *SI Vault* website: https://vault.si.com/vault/1954/10/18/college-football-is-an-infernal-nuisance.

38. Bernard W. Bierman, "You Don't Have to Subsidize to Win," 1941, 6, Bierman, Bernard W., Information files collection, ua-01158, University Archives, Elmer Andersen Library.

39. Joe Hendrickson, *Esquire*, September 1945, 98.

40. "Jackie Robinson, UCLA football star, #28, 1939," UCLA Film & Television Archive, 2:10 mark on official "UCLAFilmTVArchive" YouTube video, https://www.youtube.com/watch?v=SKOKu_P6pSE. Note: This archive shows a newsreel, presented by NBC's Bill Stern as a highlight package. It is unclear if the audio, which includes natural crowd noise, comes from the live broadcast of the UCLA–USC game. However, this author believes the announcer's verbal description of Robinson's first down (whether live or after the fact) helps

the reader understand the power of mass media in college football during this time period.

41. J. Cullen Fentress, "UCLA's Exciting Bruins and USC's Trojans Battle to 0–0 Deadlock," *California Eagle*, December 14, 1939, 12.

42. Radio listings, *Salt Lake Telegram*, September 26, 1941, 20.

2. FARIBAULT FLASH

1. Grantland Rice, "Minnesota's Bruce Smith May Be Star of Season," *Hartford Daily Courant*, September 3, 1941, 14.

2. Bert McGrane, "Fans Offer to Wager No Foe Checks Norse," *Des Moines Register*, September 12, 1941, 9.

3. Johnny Kerr, "Kerr-ent Sports by Johnny Kerr," *Faribault Journal Weekly*, July 10, 1941, 2.

4. *Faribault Journal*, February 18, 1920, 1, accessed via Minnesota Historical Society Digital Newspaper Hub.

5. Tom and Sam Akers, *The Game Breaker* (Wayzata, MN: Ralph Turtinen Pub. Co., 1977), 24.

6. Author interview with June Smith, August 2019.

7. The Dalby Database, accessed through the Rice County Historical Society website, served as an outstanding resource, in addition to the physical archives in Faribault. This author made use of the obituaries, birth records, newspaper articles, and "People in Books" sections made available by the database. The Dalby Database also provided online access to text from the "Rice County Families" book published in 1981, in which Lucius Smith described key details from his life. http://www.dalbydata.com/.

8. "Faribault Athlete Makes Reputation," *Faribault Journal*, December 27, 1911, 1, reprinted from *Pioneer Press*, accessed via Minnesota Historical Society Digital Newspaper Hub.

9. Akers, *The Game Breaker*, 15.

10. Lucius Smith, "Smith Family Story," 56, from the Rice County Historical Society Collection in Faribault, Minnesota.

11. Greg Zurn, "Brockmeyer Legacy to Wausau Is a Football Tradition," *Wausau Daily Record-Herald*, April 28, 1941, 17.

12. Akers, *The Game Breaker*, 35.

13. "Mal Eiken Directs Faribault Gridders," *Minneapolis Tribune*, September 5, 1937, 19.

14. "Second Generation of Smiths at Faribault," *Minneapolis Star*, October 15, 1937, 23.

15. *Faribault Daily News*, October 30, 1937.

16. Author interview with June Smith, August 2019.

17. Akers, *The Game Breaker*, 38.

18. Ben Petry and Andy Wilhide, "Minnesota's Greatest Generation, Transcript: Millie Bowers Johnson Oral History Interview," July 18, 2008, in Northfield, Minnesota, accessed online via Minnesota Historical Society, http://www.mnhs.org/mgg/artifact/mjohnsonoh.

19. *Minneapolis Tribune Sports*, September 27, 1938, 14.

20. Gordon Gilmore, "Nagurski-Cleated Turf Drew Smith to U," *St. Paul Pioneer Press*, September 14, 1941, 3.

21. "Gopher Eleven Routs Arizona," Associated Press via *Sioux City Journal*, October 1, 1939, 21.

22. Gilmore, "Nagurski-Cleated Turf," 3.

3. THE SUPPORTING CAST

1. Bob Husted, "The Referee," *Dayton Herald*, September 3, 1941, 12.

2. "Clark Honors Its All-American," *Daily Argus-Leader*, January 15, 1941, 8.

3. "129 to Try Out for Freshman Football at Minnesota," Associated Press via *Eau Claire Leader*, September 28, 1937, 6.

4. Bob Beebe, "Introducing New Gophers," *Minneapolis Tribune*, September 23, 1938, 23.

5. "Just a Big Boy," *Minneapolis Tribune*, August 16, 1941, 7.

6. Author interview with Bruce Odson, April 2019.

7. Bob Beebe, "'11' Improved Says Mentor," *Minneapolis Tribune*, October 15, 1939, 4.

8. Author interviews with son Dave Wildung, May 2019, brother Hal Wildung, July 2020, and niece Jane Wildung Lanphere, July 2020.

9. Al McIntosh, "More or Less Personal Chaff," *Rock County Star*, November 27, 1941, 1.

10. "Introducing—Star's All-State Outstate," *Minneapolis Star*, November 19, 1938, 8.

11. Letter from Dallas Ward to Dick Wildung, June 15, 1939, provided by Jane Wildung Lanphere from the Wildung family scrapbook.

12. Author interviews and correspondence with son Dave Wildung, May 2019, brother Hal Wildung, July 2020, and niece Jane Wildung Lanphere, July 2020.

13. "400 Honor 'Capt. Dick' at Testimonial Dinner," *Rock County Star*, December 25, 1941, 1.

14. Bernie Bierman letter to Dick Wildung, June 27, 1940, provided by Jane Wildung Lanphere from the Wildung family scrapbook.

15. "Mother," provided by Jane Wildung Lanphere from the Wildung family scrapbook.

16. "The 1940 Gophers," University of Minnesota News Service, athletics archive, 6.

17. McIntosh, "More or Less Personal Chaff," 1.

18. Minnesota 1940 Census, Census.gov, https://www2.census.gov/library/publications/decennial/1940/population-volume-1/33973538v1ch06.pdf.

19. Dick Gordon, "'U' Has Most Local Grid Starters Since 1941," *Minneapolis Star*, 1959, via the scrapbook of Bob Garnaas.

20. Bill Carlson, "Fumble!" *Minneapolis Star*, October 2, 1937, 4.

21. Author interview with Peter Levy, May 2019.

22. Carey McWilliams, "Minneapolis: The Curious Twin," *Common Ground*, Autumn 1946, 61, accessed from link posted by the Hennepin County Library, https://hclib.tumblr.com/post/18024468678/minneapolis-the-curious-twin-the-link-above-is.

23. Sarah Atwood, "This List Is Not Complete, Minnesota's Jewish Resistance to the Silver Legion of America, 1936–1940," Minnesota Historical Society's *Minnesota History* magazine (Winter 2018–2019): 142–55 (specific quote on 143), accessed online via http://collections.mnhs.org/MNHistoryMagazine/articles/66/v66i04p142-155.pdf.

24. McWilliams, "Minneapolis: The Curious Twin," 61–62.

25. *"Gentile Married"*: "Executives and Managers," *Minneapolis Tribune*, May 24, 1937, 16.

26. Ad appears under "Grocery Store," *Minneapolis Tribune*, September 11, 1938, 4, Classifieds.

27. "Kristallnacht," United States Holocaust Memorial Museum, last accessed December 2020, https://encyclopedia.ushmm.org/content/en/article/kristallnacht.

28. Peter Vaughan, "The Immigrants: Minnesota Was Their Doorway to Freedom," *Minneapolis Star*, October 5, 1973, 17, Variety 1B.

29. Author interview with Peter and Rand Levy, May 2019.

30. Bernie Bierman letter to Butch Levy, March 6, 1939, Leonard (Butch) Levy papers, Nathan and Theresa Berman Upper Midwest Jewish Archives, University of Minnesota Libraries, Minneapolis, Folder 3.

31. George Hauser letter to Butch Levy, August 4, 1939, Leonard (Butch) Levy papers, Nathan and Theresa Berman Upper Midwest Jewish Archives, University of Minnesota Libraries, Minneapolis, Folder 3.

32. Charles Johnson, "Johnson's Lowdown on Sports," February 15, 1940, 22.

33. Leonard Levy, "Leonard 'Butch' Levy LBL Scrapbook," University of Minnesota Libraries, Nathan and Theresa Berman Upper Midwest Jewish Archives, accessed digitally, umedia.lib.umn.edu/item/p16022coll475:5728.

34. Charles Johnson, "Lowdown on Sports," *Minneapolis Star*, November 18, 1940, 19.

35. "West High Yearbook 1938," Hennepin County Library, 1938, 73, https://digitalcollections.hclib.org/digital/collection/Yearbooks/id/78878/rec/41.

36. Charles Johnson, "Johnson's Lowdown on Sports," *Minneapolis Star*, October 27, 1937, 18.

37. Bill Carlson, "Washington Ends Long Local Grid Reign," *Minneapolis Star*, November 12, 1937, 23.

38. "Central High Yearbook 1938," Hennepin County Library, 1938, 61, https://digitalcollections.hclib.org/digital/collection/Yearbooks/id/10844/rec/36.

39. "Central High Yearbook 1938," 104, https://digitalcollections.hclib.org/digital/collection/Yearbooks/id/10887/rec/36.

40. R. A. Lofstrom, "Right and Left in Sports," *St. Cloud Times*, October 9, 1940, 8.

41. Joel A. Rippel, *Game of My Life Minnesota Gophers: Memorable Stories of Gopher Football* (New York: Sports Publishing, 2007), 14.

42. Roger Paschke, "Oral history with Bill Daley, Minneapolis, Minnesota," Melrose Area Historical Society, October 16, 1992, https://reflections.mndigital.org/catalog/p16022coll28:344.

43. "University of Minnesota Sports Release," University of Minnesota athletics archive, October 1941.

44. Bernard Swanson, "Thanks, Fellas; Let's Not Play," *Minneapolis Tribune*, August 26, 1941, 13. Quote attributed to George Kirksey in *Look* magazine as reprinted by the *Tribune*.

45. *Minneapolis Tribune,* March 7, 1941, 19.

46. "Marshall Yearbook 1939," Hennepin County Library, 1939, 64, https://digitalcollections.hclib.org/digital/collection/Yearbooks/id/28316/rec/16.

47. George A. Barton, "Sportographs," *Minneapolis Tribune*, November 28, 1939, 20.

48. Interview with Bob Garnaas, September 2019.

49. "The 1940 Gophers," University of Minnesota News Service and athletics archive, retrieved through the University of Minnesota Digital Conservancy.

50. "University of Minnesota Sports Release," University of Minnesota athletics archive, September 24, 1942.

51. "University of Minnesota News Service Sports Release," August 11, 1941.

52. Gordon Gammack, "Says Coach Bierman—Gopher Freshman Squads Mediocre," *Des Moines Tribune*, August 19, 1941, 12.

53. "Grid Coaches Expect Normal Year," Associated Press via *Ithaca Journal*, August 28, 1941, 16.

4. "FOOTBALL IS ONLY A GAME"

1. "The Holocaust and World War II: Key Dates," United States Holocaust Memorial Museum, served as a helpful resource and reminder of well-documented international events, https://encyclopedia.ushmm.org/content/en/article/the-holocaust-and-world-war-ii-key-dates.

2. Karissa White and Brian Horrigan, "Minnesota's Greatest Generation Oral History Project: Minnesota Native American Interviews: Interview with William N. Amyotte," August 11, 2006, Minnesota Historical Society, http://collections.mnhs.org/cms/display?irn=10803307.

3. "How Did Public Opinion about Entering World War II Change between 1939 and 1941?" United States Holocaust Memorial Museum, https://exhibitions.ushmm.org/americans-and-the-holocaust/us-public-opinion-world-war-II-1939-1941.

4. "America's Wars," United States Department of Veterans Affairs, https://www.va.gov/opa/publications/factsheets/fs_americas_wars.pdf.

5. Michael Greenberg, "Minnesota Liberators of Concentration Camps Oral History Project, Transcript: Wayne D. Hanson Oral History Interview," April 20, 1982, Minnesota Historical Society, https://media.mnhs.org/things/cms/10264/364/AV1996_48_3_M.pdf.

6. Edward S. Shapiro, "The Approach of War: Congressional Isolationism and Anti-Semitism, 1939–1941," *American Jewish History*, vol. 74, no. 1 (1984): 64, www.jstor.org/stable/23882497.

7. Text of Roosevelt's July 19, 1940, DNC speech, Miller Center for Public Affairs, University of Virginia, https://millercenter.org/the-presidency/presidential-speeches/july-19-1940-democratic-national-convention.

8. Eleanor Roosevelt, "My Day" column, November 21, 1944, verbatim reference to October 30, 1940, speech by president, the Eleanor Roosevelt Papers Digital Edition, https://www2.gwu.edu/~erpapers/myday/display-doc.cfm?_y=1944&_f=md056954.

9. Jack Cuddy, "Famed Stars Register for Conscription," United Press via *San Bernardino Daily*, 18.

10. "Joe Cronin and Billy Conn Get Their Cards," Associated Press via *Burlington Free Press and Times*, October 17, 1940, 13.

11. Cuddy, "Famed Stars Register," 18.

12. The National Archives in St. Louis, Missouri; *WWII Draft Registration Cards for Minnesota, 10/16/1940–03/31/1947*; Record Group: *Records of the Selective Service System, 147*; Box: *218*, accessed via Hennepin County Library's subscription to Ancestry Library Edition.

13. Charles Johnson, "Lowdown on Sports," *Minneapolis Star Journal*, May 12, 1941, 20.

14. Letter from Edgar M. Jaeger to Seeman Kaplan of Minneapolis, June 4, 1941, Joseph H. Ball, Theodor Broch, Stephen T. Early, Clark M. Eichelberger, Douglas Fairbanks, Richard P. Gale, Ernest W. Gibson, et al. *Committee Records, 1940–1942*, 1941, accessed in the Reading Room at the Minnesota History Center.

15. Robert E. Sherwood, *Roosevelt and Hopkins: An Intimate History* (New York: Harper and Brothers, 1948), 344.

16. May 29, 1941, speech, printed in *Minnesota Alumni Weekly*, May 31, 1941, 511.

17. "University of Minnesota News Service Sports Release," athletics archive, July 16, 1941.

18. "Jobs for Football Men Are Too Good," *National Enterprise Association* via *Billings Gazette*, June 1, 1941, 9.

19. "Bill Diehl Is Hit by Cupid and U.S. Draft," *Quad-City Times*, January 8, 1941, 10, and "College Lose Few Gridders Due to Draft," Bill Boni, Associated Press via *Gettysburg Times*, August 19, 1941, 3.

20. Associated Press, May 20, 1941.

21. Leo Kautz, *Daily Times*, May 20, 1941, 17.

22. Bob Beebe, "Van't Hull Will Report to Naval Academy Tuesday," *Minneapolis Tribune*, June 19, 1941, 18.

23. Edgar Lechner, *Dr. Edgar Lechner: A North Dakota Farm Boy Finds His Way to Gopher Football, Dentistry, and Family: A Memoir* (Eden Prairie, MN: Lilja Press, 2016), 43.

24. "Draft Takes Lundeen, Promising Gopher End," *Minneapolis Tribune*, July 22, 1941, 13.

25. Charles Johnson, "Lowdown on Sports," July 6, 1941, 32.

26. Bernard Swanson, "Draft Threatens to Snatch Bruce Smith from Gophers," *Minneapolis Tribune*, July 18, 1941, 13.

27. This author uses the term "half-dozen" based on Bierman's August 15 statement to Charles Johnson ("Lowdown on Sports," *Minneapolis Star*, August 15, 1941, 29) that estimated four losses due to the draft to that point. Adding Jim Shearer in September and possibly another defection or two, this author felt "half-dozen" was the most accurate description.

28. Charles Johnson, "Pukema Back as 64 Report for Practice," *Minneapolis Star*, September 10, 1941, 26.

29. "Heavy Demand for 'U' Season Grid Tickets," *Minneapolis Star Journal*, June 26, 1941, 35.

5. "WASHINGTON FIRST"

1. "With Minneapolis Marines in Iceland," *Minneapolis Star Journal*, September 11, 1941, 4; "Iceland Duty 'Vacation' to Marines from City," *Minneapolis Star Journal*, September 9, 1941, 22.

2. "Text of *Greer* Incident Report," Associated Press via *Boston Globe*, October 15, 1941, 14; John L. Zimmerman, "The First Marine Brigade (Provisional), Iceland 1941–1942," United States Marine Corps, 1946, accessed online, https://www.usmcu.edu/Portals/218/firstmarinebriga00unit.pdf.

3. Text of Roosevelt's September 11 fireside chat, Miller Center for Public Affairs, University of Virginia, https://millercenter.org/the-presidency/presidential-speeches/september-11-1941-fireside-chat-18-greer-incident#dp-expandable-text.

4. "The Text of Lindbergh's Address in Des Moines Coliseum," *Des Moines Tribune*, September 12, 1941, 8.

5. "Lindy's Talk Likened to Nazi Propaganda," United Press via *Brooklyn Daily Eagle*, September 12, 1941, 1.

6. "How Did Public Opinion about Entering World War II Change between 1939 and 1941?" United States Holocaust Memorial Museum, https://exhibitions.ushmm.org/americans-and-the-holocaust/us-public-opinion-world-war-II-1939-1941.

7. "Entire City Listened to Roosevelt Speech," *Philadelphia Inquirer*, September 12, 1941, 11.

8. Gordon Gilmore, "Nagurski-Cleated Turf Drew Bruce Smith to U," *Saint Paul Pioneer Press*, September 14, 1941, 3, Second Section.

9. Charles Johnson, "65 Gridders Report, Set to Start Drill," *Minneapolis Star*, September 8, 1941, 18.

10. "First 'U' Drills 17 Days Off," *Minneapolis Star Journal*, August 24, 1941, 32.

11. Bruce Smith letter to teammates, August 23, 1941, from the Rice County Historical Society Collection.

12. Charles Johnson, "Lowdown on Sports," *Minneapolis Star Journal*, September 9, 1941, 19.

13. Joe Hendrickson, "Injured Odson out of Scrimmages," *Minneapolis Star Journal*, September 12, 1941, 30.

14. Charles Johnson, "Lowdown on Sports," *Minneapolis Star Journal*, September 12, 1941, 31.

15. George Barton, "Sportographs," *Minneapolis Tribune*, September 18, 1941, 17.

16. Smith letter to teammates, August 23, 1941.

17. "Football Program, University of Washington vs. University of Minnesota, September 27, 1941," 3, University of Washington Libraries, Special Collections, https://digitalcollections.lib.washington.edu/digital/collection/pioneerlife/id/7109.

18. "Minnesota Coach Rates Line as One of Greatest," Associated Press via *Spokesman-Review*, September 16, 1941, 13.

19. Perry Dotson, "Huskies Have 24 Lettermen to Face Minnesota Saturday," *Saint Paul Pioneer Press*, September 21, 1941, 3, Second Section.

20. Perry Dotson, "Towns Cheer Gophers," *St. Paul Pioneer Press*, September 24, 1941, 13.

21. The information about the players' food comes from both Perry Dotson's article in the *St. Paul Dispatch*, September 24, 1941, as well as a press release from the University of Minnesota News Service. Additional information about the Gophers' trek and logistics comes from a variety of press clippings and U of M news releases, including but not limited to *Minnesota Alumni Weekly*, *St. Paul Dispatch*, *St. Paul Pioneer Press*, *Minneapolis Tribune*, and *Minneapolis Star*.

22. Perry Dotson, *St. Paul Dispatch*, September 24, 1941, 41.

23. "University of Minnesota Football Team and Party en route to Seattle, Wash.," pamphlet found in Leonard (Butch) Levy papers, Nathan and Theresa Berman Upper Midwest Jewish Archives, University of Minnesota Libraries, Minneapolis, Folder 4.

24. Road trip pamphlet.

25. Lechner, *Dr. Edgar Lechner: A North Dakota Farm Boy*, 45.

26. July 1941–October 25, 1941, edition.

27. "Mayor Returns, Praises Seattle for Hospitality," *Minneapolis Star*, September 29, 1941, 17.

28. Quintard Taylor, "Swing the Door Wide: World War II Wrought a Profound Transformation in Seattle's Black Community," Washington State Historical Society, *Columbia Magazine*, vol. 9, no. 2 (Summer 1995): https://www.washingtonhistory.org/wp-content/uploads/2020/04/swing-door-wide.pdf.

29. Perry Dotson, "King's Navy Pulls for Huskies," *St. Paul Pioneer Press*, September 27, 1941, 12.

30. Henry J. McCormick, "No Foolin'!" *Wisconsin State Journal*, September 26, 1941, 19.

31. "Husky Stadium," https://static.gohuskies.com/old_site/pdf/m-footbl/03guide-husky-stadium.pdf.

32. "Soldiers See Game," Associated Press via *Spokesman-Review*, September 28, 1941, 9.

33. Telegram to Butch Levy, "Leonard 'Butch' Levy LBL Scrapbook," University of Minnesota Libraries, Nathan and Theresa Berman Upper Midwest Jewish Archives, https://umedia.lib.umn.edu/item/p16022coll475:5728.

34. George Edmond, "Gophers Beat Huskies, 14–6, in Battle of Football Titans," *St. Paul Pioneer Press*, September 28, 1941, 1, Second Section.

35. Charles Johnson, "Halfback Scoots to Two Scores," *Minneapolis Star Journal*, September 28, 1941, 28.

36. Perry Dotson, "Better Than '40—Bernie," *St. Paul Pioneer Press*, September 28, 1941, 1, Second Section.

37. Lucius Smith, "Smith Family Story," 102, from the Rice County Historical Society Collection in Faribault, Minnesota.

38. Gail Fowler, Associated Press via *Sioux City Journal*, September 28, 1941, 28.

39. Bernie Bierman, "Gopher Star End Lost; Teamwork Pleases Bierman," Bierman column via *Des Moines Tribune*, September 29, 1941, 13.

40. Bob Beebe, "Greatest Gopher Team We've Played—Phelan," *Minneapolis Star*, September 28, 1941, 30.

41. Perry Dotson, "Better Than '40—Bernie," *St. Paul Pioneer Press*, September 28, 1941, Sports Page 1.

42. Letter to Butch Levy, Leonard (Butch) Levy papers, Nathan and Theresa Berman Upper Midwest Jewish Archives, University of Minnesota Libraries, Minneapolis, Folder 4.

43. *Minneapolis Sunday Tribune and Star Journal*, September 28, 1941.

44. "Gophers Greeted at Havre Stop," *Great Falls Tribune*, September 30, 1941, 10.

45. Lechner, *Dr. Edgar Lechner: A North Dakota Farm Boy*, 45.

46. "Golden Gophers Get Angel Food Cake as Gift from Lechners," *Wells County Free Press* via *Hope Pioneer*, October 16, 1941, 2.

47. George Edmond, "Gophers Tops in Toughness, Huskies Say," *St. Paul Dispatch*, September 29, 1941.

48. "Opening Convocation Address," *Minnesota Alumni Weekly*, October 11, 1941, 69.

49. Information on campus war preparations and the Ordnance Plant comes from various editions of *Minnesota Alumni Weekly*, as well as Kara Sorensen, "Twin Cities Army Ammunition Plant," MNopedia, Minnesota Historical Society, http://www.mnopedia.org/place/twin-cities-army-ammunition-plant.

50. "Ball That Beat Illini in 1924," *St. Paul Pioneer Press*, October 10, 1941, 15.

6. RIVALRY RENEWED

1. The University of Minnesota's entire online archive of Memorial Stadium can be found at "The Brickhouse" site, https://gallery.lib.umn.edu/exhibits/show/memorial-stadium-1924-1992/brickhouse.

2. University of Minnesota, "Memorial Stadium Dedication Program," *Gallery*, "The New Stadium—What and Why," 5, https://gallery.lib.umn.edu/items/show/4515.

3. George A. Barton, "Clarence Schutte Outshines Grange," *Minneapolis Tribune*, November 16, 1924, 35.

4. "Revenge in His Heart: Zupzet?" *Minneapolis Daily Times*, October 9, 1941, clippings provided by the University of Illinois Archives.

5. Letter from President Willard to Robert Zuppke, Robert Zuppke Papers 1879–1957, Box 2, University of Illinois Archives, July 1, 1941.

6. *Champaign News-Gazette*, September 9, 1941, provided by the University of Illinois Archives.

7. "Bierman Sees Zuppkes as Most Versatile," *Minnesota Daily*, October 7, 1941, 6.

8. Dick Cullum, "Thinkers! That Is What Bernie Wants," *Minneapolis Daily Times*, October 9, 1941, clippings provided by the University of Illinois Archives.

9. Dave Hoff, "Bierman Warns His Gopher Goliaths to Beware Illini Speed," Associated Press via *Alton Daily Telegraph*, October 9, 1941, 11.

10. Wilfrid Smith, "Illini Davids Brave Gopher Goliath Today," *Chicago Tribune*, October 11, 1941, 19.

11. "Higgins Routes Plebes," *Minnesota Daily*, October 1, 1941, 7.

12. "Must Win in Line—Bierman," *Minneapolis Star Journal*, October 10, 1941, 28.

13. Jack Guenther, "Zuppke May Wish He Had a Pension," United Press via *Minneapolis Tribune*, October 10, 1941, 19.

14. David V. Felts, "Second Thoughts," *Decatur Herald*, October 11, 1941, 4.

15. *Minneapolis Tribune*, October 11, 1941, 1.

16. "Early Recollections of Minnesota Football," Price Wickersham, 1877–1946, University of Minnesota Archives, Elmer Andersen Library.

17. "With the Sideliner," *Minnesota Daily*, October 14, 1941, 7.

18. Halsey Hall, "Bierman Pleased by Gopher Power," *Minneapolis Star*, October 12, 1941, 30.

19. Wilfrid Smith, "Illini Crushed, 34–6, under Gopher Attack," *Chicago Tribune*, October 12, 1941, 33.

20. *St. Paul Dispatch*, October 13, 1941, 14.

21. George Edmond, *St. Paul Dispatch*, October 13, 1941, 13.

22. "Gophers Lick Little Illini," Associated Press via *Lansing State Journal*, October 12, 1941, 18.

23. Bernie Bierman, "Coach Notes Letdown in Second Half," Bernie Bierman column via *Minneapolis Star*, October 13, 1941, 18.

7. THE LITTLE MAN

1. Alex Zelenski, "Wolverines Crush Pitt Panthers, 40–0," *Pitt News*, October 13, 1941, 6, accessed online via Documenting Pitt, Historic Records of the University of Pittsburgh.

2. "Panthers Not Awed by Minnesota Team; Face Gophers Saturday," *Morning Call*, Allentown, Pennsylvania, October 15, 1941, 17.

3. "Panthers Not Awed," 17.

4. "40,000 to Watch Woefully Weak Panthers Face Mighty Gophers," *Pittsburgh Press*, October 18, 1941, 11.

5. "Bierman Warns of Pitt Strength," *Minnesota Daily*, October 16, 1941, 1.

6. Charles Johnson, "Team Better, Morale Okay upon Arrival," *Minneapolis Star Journal*, October 17, 1941, 26.

7. "Bob Sweiger May Miss Panther Tilt," *Minnesota Daily*, October 14, 1941, 7.

8. "Governor of Minnesota Sees Fundamentals Return," *Pittsburgh Post-Gazette*, October 18, 1941, 13.

9. "Pepper Urges U.S. to Avenge Ship Attack," United Press via *St. Louis Star and Times*, October 17, 1941, 2.

10. "Confidential, Press Conference #776," Press Conferences of President Franklin D. Roosevelt, 1933–1945, Franklin D. Roosevelt Presidential Library and Museum, 774–78, "October 10, 1941–October 24, 1941," 29, http://www.fdrlibrary.marist.edu/_resources/images/pc/pc0124.pdf.

11. "Hull and Welles in Lengthy Talk with Tokyo Envoy," Associated Press via *St. Louis Post-Dispatch*, October 18, 1941, 1.

12. "Governor of Minnesota Sees Fundamentals Return," 13.

13. Alex Zelenski, "Gophers Rout Clawless Panthers, 39–0," *Pitt News*, October 20, 1941, 5.

14. "Washburn Yearbook 1939," Hennepin County Library, 1939, 113, https://digitalcollections.hclib.org/digital/collection/Yearbooks/id/74479/rec/4.

15. Charles Johnson, "Higgins Is Sensation in Victory," *Minneapolis Star Journal*, October 18, 1941, 28.

16. Chester L. Smith, *Pittsburgh Press* via *Minneapolis Star* reprint of game reactions from visiting writers, October 20, 1941, 16.

17. Harry Keck, "Minnesota Runs Wild against Pitt, 39–0," *Pittsburgh Sun-Telegraph*, October 19, 1941, 28.

18. Bernie Bierman, "Gophers off Stride for 20 Minutes," Bernie Bierman column via *Minneapolis Star*, October 20, 1941, 15.

19. Joe Hendrickson, "'Guess They Couldn't See Me behind All the Interference,' Says Higgins," *Minneapolis Star*, October 20, 1941, 15.

20. Bernie Bierman, "Wolverines a Surprise—Bierman," *Minneapolis Star Journal*, October 20, 1941, 15.

21. Halsey Hall, "Higgins, Wildung Gophers' Heroes," *Minneapolis Star*, October 19, 1941, 30.

22. Bill Boni, "Upsurge of Texas 'U' Features U.S. Grids," Associated Press via *Minneapolis Tribune*, October 20, 1941, 14.

23. Art Hill, "High and Inside," *Michigan Daily*, October 16, 1941, 3, accessed via Michigan Daily Digital Archives, University of Michigan-Bentley Historical Library.

8. LITTLE BROWN JUG ARMAGEDDON

1. "The Michigan Stadium Story," Exhibit, Bentley Historical Library, University of Michigan, https://bentley.umich.edu/athdept/stadium/stadtext/stadbild.htm.

2. Joel Stone, "Detroit: The Arsenal of Democracy," Detroit Historical Society, https://detroithistorical.org/sites/default/files/lessonPlans/J.Stone_.pdf.

3. Herb Baker, "Navy, Northwestern Picked to Take Big Grid Games," Associated Press via *Evening Star*, Washington, D.C., October 24, 1941, C-2.

4. "Ticket Lack Blame Laid to Students," *Michigan Daily*, October 22, 1941, 1.

5. Special to the *Star Journal*, "110,000 Want to See Contest; Wolverines Battered, but Unhurt," *Minneapolis Star Journal*, October 21, 1941, 21.

6. Homer Swander and Hale Champion, "Tickets for Gopher Tilt Bring Students Distress," *Michigan Daily*, October 21, 1941, 1.

7. "Kuzma, New Michigan Hero, No Harmon and Knows It," dateline Ann Arbor, via *Kenosha News*, October 24, 1941, 12.

8. "Gophers Respect Westfall," Associated Press via *Montana Standard*, October 24, 1941, 10.

9. Jack Guenther, "Smith Only Back with U.S. Fame," United Press via *Minneapolis Star Journal*, October 21, 1941, 22.

10. "Crisler Says Michigan Low but Talks Favorably," Associated Press via *Montana Standard*, October 24, 1941, 10.

11. George A. Barton, "Rathbun and Oss Quit Minnesota Board in Rumpus over Coaches," *Minneapolis Tribune*, February 12, 1930, 18.

12. Fritz Crisler to Bernie Bierman, April 27, 1931, H. O. Crisler papers 1922–1978, Box 1, Bentley Historical Library, University of Michigan.

13. Bernie Bierman letter to Fritz Crisler, June 13, 1931, H. O. Crisler papers 1922–1978, Box 1, Bentley Historical Library, University of Michigan.

14. "Two University Officials Deny Bierman Rumor," *Minneapolis Star*, September 23, 1931, 14.

15. "Tulane Coach to Minnesota," Associated Press via *Huntsville Times*, December 6, 1931, 13.

16. "Princeton Grid Position Offered to Fritz Crisler," *Chicago Tribune*, February 23, 1932, 19.

17. H. O. Crisler papers 1922–1978, Box 1, Bentley Historical Library, University of Michigan.

18. Fritz Crisler to Lotus Coffman, March 7, 1932, H. O. Crisler papers 1922–1978, Box 1, Bentley Historical Library, University of Michigan.

19. Perry Dotson, "Lack of Pep Worries Coaches," *St. Paul Pioneer Press*, October 24, 1941, 15.

20. Hal Wilson, "Capacity Crowd to See Thriller," *Michigan Daily*, October 25, 1941, 1.

21. Charles Johnson, "'Beat Minnesota' Posters Greet Gophers; Daley Back at Fullback, Sweiger at Half," *Minneapolis Star Journal*, October 24, 1941, 24.

22. Perry Dotson, "Ann Arbor Population Tripled," *St. Paul Pioneer Press*, October 25, 1941, 10.

23. Multiple newspapers reported an attendance record at Michigan Stadium in the fall of 1941, but current University of Michigan archives show a revised figure of 84,658. Regardless, it is still fair to say the game attracted *one* of the largest crowds in history. Source: https://bentley.umich.edu/athdept/football/fbteam/1941fbt.htm.

24. Leonard Levy, "Leonard 'Butch' Levy LBL Scrapbook," University of Minnesota Libraries, Nathan and Theresa Berman Upper Midwest Jewish Archives, https://umedia.lib.umn.edu/item/p16022coll475:5728.

25. Halsey Hall, "Minnesota's Sig Harris Sort of Little Brown Jug, Himself," *Minneapolis Star Journal*, September 17, 1941, 30.

26. Rachel Reed, Brian Williams, and Greg Kinney, "The Origins of the Little Brown Jug," Bentley Historical Library, University of Michigan, https://bentley.umich.edu/features/the-origins-of-the-little-brown-jug/; "The Little Brown Jug –– Minnesota vs. Michigan," University of Minnesota Athletics,

https://gophersports.com/sports/2018/5/21/sports-m-footbl-spec-rel-brown-jug-html.aspx.

27. R. A. Lofstrom, "Right and Left in Sports," *St. Cloud Times*, October 28, 1941, 9.

28. Charles Johnson, "Gophers March On, Rip Michigan, 7–0," *Minneapolis Sunday Tribune and Star Journal*, October 26, 1941, 26.

29. Johnson, "Gophers March On," 26.

30. Hal Wilson, "Wolverines Edged Out by Minnesota, 7–0," *Michigan Daily*, October 26, 1941, 1 and 7.

31. Bernie Bierman, "Gophers Go at Best in Tight Jams," Bernie Bierman column via *Minneapolis Star Journal*, October 27, 1941, 17.

32. Wilson, "Wolverines Edged Out," 1 and 7.

33. John Sabo, "Minnesota Edges Out Michigan on Second-Period Score," *Detroit Free Press*, October 26, 1941, 1.

34. Quirk, *The Golden Years*, 248.

35. Tom O'Brien, "Gophers Tally Single Marker to Win Game," *Lansing State Journal*, October 26, 1941, 15.

36. Wilson, "Wolverines Edged Out," 1 and 7.

37. Rippel, *Game of My Life*, 18.

38. Halsey Hall, "'Sweiger's Pinch Plunge Saved Game'—Bierman," *Minneapolis Sunday Tribune and Star Journal*, October 26, 1941, 30.

39. William Weatherby, Associated Press via *Minneapolis Star Journal*, October 26, 1941, 26.

40. Stanley Woodward, "Northwestern Has Good Chance to Beat Minnesota," comments printed in *Boston Globe*, October 29, 1941, 24.

9. THE TALKING PLAY

1. "String Breaks," *Minneapolis Tribune*, November 1, 1941, 3.

2. Franklin D. Roosevelt, Statement Denouncing the Nazi Murder of French Hostages, posted online by Gerhard Peters and John T. Woolley, The American Presidency Project, https://www.presidency.ucsb.edu/node/210161.

3. Text of Roosevelt's Navy Day speech printed by Associated Press, October 28, 1941.

4. "Tokio Silent after Speech by President," Associated Press via *Iowa City Press-Citizen*, October 28, 1941, 1.

5. "Prelude to War, The U.S.S. *Reuben James*," National Archives and Records Administration, https://www.archives.gov/exhibits/a_people_at_war/prelude_to_war/uss_reuben_james.html; other information on the *Reuben*

James came from multiple press reports, including Doris Fleeson, "44 Saved in Destroyer Sunk in Convoy off Iceland," *Daily News*, November 1, 1941, 99.

6. Inquirer Washington Bureau, "Congressmen Believe Sinking of Destroyer Brought War Nearer," *Philadelphia Inquirer*, November 1, 1941, 4.

7. "Nazis Smash Deeper into Donets Basin," Associated Press via the *Capital Times*, November 1, 1941, 1.

8. "Army–Notre Dame Football Game," Sherwood, *Roosevelt and Hopkins*, 382.

9. Charles Johnson, "Lowdown on Sports," *Minneapolis Star Journal*, November 1, 1941, 7.

10. Bill Boni, "Minnesota and Texas Tied in Poll for Nation's Top Grid Team," Associated Press via *Battle Creek Enquirer*, October 28, 1941, 13.

11. Charles Dunkley, "Gophers, 'Cats Top Slate," Associated Press via *Sioux City Journal*, October 28, 1941, 11.

12. Gordon Gilmore, "High and Inside," *St. Paul Pioneer Press*, October 27, 1941, 11.

13. Lucius Smith, "Smith Family Story," 106, from the Rice County Historical Society Collection in Faribault, Minnesota.

14. Joe Hendrickson, "Sweiger 'Talks' Pain out of Gophers Cripples," *Minneapolis Star Journal*, October 28, 1941, 19.

15. Jim F. Scott, "Hot Reserve Eleven Defeats Plebes in Chilly Grid Tilt, 24–6," *Minnesota Daily*, October 28, 1941, 7.

16. Charles Johnson, "Bierman Sifts Reserves for Left Half Depth," *Minneapolis Star Journal*, October 28, 1941, 19.

17. "Northwestern 'Toughest,'" *Minnesota Daily*, October 30, 1941, 3.

18. Herb Barker, "Barker . . . Picks 'Em," Associated Press via *Sioux City Journal*, November 1, 1941, 14.

19. The attendance figure of 64,464 appeared in the *Minneapolis Star*, November 2, 1941, 17. The University of Minnesota now reports a revised attendance of 61,784, slightly smaller than crowds against Michigan (1940) and Notre Dame (1937) in prior years. Source: https://gophersports.com/sports/2018/5/21/sports-m-footbl-spec-rel-attendance-records-html.aspx.

20. George A. Barton, "Sportographs," *Minneapolis Star Journal*, November 9, 1941, 30.

21. Gordon Gilmore, "Tears and Sweat Forge New Link," *St. Paul Pioneer Press*, November 2, 1941, 5 Sports.

22. George A. Barton Papers, Minnesota Historical Society.

23. Bud Higgins, "Higgins, Gophers Beat Cats on 'Silly' Talking Play," *Minneapolis Star*, September 23, 1948, 42.

24. Bernie Bierman as told to Frank Mayer, "Sideline Director," *Esquire*, November 1939, 186.

25. George A. Barton Papers, Minnesota Historical Society.

26. McCallum, *Big Ten Football Since 1895*, 69–70.

27. Wilfrid Smith, "Minnesota Beats N.U., 8–7," *Chicago Tribune*, November 2, 1941, 32.

28. Joe Hendrickson, "Fullback 'Argues' with Cats in Trick to Aid Higgins Run," *Minneapolis Star Journal*, November 2, 1941, 33.

29. Ted Williams, "Williams Thrilled, Lauds Higgins, Garnaas; Sorry for Punt Catchers," *Minneapolis Tribune*, November 3, 1941, 13.

30. Bob Beebe, "'We Deserve to Win'—Waldorf," *Minneapolis Star Journal*, November 2, 1941, 31.

31. Associated Press, November 4, 1941.

32. "Avers Purple Watchers Saw Rules Broken," International News Service via the *Hammond Times*, November 3, 1941, 9.

33. "Lynn Waldorf Protests Touchdown Play; Bierman Answers," *Minneapolis Star Journal*, November 3, 1941, 18.

34. Bob Brachman, "Just a Minute," *San Francisco Examiner*, November 8, 1941, 23.

35. "Gophers Nip Wildcats, 8–7, in Bitterly Fought Conference Contest," Associated Press via *Palladium-Item*, November 2, 1941, 11.

36. Weldon Hart, "Steers Crush Mustangs to Bury 8-Year Jinx," *Austin American-Statesman*, November 2, 1941, 1.

37. Bernard Swanson, "Roamin' Round," *Minneapolis Tribune*, November 5, 1941, 14.

10. "ONLY HUMAN"

1. Charles Johnson, "Cornhuskers Promise a 'Revival,'" *Minneapolis Star Journal*, November 5, 1941, 29.

2. "Nebraska's 110th Wins Laurels," *State Journal*, Lincoln, Nebraska, November 10, 1941, 4, and "Huskers Gain Quarterback and Coach for Game," Associated Press via *Minneapolis Tribune*, November 5, 1941, 13.

3. John Bentley, "I May Be Wrong," *State Journal*, Lincoln, Nebraska, November 5, 1941, 16.

4. "Coach Bernie Bierman—Wants 'Bowl Ban' Lifted," Associated Press via the *Des Moines Register*, December 23, 1937, 8.

5. Mel Larson, "Bruce Smith on Crutches," *Minneapolis Tribune*, November 4, 1941, 13.

6. Maury Diamond, "Smith on Crutches as Gophers Begin Work for Cornhuskers," *Minnesota Daily*, November 4, 1941, 6.

7. Bernard Swanson, "Roamin' Round," *Minneapolis Tribune*, November 7, 1941, 17.

8. Jack Guenther, "Guenther Still Cheers Fordham, Slaps Gophers," United Press via *Minneapolis Tribune*, November 4, 1941, 14.

9. University Alumni Association, et al., "Open Letter to the Team!," *Daily Nebraskan*, November 7, 1941, 4, accessed online via University of Nebraska–Lincoln Libraries.

10. Bernie Bierman, "I Have My Fingers Crossed—Bierman," Bernie Bierman column via *Minneapolis Star Journal*, November 7, 1941, 27.

11. John Bentley, *State Journal*, Lincoln, Nebraska, November 8, 1941, 11.

12. "Minnesota Defeats Nebraska, Honor Service Men," *Minnesota Alumni Weekly*, November 15, 1941, 161.

13. "Proposal Called Final Effort," United Press via *Dayton Herald*, November 6, 1941, 29.

14. "Minnesota Defeats Nebraska," 161.

15. Bob Miller, "Inspired Cornhuskers Fall before Mighty Minnesota," *Daily Nebraskan*, November 9, 1941, 3.

16. Joe Hendrickson, "Gophers Hit All Time Low in 'Stock Market,'" *Minneapolis Star Journal*, November 9, 1941, 28.

17. Don Kellog, "Write Up Blue, He Was Great—Herndon," *Sunday Lincoln Journal and Star*, November 9, 1941, 14.

18. Joe Morgan, "Gophers Edge Nebraska, 9–0," United Press via *Oakland Tribune*, November 9, 1941, 14.

19. Gordon Gilmore, "Wildung Is Smith's All-American Choice," *St. Paul Pioneer Press*, November 9, 1941, 3.

20. Weldon Hart, "Monday Morning Quarterback," the *Austin American-Statesman*, November 10, 1941, 9.

21. Perry Dotson, "Bierman Orders Full Practice Monday," *St. Paul Pioneer Press*, November 9, 1941, 3.

22. Halsey Hall, "Errors Stir Bierman Ire," *Minneapolis Star Journal*, November 9, 1941, 27.

23. Bill Mandelcorn, "Top O' the Morn," *Sentinel-Star*, November 9, 1941, 8.

I I. FLOYD OF ROSEDALE

1. "Rock Island Explains Faribault Gopher Stop," *Minneapolis Star Journal*, November 16, 1941, 35.

2. George Edmond, "Smith Runs Half of Last Drill Session," *St. Paul Pioneer Press*, November 14, 1941, 16.

3. "'Dem Gopher Bums' Next on Hawks' Grid List," *Daily Iowan*, November 11, 1941, 4, accessed online via the University of Iowa Libraries.

4. Gordon Gilmore, "Farmer Better Than Kinnick, Says Mentor," *St. Paul Pioneer Press*, November 11, 1941, 10.

5. Brad Wilson, "Iowan 12th Man for Gophers?," *Des Moines Register*, November 15, 1941, 1.

6. Matt Trowbridge, "The Man behind Floyd of Rosedale," *Iowa City Press-Citizen*, November 25, 1989, 38.

7. "As Iowa's 'Texas Tornado' Withered Northwestern," *Pittsburgh Courier*, October 13, 1934, 5, Second Section.

8. George Barton, "Stan Kotska Scores Three Touchdowns in Furious Attack," *Minneapolis Tribune*, October 28, 1934, 14.

9. Irvin Rudick, "Minnesota Power Plays Perfect, Solem Declares," *Minneapolis Tribune*, October 28, 1934, 12.

10. "Disappointed Iowa Homecomers Leave after Slaughter," Associated Press via *Sioux City Journal*, October 28, 1934, 22.

11. Jack Gurwell, "Gophers Trounce Hawks, 48–12," *Daily Iowan*, October 28, 1934, 1.

12. Chester Washington, "In the Melting Pot of Sports," *Pittsburgh Courier*, November 3, 1934, 15.

13. "Will Minnesota's Gophers 'Simmons' Him?," *Minneapolis Spokesman*, November 2, 1934, 1.

14. "Gopher Coach Says He's 'Fed Up' with Talk," Associated Press via *Iowa City Press-Citizen*, November 9, 1935, 12.

15. George A. Barton, "Bierman Asks Police Guards for Men Today," *Minneapolis Tribune*, November 9, 1935, 1 and 19.

16. "Upbraids Herring," Associated Press via *Gazette*, Cedar Rapids, Iowa, November 9, 1935, 1.

17. Gov. Olson's messages to Gov. Herring and Bierman were printed, in full, on the first page of the *Minneapolis Star Journal* on November 9, 1935.

18. Bernie Bierman, "Gopher Ability to Keep Heads Won—Bierman," *Minneapolis Star*, November 11, 1935, 14.

19. Bert McGrane, "Gopher Power Nips Iowa, 13–6," *Des Moines Register*, November 10, 1935, 18.

20. Tom Snee, "The Pig and the Politician," University of Iowa Office of Strategic Communication, posted 2010, https://stories.uiowa.edu/pig-and-politician.

21. Matt Trowbridge, "The Man behind Floyd of Rosedale," *Iowa City Press-Citizen*, November 25, 1989, 38.

22. Kim Briggeman, "Missoula's James Dorsey Raised His Voice for Racial Justice," *Missoulian*, January 19, 2020, https://missoulian.com/news/local/mis-

soulas-james-dorsey-raised-his-voice-for-racial-justice/article_c726f790-55b4-
5579-bdbe-079976b73001.html.

23. Mike Soffin, *Minnesota Daily*, February 8, 1951, article accessed through the Bernie Bierman file, Elmer Andersen Library, University of Minnesota.

24. "Twin Town Post," *Minneapolis Spokesman*, October 4, 1936, 2.

25. Curator Riv-Ellen Prell, University of Minnesota Professor Emerita of American Studies, Curator Sarah Atwood, PhD candidate in American Studies, and research team, "Segregated Student Housing and the Activists Who Defeated It," last accessed December 2020, http://acampusdivided.umn.edu/index.php/essay/segregated-student-housing/.

26. "Coach Bierman Silent on Courier Inquiry on Why Bell and Reid Weren't Used in Game with Texas," *Pittsburgh Courier*, November 21, 1936, 15.

27. Nellie Dodson, *Minneapolis Spokesman* column, October 18, 1935, 1.

28. The impact of UCLA's team in the late 1930s has been written about at length, but the Cynthia Lee story for UCLA's news service on August 21, 2014 (https://newsroom.ucla.edu/stories/forgotten-story-of-four-who-broke-color-barrier-in-pro-football-to-screen-at-royce) was quite helpful for these purposes.

29. "Mrs. Franklin D. Roosevelt Named Honorary Chairman of All-Star Football Game," *New York Age*, November 15, 1941, 11; "Irish, Wildcat Aces Face Negro Stars in Charity Game," International News Service via *Courier-Post*, Camden, New Jersey, November 24, 1941, 25.

30. Morgan Jensen, "Lillard, Walker Signed by Pros," *Pittsburgh Courier*, November 15, 1941, 15.

31. Bert McGrane, "On the Sideline," *Des Moines Register*, November 28, 1941, 9.

32. Bernie Bierman, "Gophers Sunk if They Play Like They Did in Husker Tiff," Bernie Bierman column via *Des Moines Tribune*, November 14, 1941, 32.

33. Bill Buckley, "Hawkeyes Face Gopher Might," *Daily Iowan*, November 15, 1941, 1; "Kinnick Stadium," Iowa Athletics, https://hawkeyesports.com/kinnick-stadium/.

34. Joe Hendrickson, "Hardest Sock: Odson Rammed by Sweiger," *Minneapolis Star Journal*, November 17, 1941, 23.

35. Ray Christensen, *Tales from the Minnesota Gophers: A Collection of the Greatest Gopher Stories Ever Told* (New York: Sports Publishing, 2014), e-book 288–89; "1941 National Champions," GopherSports.com, https://gophersports.com/sports/2018/5/21/sports-m-footbl-spec-rel-1941-champions-html.aspx.

36. "Hawks," *Daily Iowan*, November 16, 1941, 6.

37. Edwin Moore Jr., "Gophers Overpower Game Hawkeyes, 34–13," *Courier*, Waterloo, Iowa, November 16, 1941, 26.

38. Perry Dotson, "Bruce Comes Out Unharmed," *St. Paul Pioneer Press*, November 16, 1941, 3, Section Two.

39. Moore Jr., "Gophers Overpower Game," 26.

40. Moore Jr., "Gophers Overpower Game," 26.

41. "'Happiest Day,' Admits Smith," Special to the Pioneer Press, published in *St. Paul Pioneer Press*, November 16, 1941, 3, Section Two.

42. Bert McGrane, "Hawks Hit First; Once Tied, 13–13," *Des Moines Register*, November 16, 1941, 54.

43. "The U.S.–Japan War Talks as Seen in Official Documents," Japan Center for Asian Historical Records, National Archives of Japan, https://www.jacar.go.jp/english/nichibei/popup/pop_23.html.

44. "Will Wed Saburo Kurusu," *New York Times*, August 18, 1914.

45. "Marine Withdrawal from China Clears Decks for Jap War," Associated Press via *Minneapolis Tribune*, November 15, 1941, 11.

46. "Confidential, Press Conference #783," Press Conferences of President Franklin D. Roosevelt, 1933–1945, Franklin D. Roosevelt Presidential Library and Museum, November 14, 1941, 41, http://www.fdrlibrary.marist.edu/_resources/images/pc/pc0125.pdf.

47. Max W. Schmidt and Chief Hamilton to State Department, "Memorandum Prepared in the Division of Far Eastern Affairs," Foreign Relations of the United States Diplomatic Papers, 1941, The Far East, Volume IV, Department of State, Office of the Historian, https://history.state.gov/historicaldocuments/frus1941v04/d444.

48. "November 17th, 1941, Transcript," Franklin D. Roosevelt Day by Day, A Project of the Pare Lorentz Center at the FDR Presidential Library, http://www.fdrlibrary.marist.edu/daybyday/daylog/november-17th-1941/.

49. William C. Murphy Jr., "War, Peace in Balance for U.S. and Japan as Kurusu Sees Roosevelt," *Philadelphia Inquirer*, November 18, 1941, 12.

50. "Japs Hopeful after Washington Parley," Associated Press via *Boston Globe*, November 18, 1941, 8.

12. ON WISCONSIN

1. "For the Last Year—Thanksgiving Series Begins," *Pittsburgh Press*, November 20, 1941, 1–2.

2. "City Observes Thanksgiving with Worship," *Minneapolis Tribune*, November 20, 1941, 1.

3. Bob Considine, "Gophers One of Great Football Teams of Our Time," International News Service via *Minneapolis Tribune*, November 21, 1941, 13.

4. Bernard Swanson, "Smith, Frickey Ready; Pukema in Poor Shape," *Minneapolis Tribune*, November 18, 1941, 13.

5. Leonard Levy, "Leonard 'Butch' Levy LBL Scrapbook," University of Minnesota Libraries, Nathan and Theresa Berman Upper Midwest Jewish Archives, https://umedia.lib.umn.edu/item/p16022coll475:5728.

6. Hank Casserly, "36 Inspired Badgers Trek to Minnesota," *Capital Times*, Madison, Wisconsin, November 20, 1941, 41.

7. Bob Beebe, "Minnesota Picked over Badgers in Offense Duel," *Minneapolis Tribune*, November 22, 1941, 7.

8. Roundy Coughlin, "Roundy Says," *Wisconsin State Journal*, November 22, 1941, 8.

9. Dave Anderson, *Minnesota–Wisconsin College Football Rivalry* (Charleston, SC: Arcadia Publishing, 2015), Kindle 51.

10. "Stassen and Heil Churned Up over 'Dairy Bowl' Game," *Minneapolis Tribune*, November 22, 1941, 1.

11. James Lucier, "Finish Studies before Draft," *Minnesota Daily*, November 22, 1941, 8.

12. "Army Call Is 'Delayed' for Bob Sweiger," *Minneapolis Star*, November 20, 1941, 29.

13. Charles Johnson, "Lowdown on Sports," *Minneapolis Star Journal*, November 21, 1941, 26.

14. Harry Ferguson, "Minnesota Only One of Four Perfect-Record Elevens in for Trouble Today," United Press via *Wisconsin State Journal*, November 22, 1941, 10.

15. Robert Weed, "English Miss Thrilled as Bruce Smith 'Pushes People Aside with His Hands,'" *Minneapolis Star Journal*, November 23, 1941, 27.

16. Joe Hendrickson, "Smith Salaams as Pass Hits," *Minneapolis Sunday Tribune and Star Journal*, November 23, 1941, 36.

17. Charles Johnson, "Gophers Tip Badgers, 41–6, Win Big Ten, U.S. Titles," *Minneapolis Star Journal*, November 23, 1941, 29.

18. Halsey Hall, "'All Share Glory'—Bernie," *Minneapolis Sunday Tribune and Star Journal*, November 23, 1941, 33.

19. Perry Dotson, "Former Wildcat Coach Lauds Team," *St. Paul Pioneer Press*, November 23, 1941, 3.

20. Gordon Gilmore, "Fine a Half as Country Has Known—Stuhldreher," *St. Paul Pioneer Press*, November 23, 1941, 3.

21. Hall, "'All Share Glory'—Bernie," 33.

22. Bob Beebe, "'Bruce Is All-American,'" *Minneapolis Sunday Tribune and Star Journal*, November 23, 1941, 33.

23. Earl Hilligan, "Smith Is Minnesota Spearhead as Wisconsin Is Crushed, 41–6," Associated Press via *Evening Star*, Washington, D.C., November 23, 1941, C-3.

24. Dotson, "Former Wildcat Coach," 3.

13. CHAMPIONS AGAIN

1. Joe Hendrickson, "Bruce Smith, Who'd Do It All Over Again, Wants to Try Pro Ball," *Minneapolis Star Journal*, November 25, 1941, 19; "Gopher Frosh Look Good," *Minneapolis Star Journal*, November 25, 1941, 13.

2. George A. Barton, "Bierman Lauds Line for 'Clutch' Roles," *Minneapolis Tribune*, November 25, 1941, 15.

3. Bob Beebe, "41 Gophers Honored at Convocation," *Minneapolis Tribune*, November 26, 1941, 13.

4. *Rock County Star* clippings and family scrapbook provided by Jane Wildung Lanphere.

5. "Reserves 1942 Problem—Wildung," *Minneapolis Star Journal*, November 26, 1941, 28.

6. Joe Hendrickson, "Biggest Thrill," *Minneapolis Star Journal*, November 26, 1941, 28.

7. Hendrickson, "Bruce Smith, Who'd Do It All Over Again," 19.

8. U.S. Secretary of State, "Document Handed by the Secretary of State to the Japanese Ambassador (Nomura) on November 26, 1941," Papers Relating to the Foreign Relations of the United States, Japan, 1931–1941, Volume II, U.S. Department of State, Office of the Historian, https://history.state.gov/historicaldocuments/frus1931-41v02/d409.

9. "The US–Japan War Talks as Seen in Official Documents," Japan Center for Asian Historical Records, National Archives of Japan, https://www.jacar.go.jp/english/nichibei/digest/.

10. Eri Hotta, *Japan 1941: Countdown to Infamy* (New York: Knopf Doubleday, 2013), e-book, 314, accessed via Saint Paul Public Library.

11. Joe Hendrickson, "'What Those Fellows Did Means More Than Anything That Happened to Me in Football'—Sweiger," *Minneapolis Star Journal*, November 26, 1941, 28.

12. Eddie Dooley, "Gophers Best; Smith Called Standout Star," International News Service via *Minneapolis Tribune*, November 24, 1941, 14.

13. These results were posted in newspapers across the country including the *Wilmington Morning Star*, November 26, 1941.

14. "National Poll Rankings," 116 (shows various ranking systems); "Major Selectors since 1936" and "National Poll Champions in Bowl Games," 119 and

122 (shows Minnesota as NCAA-designated champion for 1941), last accessed October 2020, http://fs.ncaa.org/Docs/stats/football_records/2020/FBS.pdf.

15. Dwight Pelkin, "It's This Way," *Sheboygan Press*, Wisconsin, November 21, 1941, 16.

16. *Casper Tribune-Herald* (November 20, 1941, 6), *Medford Mail Tribune* (November 19, 1941, 4), and Al Warden, *Ogden Standard-Examiner* (November 18, 1941, 7).

17. Lynn Callaway, "From the Press Box," *Daily Dispatch*, Moline, Illinois, November 18, 1941, 16.

18. Edwin Moore Jr., "Off the Cuff," *Waterloo Daily Courier*, November 19, 1941, 13.

19. William Tucker, "Gopher Star Standout of Grid Season," United Press via *Dayton Herald*, November 29, 1941, 8.

20. "Smith Modest about the Heisman Trophy," Associated Press via *Minneapolis Star Journal*, November 30, 1941, 27.

21. "Smith Selected Player of Year," *Minneapolis Tribune*, November 29, 1941, 7.

22. Ed Dahl, *Faribault Journal Weekly*, December 4, 1941, 2.

23. *Faribault Journal Weekly* and *Faribault Daily News*, November 1941 and December 1941.

24. "The Smiths Go to New York," *Faribault Daily News*, December 8, 1941. Full quote: "The Smiths went to New York yesterday. Off early Sunday morning . . ."

14. PEARL HARBOR

1. "Record Crowd Takes in Colorful Shrine Show," *Honolulu Star-Bulletin*, December 8, 1941, 18.

2. "Remembering Pearl Harbor, A Pearl Harbor Fact Sheet," The National World War II Museum, https://www.census.gov/history/pdf/pearl-harbor-fact-sheet-1.pdf.

3. "3,000 Casualties Are Indicated on Oahu" and "Dead, Injured," *Honolulu Star-Bulletin*, December 8, 1941, 1.

4. "Visiting Grid Players Given Police Duties," *Honolulu Star-Bulletin*, December 8, 1941, 18.

5. WOR broadcast on December 7, 1941: "WOR Newsflash," Newseum, accessed via YouTube, https://www.youtube.com/watch?time_continue=2&v=cYDg4FqlBEc&feature=emb_logo.

6. Tommy Holmes, "Giants Champ in East but Not in Brooklyn!" *Brooklyn Daily Eagle*, December 8, 1941, 15.

7. *Minnesota Alumni Weekly*, December 13, 1941, 213.

8. Gareth Hiebert, "U Students Hear President in Grim Silence," *Minnesota Daily*, December 9, 1941, 3.

9. "Jap Attack Brings Mingled Emotions," *Minnesota Daily*, December 8, 1941, 1.

10. "Alumnus Loses Life at Pearl Harbor," *Minnesota Alumni Weekly*, December 13, 1941, 221.

11. Max Schulman column, *Minnesota Daily*, December 8, 1941, 8.

12. "Named Football Man of the Year, Smith Arrives at 'Tuxedo Junction' (New York) Today," *Faribault Daily News*, December 8, 1941, 8.

13. Bernard Swanson, "Sports Editor on N.Y. Junket Runs into War," *Minneapolis Tribune*, December 10, 1941, 1.

14. Bernard Swanson, "Bruce Permits Heisman Donor to Make Dates," *Minneapolis Tribune*, December 9, 1941, 18.

15. Author interview with June Smith, August 2019.

16. On Page 12 of the *Faribault Daily News* on December 10, 1941, the article "Heisman Trophy for Entire Team—Smith," reveals that people in Faribault were "disappointed" that the live broadcast of Smith's speech was "called off" the night before. However, the article also mentions that people in Faribault heard the recorded speech, thanks to transcription, after Roosevelt's fireside chat.

17. "Fireside Chat 19: On the War with Japan," University of Virginia Miller Center, https://millercenter.org/the-presidency/presidential-speeches/december-9-1941-fireside-chat-19-war-japan.

18. Bernard Swanson, "Smith Wows Them at Heisman Fete," *Minneapolis Tribune*, December 10, 1941, 17–18.

19. Special to the Star Journal, "'Bruce Smith for Mine,' Says New York," *Minneapolis Star Journal*, December 10, 1941, 33.

20. Whitney Martin, "Worth of Football Gets Boost from Cup Winners," Associated Press via *The News and Observer*, December 11, 1942, 14.

21. Reprinted with permission from the Rice County Historical Society Collection in Faribault, Minnesota. The full speech published in this chapter takes Smith's spoken variations into account.

22. "Impresses," *World-Telegram* excerpt printed in *The Tablet*, Brooklyn, New York, December 13, 1941, 15.

23. "'Bruce Smith for Mine,'" 33.

24. Smith postcard to family, from the Rice County Historical Society Collection in Faribault, Minnesota.

25. Associated Press, December 12, 1941, accessed via *Muncie Evening Press*, December 12, 1941, 18.

26. "1942 National Football League Draft," Pro Football Hall of Fame, posted January 1, 2005, https://www.profootballhof.com/news/1942-national-football-league-draft/.

27. DeWitt's letter to U.S. Army Chief of Staff, with a mention of Executive Order 9066, published by the Museum of the City of San Francisco, available publicly online via http://www.sfmuseum.org/war/dewitt0.html.

28. "Rose Bowl Game Ordered Canceled," Associated Press via *Chattanooga Daily Times*, December 14, 1941, 18.

29. Joe B. Carter, "35,000 Witness Charity Game Played in Mud," *Times*, Shreveport, Louisiana, January 4, 1942, 17.

30. George Barton, "Bernie Gets $1,600 Defense Bond Gift," *Minneapolis Tribune*, January 17, 1942, 7.

15. A NEW REALITY

1. Hugh Fullerton, "Sports Roundup," *Globe-Gazette*, Mason City, Iowa, March 5, 1942, 14.

2. Gayle Talbot, "Football Closest Thing to War Explains Tom Hamilton," Associated Press via *Des Moines Tribune*, May 21, 1942, 23.

3. "Pre-Flight Training Bill at Iowa No Picnic," Associated Press via *Des Moines Tribune*, May 7, 1942, 23.

4. "Bierman Toots Iowa Whistle on May 28," *Minneapolis Tribune*, April 25, 1942, 7.

5. "70 Seahawks Expected for First Grid Workout Monday," *Muscatine Journal*, Muscatine, Iowa, August 29, 1942, 5.

6. Hugh Fullerton Jr., "Sports Roundup," *Des Moines Tribune*, September 8, 1942, 11.

7. Eddie Dooley, "The Service Teams," *Football Illustrated*, 1942, 21.

8. "History," Naval Station Great Lakes, https://www.cnic.navy.mil/regions/cnrma/installations/ns_great_lakes/about/history.html.

9. "Bruce Back," *Minneapolis Star Journal*, July 1, 1942, 27.

10. Levy letter to parents, multiple letters during summer 1942, exact dates not marked/unknown, Leonard (Butch) Levy papers, Nathan and Theresa Berman Upper Midwest Jewish Archives, University of Minnesota Libraries, Minneapolis, Folder 6.

11. Bierman letter to Levy, March 24, 1942, Leonard (Butch) Levy papers, Nathan and Theresa Berman Upper Midwest Jewish Archives, University of Minnesota Libraries, Minneapolis, Folder 6.

12. Levy to parents, multiple letters during summer 1942, exact dates not marked/unknown, Leonard (Butch) Levy papers, Nathan and Theresa Berman

Upper Midwest Jewish Archives, University of Minnesota Libraries, Minneapolis, Folder 6.

13. Eddie Dooley, "The Service Teams," *Football Illustrated*, 1942.

14. Hugh Fullerton, "Sports Roundup," Wide World via *Burlington Daily News*, May 1, 1942, 6.

15. Through services like the AP, this quote from Tunney circulated widely in dozens of U.S. newspapers in late August 1942.

16. "Bob Zuppke Peeved at Mr. Gene Tunney," Associated Press via *Ironwood Daily Globe*, Ironwood, Michigan, August 22, 1942, 8.

17. "Beamish Advocates Dropping of Sports," International News Service, via *Pittsburgh Sun-Telegraph*, September 30, 1942, 23.

18. "Reply of Waldorf," International News Service via *The Times-Tribune*, Scranton, Pennsylvania, October 1, 1942, 25.

19. Wilfrid Smith, "Great Lakes Prepares for Football Card of 12 Games," *Chicago Tribune*, September 1, 1942, 21.

20. Eddie Dooley, *Football Illustrated*, 1942, 2.

21. *Football Illustrated*, 1942.

22. Tommy Devine, "Gophers Pitted against Field; 20 Vets Return," United Press via *Quad-City Times*, Davenport, Iowa, September 1, 1942, 9.

23. Danzig, *History of American Football*, 368.

24. "M Recognition Banquet, Honoring Members of the 1942 Minnesota Football Squad," saved in the archives of Jack and Virginia Spewak.

25. Bernard Swanson, "Like '34 Pitt Game, Shouts Svendsen," *Minneapolis Star Journal*, October 4, 1942, 34.

26. Joe Hendrickson, "Just a Superman," *Minneapolis Star Journal*, October 4, 1942, 34 (4, Peach Section).

27. Halsey Hall, "Daley's Greatest Game—Bierman," *Minneapolis Star Journal*, October 4, 1942, 34.

28. "Big Ten Tables Frosh Plan, Minnesota Wants One Provision," from Late Dispatches, *Minneapolis Star Journal*, December 9, 1942, 30.

29. Author interview with June Smith, August 2019.

30. All information on Smith's movie and quotes from the film come from author's viewing of "Smith of Minnesota," released October 15, 1942, Columbia Pictures, accessed via DVD.

31. Fan letter to Bruce Smith, November 21, 1942, from the Rice County Historical Society Collection in Faribault, Minnesota.

32. "At Local Theatres," *Republican and Herald*, Shenandoah, Pennsylvania, October 22, 1942, 3.

33. "Bruce Smith Picked for Touchdown Club Service Team Award," *Sandusky Register* (Sandusky, Ohio), wire services, January 4, 1943, 7.

34. "3 Outstanding Gridders Modestly Give Coaches Credit," Associated Press via *Des Moines Tribune*, January 6, 1943, 14.

35. "Induction Statistics," Selective Service System, Official Site of the United States Government, https://www.sss.gov/About/History-And-Records/Induction-Statistics.

36. *Minnesota Alumni Weekly*, January 16, 1943, 237; information on female enrollment, February 20, 1943, 299.

37. "Military Information," *Minnesota Alumni Weekly*, January 16, 1943, 236.

38. Charles Johnson, "Lowdown on Sports," June 5, 1943, 5.

39. "Ohio State's Hopes Rest on 60 Frosh," Associated Press via *Arizona Republic*, September 2, 1943, 12.

40. R. A. Lofstrom, "Right and Left in Sports," *St. Cloud Times*, October 23, 1943, 8.

41. Bernard Swanson, "Daley Called His Shot!" *Minneapolis Tribune*, October 24, 1943, 24.

42. Levy letter to parents, exact date not marked/unknown, Leonard (Butch) Levy papers, Nathan and Theresa Berman Upper Midwest Jewish Archives, University of Minnesota Libraries, Minneapolis, Folder 6.

43. Akers, *The Game Breaker*, 150.

16. NORMANDY

1. Midshipman First Class Troy A. Shoulders, "The U.S. Navy in Operation Overlord under the Command of Rear Admiral Alan G. Kirk," A Trident Scholar Project Report, No. 221, September 27, 1994, 96, https://apps.dtic.mil/dtic/tr/fulltext/u2/a284910.pdf.

2. Mark Zangara, *The Fate of the USS Tide: The Forgotten Sailors of D-Day* (WW2 History Archive, 2019), 271.

3. Weldon Payne, "Local Man's Ship Sank Day after D-Day Landing," *Huntsville Times*, June 7, 1959, 10.

4. Payne, "Local Man's Ship Sank," 10.

5. Zangara, *The Fate of the USS Tide*, 274.

6. Zangara, *The Fate of the USS Tide*, 264.

7. Author interview with Deb Welch, June 2019.

8. "Heroes of Europe and Pacific in Fort Eustis Naval Hospital Relate Some Grim Experiences," *Daily Press*, Newport News, Virginia, December 24, 1944, 29.

9. Payne, "Local Man's Ship Sank," 10.

10. Zangara, *The Fate of the USS Tide*, 275.

11. "Sixty Years Later, A Hero's Reception, Member Profile: Mike Welch," University of Minnesota, University Relations (2004), M, 2004, University of Minnesota, retrieved from the University of Minnesota Digital Conservancy.

12. Zangara, *The Fate of the USS Tide*, 276.

13. "Sixty Years Later, A Hero's Reception, Member Profile: Mike Welch," University of Minnesota, University Relations, 2004.

14. Zangara, *The Fate of the USS Tide*, 279.

15. Zangara, *The Fate of the USS Tide*, 293.

16. Author interview with Deb Welch, June 2019.

17. University of Minnesota Alumni Association, *Minnesota Magazine*, vol. 103, nos. 5–6 (May–August 2004): 53, retrieved from the University of Minnesota Digital Conservancy.

18. Author interview with Charles Ringer, November 2019.

19. Author interview with Bruce Odson, April 2019.

20. Oral history interview with Warren Francis Plunkett, Veterans History Project, Library of Congress, American Folklife Center, http://memory.loc.gov/diglib/vhp/story/loc.natlib.afc2001001.05809/.

21. Author interview with Ann Waits, January 2020.

17. I-W-O J-I-M-A

1. Author interview with Kristy Bierhaus, September 2019.

2. Halsey Hall, "Gophers' Best Game," *Minneapolis Star Journal*, November 17, 1940, 24.

3. Joe Hendrickson, "Bierhaus Likes Switch," *Minneapolis Star Journal*, September 18, 1942, 28.

4. "1,176 Practice Hours? Worth It, Recall 7 Gopher Seniors," *Minneapolis Tribune*, November 25, 1942, 11.

5. James Bradley and Ron Powers, *Flags of Our Fathers* (New York: Bantam Books, 2000), 285, e-book version accessed through the Hennepin County Public Library.

6. Bernard C. Nalty and Danny J. Crawford, "The United States Marines on Iwo Jima," Department of the Navy, United States Marine Corps, History and Museums Division, 1, https://www.marines.mil/Portals/1/Publications/The%20United%20States%20Marines%20On%20Iwo%20Jima_The%20Battle%20and%20the%20Flag%20Raisings%20%20PCN%2019000316600.pdf.

7. "'Invading Island Like Grid Game'—Bierhaus," *Minneapolis Star Journal*, July 31, 1945, 17.

8. Frank Litsky, "Angelo Bertelli, 78, Is Dead; Quarterback for Notre Dame," *New York Times*, June 29, 1999, https://www.nytimes.com/1999/06/29/sports/angelo-bertelli-78-is-dead-quarterback-for-notre-dame.html.

9. "First Lieutenant Jack Lummus, USMCR (Deceased)," Marine Corps University, https://www.usmcu.edu/Research/Marine-Corps-History-Division/Information-for-Units/Medal-of-Honor-Recipients-By-Unit/1stLt-Jack-Lummus/.

10. Roger Rosenblum, "Spotlight Sports," *Mason City Globe-Gazette*, May 19, 1945, 6.

11. Bernard Swanson, "Introducing—Star's Outstate All-State," *Minneapolis Star*, November 19, 1938, 8.

12. "Just Reward," *Minneapolis Tribune*, November 11, 1942, 15.

13. Author interview with Ann Waits, January 2020.

14. Keith Wheeler, *We Are the Wounded, The Illustrated Edition* (Originally published: 1945, e-book accessed January 2020), 227.

15. Wheeler, *We Are the Wounded*, 234.

16. Keith Wheeler, "Keith Wheeler Pays Big Tribute, Val Hollingsworth, Joe Lauterbach Lose Legs," *Honolulu Star-Bulletin*, Wednesday, March 27, 1946, 10.

17. Author interview with Joe Lauterbach's son (also named Joe), January 2020.

18. Author interview with Ann Waits, January 2020.

19. "'Invading Island Like Grid Game'—Bierhaus," 17.

20. Nalty and Crawford, "The United States Marines on Iwo Jima," 5, 9.

18. COMING HOME

1. "USS Amsterdam – War History," Record Group 38: Records of the Office of the Chief of Naval Operations, 1875–2006, Series: World War II War Diaries, Other Operational Records and Histories, ca. 1/1/1042–ca. 6/1/19, page 2, Fold3 File #301052341, accessed via the National Archives, https://catalog.archives.gov/id/77526063.

2. "USS Amsterdam – War Diary, 8/1/45–9/30/45," Record Group 38: Records of the Office of the Chief of Naval Operations, 1875–2006, Series: World War II War Diaries, Other Operational Records and Histories, ca. 1/1/1042–ca. 6/1/19, August 31, 1945, page 7, Fold3 File #300846201, accessed via the National Archives, https://catalog.archives.gov/id/77529223.

3. The 200,000 figure is commonly cited. For example, see Thomas Holmes, "The Dropping of Atomic Bombs on Japan," *Social Education*, vol. 69, no. 4 (2005): 209+. National media outlets have also recently used that

figure, including *The New York Times* (https://www.nytimes.com/2020/08/06/world/asia/hiroshima-nagasaki-japan-photos.html) and NBC News (https://www.nbcnews.com/news/asian-america/japanese-american-hiroshima-victim-reality-being-bombed-his-own-country-n1235912).

4. *Minnesota Alumnus*, vol. 45, nos. 1–3 (September–November 1945): 3, retrieved from the University of Minnesota Digital Conservancy, http://hdl.handle.net/11299/52369.

5. "World War II, Korea and Vietnam Casualties Listed by State," U.S. Army Center of Military History, https://history.army.mil/html/documents/casualties/stcas.html.

6. Various press reports covered these stories extensively, including the *Minneapolis Tribune* and *Minneapolis Star Journal.*

7. "USS Amsterdam – War History," Record Group 38: Records of the Office of the Chief of Naval Operations, 1875–2006.

8. "USS *Serpens* Memorial," Arlington National Cemetery, https://www.arlingtoncemetery.mil/Explore/Monuments-and-Memorials/USS-Serpens.

9. Emailed correspondence with Bruce Pukema, January 2020.

10. "Oral history with Bill Daley, Minneapolis, Minnesota," Melrose Area Historical Society, October 16, 1992, https://reflections.mndigital.org/catalog/p16022coll28:344.

11. "Famed Bruce Smith to Play with Packers," *Green Bay Press-Gazette*, February 7, 1945, 13.

12. "Today's Guest Star," *Morning-Call*, Paterson, New Jersey, comment reprinted in *St. Cloud Times*, November 2, 1945, 9.

13. Dave Yuenger, "Packers' Second-Half Drive Whips Giants, 23–14," *Green Bay Press-Gazette*, November 26, 1945, 13–14.

14. Akers, *The Game Breaker*, 154.

15. Yuenger, "Packers Second-Half Drive," 13.

16. Author interview with Peter and Rand Levy, May 2019.

17. Sid Feder, "Cleveland National Football League Franchise Shifted to Los Angeles for Next Season," Associated Press via *Morning Call*, Allentown, Pennsylvania, January 13, 1946, 12.

18. "Cleveland Rams' Franchise Moved to Los Angeles," Associated Press via *Times-Signal*, Zanesville, Ohio, January 13, 1946, 9.

19. Cliff Christl, "Dick Wildung Was Tenacious Two-Way Lineman," Green Bay Packers official site, https://www.packers.com/news/dick-wildung-was-tenacious-two-way-lineman.

20. Author interview with Dave Wildung, May 2019.

21. Maury White, "Birthplace Mystery Kept Fitch out of Hall—Until Now," *Des Moines Sunday Register*, July 7, 1991, 28.

22. Bob Brachman, "Bierman Hits Back at 'Flop of Year,'" *San Francisco Examiner*, December 22, 1945, 19.

23. "People's Column," *Minneapolis Star*, December 10, 1949, 11.

24. Charles Johnson, "Bierman Quits as 'U' Coach," *Minneapolis Star*, November 13, 1950, 1.

25. Barbara Flanagan, "Mrs. Bierman Is Sad but Relieved," *Minneapolis Tribune*, November 14, 1950, 1.

26. Rolf Felstad, "Gophers Win Last Home Game for Bierman," *Minneapolis Sunday Tribune*, November 19, 1950, 1.

19. LEGACY

1. Author interview with Peter and Rand Levy, May 2019.

2. Minnesota Gophers YouTube Account, "Watch Live: Gopher Football Defeats #5 Penn State 31–26 (Gopher Classics)," rebroadcast of ABC from November 9, 2019, and streamed live on March 28, 2020, https://www.youtube.com/watch?v=8ZKtq7oAtO0.

3. "Elite Access: Gopher Football Visits Bruce Smith's Grave at Fort Snelling," Minnesota Gophers, YouTube, https://www.youtube.com/watch?v=QAVBak9gW4o.

4. Author interview with Bruce Smith's son, also named Bruce, August 2019.

5. Akers, *The Game Breaker*, 162.

6. "Bruce Smith of Football Fame Dies of Cancer," *Minneapolis Star*, August 28, 1967, 8.

7. Bill Hengen, "Smith Voted into Grid Hall of Fame," *Minneapolis Star*, February 17, 1972, 49.

8. Author interview with Peter Levy, May 2019.

9. Author interview with Bruce Odson, April 2019.

10. Author interview with Bob Garnaas, September 2019.

11. Author interview with Dave Wildung, May 2019.

12. Author interview with Michael and Cindy Sweiger, October 2019.

13. "Oral History with Bill Daley, Minneapolis, Minnesota," Melrose Area Historical Society, October 16, 1992, https://reflections.mndigital.org/catalog/p16022coll28:344.

14. Author interview with Kristy Bierhaus, September 2019.

15. Author interview with Deb Welch, June 2019.

16. Veterans History Project oral interview with Warren Plunkett, http://memory.loc.gov/diglib/vhp/bib/loc.natlib.afc2001001.05809.

17. Author interview with Ann Waits, January 2020.

18. McCallum, *Big Ten Football since 1895*, 69.

19. "Bernie Bierman Was Genuine Minnesota Legend," Associated Press via *St. Cloud Times*, March 9, 1977, 16.

20. Millard L. Gieske, "To Minnesotans, Bierman Stood for 'U,'" *Minneapolis Tribune*, March 27, 1977, 13.

BIBLIOGRAPHY

MANUSCRIPTS AND COLLECTIONS

Barton, George A., Papers. Minnesota Historical Society.

Bierman, Bernard W. HR file and President's Office records. University of Montana Mansfield Library Archives.

Bierman, Bernard W. Information files collection, ua-01158. University of Minnesota Archives, Elmer Andersen Library.

Crisler, H. O., Papers. 1922–1978, Box 1. Bentley Historical Library, University of Michigan.

Daley, Bill. Interview by Roger Paschke. "Oral History with Bill Daley, Minneapolis, Minnesota." Melrose Area Historical Society, October 16, 1992.

Football program, University of Washington vs. University of Minnesota, September 27, 1941. Page 3. University of Washington Libraries, Special Collections.

Hanson, Wayne D. "Minnesota Liberators of Concentration Camps Oral History Project, Transcript: Wayne D. Hanson Oral History Interview." Michael Greenberg, April 20, 1982, Minnesota Historical Society.

Johnson, Millie Bowers. "Minnesota's Greatest Generation, Transcript: Millie Bowers Johnson Oral History Interview." July 18, 2008, in Northfield, Minnesota, Minnesota Historical Society.

Levy, Leonard (Butch), Papers. Nathan and Theresa Berman Upper Midwest Jewish Archives, University of Minnesota Libraries, Minneapolis.

Roosevelt, Eleanor. The Eleanor Roosevelt Papers, Digital Edition, George Washington University.

Roosevelt, Franklin D. "Day by Day." A Project of the Pare Lorentz Center at the FDR Presidential Library.

Rosenman, Samuel I. General Services Administration, National Archives and Records Services. Franklin D. Roosevelt Library and Museum Website.

Smith, Lucius, and Bruce Smith. Collection, Biography, and Obituary, Rice County Historical Society, including the online Dalby Database.

Wickersham, Price. "Early Recollections of Minnesota Football." 1877–1946, University of Minnesota Archives, Elmer Andersen Library.

BOOKS AND PERIODICALS

Akers, Tom, and Sam Akers. *The Game Breaker.* Wayzata, MN: Ralph Turtinen Pub. Co., 1977.

Anderson, Dave. *Minnesota–Wisconsin College Football Rivalry.* Charleston, SC: Arcadia Publishing, 2015. Kindle.

Atwood, Sarah. "This List Is Not Complete, Minnesota's Jewish Resistance to the Silver Legion of America, 1936–1940." Minnesota Historical Society, Winter 2018–2019, 142–55.

Barnett, Robert, and Thomas Harbrecht. "College Football During World War II: 1941–1945." *Physical Educator,* vol. 36, issue 1 (March 1, 1979).

Bierman, Bernie, and Frank Mayer. *Winning Football; Strategy, Psychology and Technique, by B. W. "Bernie" Bierman.* New York: Whittlesey House, 1937.

Bradley, James, and Ron Powers. *Flags of Our Fathers.* New York: Bantam Books, 2000. Hennepin County Public Library e-book.

Carlson, Stan W. *Dr. Henry L. Williams: A Football Biography, by Stan W. Carlson.* First edition, 1938. Stored in the Minnesota History Center's Gale Family Library.

Christensen, Ray. *Tales from the Minnesota Gophers: A Collection of the Greatest Gopher Stories Ever Told.* New York: Sports Publishing, 2014. Kindle.

Crawford, Danny J., and Bernard C. Nalty. "The United States Marines on Iwo Jima." Department of the Navy, United States Marines Corps, History and Museums Division.

Danzig, Allison. *The History of American Football.* Hoboken, NJ: Prentice-Hall, 1956.

Goodwin, Doris Kearns. *No Ordinary Time: Franklin and Eleanor Roosevelt: The Home Front in World War II.* New York: Simon & Schuster, 1995.

Holmes, Thomas. "The Dropping of Atomic Bombs on Japan." *Social Education,* vol. 69, no. 4 (2005): 209+.

Hotta, Eri. *Japan 1941: Countdown to Infamy.* New York: Knopf Doubleday, 2013. Saint Paul Public Library e-book.

Jones, Wilbur D. *"Football! Navy! War!": How Military "Lend-Lease" Players Saved the College Game and Helped Win World War II.* Jefferson, NC: McFarland, 2009. Kindle.

Lechner, Edgar. *Dr. Edgar Lechner: A North Dakota Farm Boy Finds His Way to Gopher Football, Dentistry, and Family: A Memoir.* Eden Prairie, MN: Lilja Press, 2016. Stored in the Minnesota History Center's Gale Family Library.

McCallum, John D. *Big Ten Football since 1895.* Boston: Chilton Book Company, 1976.

Miller, Patrick B. "Slouching toward a New Expediency: College Football and the Color Line during the Depression Decade." *American Studies,* vol. 40, no. 3 (Fall 1999).

Olson, Lynne. *Those Angry Days: Roosevelt, Lindbergh, and America's Fight over World War II, 1939–1941.* New York: Random House Trade Paperbacks, 2014. Hennepin County Library e-book.

Quirk, James P. *Minnesota Football: The Golden Years 1932–1941.* Grantsburg, WI: Self-published, first printing 1984.

Rippel, Joel A. *Game of My Life Minnesota Gophers: Memorable Stories of Gopher Football.* New York: Sports Publishing, 2007.

Shapiro, Edward S. "The Approach of War: Congressional Isolationism and Anti-Semitism, 1939–1941." *American Jewish History,* vol. 74, no. 1 (1984): 45–65. www.jstor.org/stable/23882497.

Sherwood, Robert. *Roosevelt and Hopkins: An Intimate History.* New York: Harper & Brothers, 1948.

Shoulders, Troy A. "The U.S. Navy in Operation Overlord under the Command of Rear Admiral Alan G. Kirk." A Trident Scholar Project Report, No. 221, September 27, 1994.

Taylor, Quintard. "Swing the Door Wide: World War II Wrought a Profound Transformation in Seattle's Black Community." Washington State Historical Society, *Columbia Magazine,* vol. 9, no. 2 (Summer 1995).

Wheeler, Keith. *We Are the Wounded, The Illustrated Edition.* New York: E. P. Dutton. Originally published: 1945. e-book.

Zangara, Mark. *The Fate of the USS Tide: The Forgotten Sailors of D-Day*. WW2 History Archive, 2019.

INDEX

178–180, 184; southern French
Indochina, occupation of, 49
Jefferson, Bernie, 147
Jeffery, Ira, 180
Johnson, Bill, 48, 170
Johnson, Charles, 36, 48, 51, 202; game
coverage, 99–100, 104, 112, 161, 166
Johnson, Don, 169
Jones, Biff, 127, 128, 131, 134, 135
Jones, Edgar "Special Delivery," 82, 86,
88
Juzwik, Steve, 173–174

Kansas State University, 126, 127
Keene, Roy, 178
Kelley, Larry, 184
Kinard, Bruiser, 178
Kinnick, Nile, 141, 184; death of, 202
Kirk, Alan, 207
Klefsaas, Kerm, 237
Konoe, Fumimaro, 85
Kreick, Ray, 166
KSTP radio, 64
Kula, Bob, 169
Kulbitski, Vic, 42, 164, 197, 202
Kuribayashi, Tadamichi, 221
Kurusu, Saburo, 132, 154–156, 171, 184
Kuusisto, Bill, 36
Kuzma, Tommy, 81, 89, 93, 103–108

Lach, Steve, 173
Lambeau, Earl "Curly," 211, 220,
231–232, 233, 235
Lauterbach, Joe, xxi; early life and college
career, 42, 78, 130, 222; Iwo Jima,
service at, 215, 222–224, 227; later life,
246
Lechner, Ed, 41, 149, 151, 165; memoir
recollections, 51, 62, 68; military
service, 203, 204; vs. Illinois, 77, 79; vs.
Michigan, 103, 105; vs. Northwestern,
119, 122–123; vs. Pittsburgh, 83, 86, 89
Lend-Lease, 2, 49, 50, 69, 76, 180
Letters from Iwo Jima, 217
LeVoir, Babe, 40, 169, 190
Levy, Leonard "Butch," xix, 41, 50; at
Great Lakes Naval Training Station,
191, 192–193, 198, 201, 210; at West
High School, 32, 33, 36, 51, 78, 201;

awards, 173; early years at Minnesota,
34–36, 115; later life, 239–240,
242–243; meeting his wife Lucky,
33–34; move to Idaho, 204; nickname,
origins of, 32; NFL career, 186,
233–235; vs. Illinois, 77; vs. Iowa, 148;
vs. Michigan, 100, 103, 106; vs.
Nebraska, 133, 134; vs. Northwestern,
119, 124; vs. Pittsburgh, 89; vs.
Washington, 63, 64, 66–67; vs.
Wisconsin, 159, 164, 165; wrestling
skills, 34–35, 58, 192, 234, 242–243
Levy, Marv, xxi
Lindbergh, Charles, 1–3, 46, 48–49;
infamous Des Moines speech, 54–55
Litchfield, Minnesota, 6–7, 46, 238
Litman, Neil, 165
"Little Brown Jug," 90, 108, 141, 145, 203;
origins, 100–102. *See also* Harris, Sig
Louis, Joe, xv
Los Angeles Dons, 231, 234, 242
Los Angeles Rams, 233, 235
Lowery, Louis, 226
Lummus, Jack, 221
Lund, Pug, 12, 38
Lundeen, Ralph, 51
Luekemeyer, Dick, 115–117
Lushine, Jim, 41
Luverne, Minnesota, 28–29, 31, 89;
Luverne Style Shop, 30. *See also*
Wildung, Dick
Lyons, Gene, 166

MacArthur, Douglas, xix, 199–200
Manion, Norbert, 28–29
Marmath, North Dakota, 61
Marquette University, 50, 178, 195
Marshall, Bobby, 144–145
Marshall High School, 32, 40–41
McCormick, Frank, 108, 168
McWilliams, Carey, 32–33
Melrose Area Historical Society, 245
Melrose, Minnesota, 38, 58, 77, 245
Memorial Stadium, xix, 1, 26, 112;
capacity of, 112, 118, 161–162, 196,
232; comparison to Michigan Stadium,
91; construction, 69, 71–72; crowd
descriptions, 76–77, 124, 166, 167,
197, 236, 237; early years, 19, 37–38,

ABOUT THE AUTHOR

Danny Spewak has a decade of experience as a news reporter at local television affiliates in Minneapolis–St. Paul, Buffalo, and mid-Missouri. He grew up in St. Louis and graduated from the University of Missouri with dual degrees in journalism and political science. Danny's late grandfather, Minneapolis native Jack Spewak, played football for the University of Minnesota and served in the South Pacific during World War II with the Army Air Corps.

CPSIA information can be obtained
at www.ICGtesting.com
Printed in the USA
LVHW081614080921
697347LV00002B/101